Schooling for Humanity

Studies in the
Postmodern Theory of Education

Joe L. Kincheloe and Shirley R. Steinberg
General Editors

Vol. 178

PETER LANG
New York • Washington, D.C./Baltimore • Bern
Frankfurt am Main • Berlin • Brussels • Vienna • Oxford

David O. Solmitz

Schooling for Humanity

When Big Brother Isn't Watching

Foreword by
Kathleen Kesson

PETER LANG
New York • Washington, D.C./Baltimore • Bern
Frankfurt am Main • Berlin • Brussels • Vienna • Oxford

Library of Congress Cataloging-in-Publication Data

Solmitz, David O.
Schooling for humanity: when Big Brother isn't watching / David O. Solmitz.
p. cm. — (Counterpoints; vol. 178)
Includes bibliographical references and index.
1. Critical pedagogy—United States. 2. Education—Aims and objectives—United States.
3. Public schools—Maine—Madison. 4. Solmitz, David O.
I. Title. II. Counterpoints (New York, N.Y.); vol. 178.
LC196.5.U6 S65   370.11'5—dc21   00-062975
ISBN 0-8204-5207-6
ISSN 1058-1634

Die Deutsche Bibliothek-CIP-Einheitsaufnahme

Solmitz, David O.:
Schooling for humanity: when Big Brother isn't watching / David O. Solmitz.
–New York; Washington, D.C./Baltimore; Bern;
Frankfurt am Main; Berlin; Brussels; Vienna; Oxford: Lang.
(Counterpoints; Vol. 178)
ISBN 0-8204-5207-6

Cover design by Dutton & Sherman Design

Author photo by Miranda Ring

The paper in this book meets the guidelines for permanence and durability
of the Committee on Production Guidelines for Book Longevity
of the Council of Library Resources.

© 2001 Peter Lang Publishing, Inc., New York

Printed in the United States of America

DEDICATION

To my dear, compassionate, insightful wife Jing Ye,

And our daughter May Ye

As well as to all those individuals worldwide who are struggling

with hope and courage to reclaim the wonder and compassion

for one another and for our mutual planet

TABLE OF CONTENTS

ACKNOWLEDGMENTS

As transnational corporations globalize the world economy, a monoculture is created in which the primary purpose of education is to prepare students to become marketable products for the prosperity of business and industry. By submitting to the demands of corporate giants, education focuses upon the accumulation of information and the development of skills required by these monoliths. It is increasingly less concerned with fostering the principles of a democratic society, human dignity, freedom, social responsibility, and the preservation of the biosphere. This book is written without optimism but with tremendous hope that together parents and educators in this country and throughout the world will continue to struggle to make our schools more human, to retain the initial wonderment of the world that young children have, to foster a global community in which people of all cultures, races, ethnicities, beliefs, age, and sexual orientations can live in compassionate harmony with one other and conserve the delicate environment that we share on planet earth.

This book would never have been possible without the tremendous support and encouragement from my wife, Jing Ye. It was she who urged me to resign from thirty years of teaching at Madison Area Memorial High School in the small, rural central Maine mill town of Madison, to write this book in order to share my experience, philosophy, and methods with teachers to be as well as with those teachers desiring recertification. With her belief in me and with the encouragement of my Goddard College professor Gus Lyn-Piluso, who felt my ideas and writings should be published, and with the extraordinary support of my mentor, a truly progressive educator, Dr. Kathleen Kesson, I developed the confidence to write this book. My cousin Frederic G. Corneel, an attorney and author in his own right, read the manuscript with a fine-toothed comb. He not only offered editorial changes, but also provided insightful critique for which I am very grateful. I would like to thank James W. Hennigar, executive director of the Good Will-Hinkley School in Hinkley, Maine, an important educator in his own right, for allowing me to quote letters he wrote to me while he was my superintendent. I owe a debt of thanks to the editor of the *Central Maine Morning Sentinel* in Waterville, Maine, for allowing me to print materials from various editions of this newspaper. I also wish to thank Houghton Mifflin Co. for permission to reprint an excerpt from *Horace's School* copyright © 1992 by Theodore R. Sizer.

I am indebted to my many students during thirty years of teaching at Madison High School. Their stories, experiences, insight, and friendship have made this book become alive. As some of their stories are quite personal, I have consistently used pseudonyms in place of all of their real names with the exception of Ayanna Booth-Athenian, the student who gave the 1999 graduation address at Madison High School, and Caitlin Malloy, the senior student whose speech I quoted from a program on harassment at Madison High School. I am also grateful to my former student, Sandy Knowles, Customer Service Representative at J.S. McCarthy/Letter Systems Printers in Augusta, ME for her dedication to make sure my manuscript was most promptly and professionally typeset.

FOREWORD

By Kathleen Kesson

Director of Teacher Education, Goddard College,
Plainfield, Vermont

Critical education scholars have been examining the relationship between schooling and the political economy since at least 1962, with the publication of *Schooling in Capitalist America: Educational Reform and the Contradiction of Economic Life,* by Samuel Bowles and Herbert Gintis. Since that time, numerous scholars and researchers, including Richard Brosio (1994), Martin Engels (1999), Jean Anyon (1980) and David Gabbard (2000) have provided us with compelling analyses of the ways that power, capital, and educational ideas intersect. If these researchers are to be believed, most educational reform initiatives of at least the past 20 years are geared toward ensuring that the United States will remain dominant in the emerging global economy. Even the most cursory reading of the 1983 document *A Nation at Risk* reveals these imperatives at the core of recent reform movements. What is lost in this rush to the top of the materialist heap is an education for the more enduring human values: for creativity, intellectual development, care, social justice, and democracy.

While researchers, theorists, and college professors have alerted us to these issues, teachers have been less vocal about the impact of these imperatives on their daily practice. With David Solmitz's *Schooling for Humanity: When Big Brother Isn't Watching?* we have a narrative that spans 30 years of the struggles of a democratic educator to teach for these higher human values in the face of the increasing corporatism of our public schools. A social studies and German teacher at a small consolidated high school in rural Maine for all of these 30 years, Solmitz documents in precise detail the ways in which the obligation of our public schools to educate citizens for a democracy has been successively overridden by the requirement to educate students to take their places as producers and consumers in a rapidly expanding global economy. This has resulted, as he so compellingly illustrates, in the loss of community, alienation, apathy, and boredom among students, heightened social class differences, and a substantial danger to the democratic principles upon which this country was founded.

To make his case for an education for democracy, David (or Dangerous Dave, as his students fondly called him) relies on historical evidence, citing Plato, Rousseau, John Dewey, Horace Mann, Thoreau, Emerson, and other upholders of the democratic ideal for schooling. Relying upon such luminaries, he reminds us that the vision for schooling in a democratic society has been that of a truly level playing field, in which children of all castes and classes might have the equal opportunity to discover and develop their practical, intellectual, and artistic passions, and utilize these to create lives of meaning and fulfillment. His firsthand account of daily life in a typical school illustrates how very far from this vision we are.

David is a dedicated collector of artifacts—a reflective journal, his letters to the editor over the years, op-ed pieces, speeches, written reprimands from principals and superintendents (these are especially illustrative), student work, letters from students—and he uses these various documents to weave together his narrative. It is a valuable collection of data that serves to reconstruct for us the life of an intellectually alive, passionate, caring, and occasionally defiant educator. In an age of conformity and acquiescence to the corporate status quo, he proves to be an outspoken advocate for students, a rebel with many causes, and a defender of the democratic ideal.

Teachers who share his values will find much to resonate with in these stories as David explores the difficulties that manifest themselves when one tries to be a liberatory educator in an authoritarian setting. Unlike many young idealists, who throw in the towel when the struggle proves too overwhelming, he hung in there for three decades, fighting the good fight against great odds. We hear in this narrative about some of the contradictions of being a democratic educator. David lets us in on his struggle to come to terms with "discipline," as he reveals, on the one hand, his efforts to empower students to think independently and challenge authority, and his desire, on the other, to maintain enough decorum in his classroom to keep from being fired. We empathize with him as he finds himself caught in the bind of whether to teach to the test, thus enabling his students to better jump through pre-ordained hoops, or to co-create, with his students, a curriculum of genuine relevance. We cheer him on as he fights, always, with the disenfranchised; victims of small town classism, sexism, racism, and homophobia. We applaud his efforts, often met with staunch resistance from administrators and conservative local citizens and parents, to bring controversial social issues to the center of his curriculum. We celebrate his efforts to spark independent and critical thinking in his students, even when it threatens his own control of the classroom. All this in the relative isolation of a small Maine mill town.

Along with the story of David's educational career, which would be worth reading in itself, David brings us an analysis that situates his story within the context of the "New World Order," the emerging global system that is attempting to integrate the peoples and cultures of the world into one homogenous economic unit. He blows the whistle on such democratic sounding euphemisms as cooperative learning, individualized education plans (IEP's) for everyone, interdisciplinary and team teaching, total quality management, high standards for all, and excellence. He deconstructs these phrases, and systematically demonstrates how they mask ever more refined forms of domination and control, and feed the corporate agenda for schools and society. He sheds light on some of the possible causes for the recent incidents of violence that have surfaced in rural, urban, and suburban schools alike, suggesting that along with finger pointing at the media, the disintegrating family, and the gun lobby, we might also look for answers at the structure and practices of schooling. The new focus, he asserts, on high standards and high stakes testing, despite the rhetoric of equity in which it has been garbed, takes place in an increasingly competitive educational environment set up to foster winners and losers, haves and have nots, and is itself a source of the kind of alienation that breeds violence. Combined with the current lack of trust in young people and a curriculum divorced from any inherent meaning for most students, the constellation of current school practices that fit the corporate agenda will not solve the problems of youth violence and alienation, but exacerbate them.

Not content with merely critiquing the system, David takes the courageous leap of laying out a plan to democratize schools. Drawing upon his own experiments in liberatory education, he generates a number of principles that teachers and administrators, school board members and parents alike, would do well to heed, if they hope to recapture the democratic imperative that has always been the unrealized potential of America's educational system. He thus ends on a note of cautious optimism, arguing that we must strive to cultivate a strong set of democratic values that foster tolerance, acceptance of differing beliefs, viewpoints and cultures. This, he says, is a "schooling for humanity."

REFERENCES

Anyon, J. 1980. Social class and the hidden curriculum of work, Journal of Education, 162: 67–92.

Brosio, R. 1994. *A radical democratic critique of capitalist education.* New York: Peter Lang.

Engels, M. 1999. *Markets vs. democracy: The struggle for control of public education.* Philadelphia: Temple University Press.

Gabbard, D. 2000. edited by *Knowledge and Power in the Global Economy: Politics and Rhetoric of School Reform.* Mahwah, NJ: Lawrence Erlbaum Associates.

PREFACE

This book is being written directly following thirty years of teaching social studies and a little German at Madison Area Memorial High School, a small consolidated high school, located in a rural, central Maine mill town. During these three decades, I have witnessed the ravaging flood of capitalist-corporate domination over our public schools that erodes the democratic imperative on which this country was founded. Even so, against many odds I have tried and remain firmly convinced that it is possible to create democratic schools within a diverse community that enhance the humanity in each and every one of us: students and adults.

Corporate Domination versus the Democratic Imperative

Emphasis upon expanding profits for business and industry at the expense of the employee and the natural environment hasn't changed since the era of the Industrial Revolution. The difference is that today hi-tech developments are making it possible for already massive corporations to merge into powerful, transnational entities that are globalizing the world to secure vast wealth for themselves. By espousing democracy, they are disguising their hierarchical structure in order to appear compassionate and win the commitment not only of their employees, but also of the governments in countries into which they are expanding.

American public education now cowers to these corporate powerhouses. Educators together with legislators and corporate leaders have created state and national standards to meet their demands. Students are being prepared to meet the new paradigm of business and industry for the postmodern, high-technological era. The standards even use the euphemistic and manipulative language that disguises corporate greed for profit with a concern for humanity. For instance, global stewardship refers to taking advantage of low wages, lack of protective legislation for laborers, and few if any laws pertaining to environmental protection in developing countries. Lifelong learning implies that a person must constantly be re-educated as s/he will hold at least eight different kinds of careers throughout a lifetime. Critical thinking is acceptable so long as employees do not criticize policies of the corporation that employs them. Teaming and problem solving refer to a team of workers solving problems for the corporation. This concept often leads to downsizing of the workforce. Therefore, some of the problem solving employees receive their pink slips.

The same management practices used by corporate America that cause the employees to feel as if they have ownership in the management of the corporation are used by public schools as a means to discipline students. By involving the entire community, parents, school personnel, and law enforcement officials using a "kinder and gentler" as opposed to a punitive approach, condition students to conformity.

Even though our public schools do teach about democracy, they rarely practice it either within the classroom or throughout the entire school itself. As the corporate domain is so powerful, demanding, and manipulative, it becomes increasingly difficult to establish balance with the democratic imperative and the biosphere.

In the spring of 1999 I resigned from Madison High School to write this book to examine and to explore solutions to these problems. Madison High School is not essentially different from many high schools in this country. By sharing my experiences and learnings from thirty years of teaching there, you, the reader, may better understand the problems my students and I faced. You will then be able to effectively participate in a dialogue by critiquing and offering other solutions.

Although I have been labeled by many of my colleagues and townspeople with the "L" word President Reagan and other conservatives used to identify their counterpart in the opposing camp, my bias in the tradition of progressive education dates to the eighteenth-century European Enlightenment. Thus, I have been influenced by such eighteenth-century educators as Johann Heinrich Pestalozzi and Jean Jacques Rousseau to our own promoters of universal schooling, Thomas Jefferson and Horace Mann, and such twentieth-century philosophers as John Dewey, the contemporary Brazilian pedagogue, Paulo Freire, as well as John Holt, bell hooks, and Neil Postman.

Both Eastern and Western theorists dating back to the ancient Buddhist traditions of the East and America's own transcendental philosophers, Henry David Thoreau and Ralph Waldo Emerson, also have influenced me. These philosophers accent appreciation for all life at the moment as opposed to rushing through life in fear of being unable to reach some fantastic, materialistic goal. Their interest is allowing people to live in harmony with each other and their natural environment.

From the onset of my employment in Madison, I have prudently kept notes, articles I have written for both the school and regional newspapers, reports about my escapades printed in the press, videotapes of projects I have created, and numerous reprimands from administrators over the years. Therefore, it seemed reasonable to write a narrative of my experiences as a democratic teacher in a traditionally authoritarian school system. I weave my theories and experiences with philosophic concepts that date back to Plato and to ancient Eastern thought, as well as with more recent and even contemporary educational theorists. I intertwine the history of education reform in the United States with the contemporary conflict of national and state mandates versus local control of the school system.

It is my intent to tell my story in as non-selfish, non-self-indulgent a manner as possible. Using this approach, I hope to encourage the reader to explore with me the need for a community that represents a wide diversity of viewpoints yet upholds and actively fights to preserve the democratic principles upon which this country was founded. If we agree with John Dewey, who believed that democracy can be a way of life, then it seems fair that as a community we can build democratic schools that hold at bay the powers of corporate capitalism.

In spite of the Goals 2000 (1994), national standards remain divorced from personality development that nurtures sensitive, caring, and accepting individuals who seek to live in harmony with their compatriots. People with these traits are also aware of and sensitive to current world problems as these unfold in that they respond actively to them.

The reader should be aware that I am bringing the same missionary zeal with which I began teaching in Madison three decades ago to different arenas. These include, you the reader, as well as prospective teachers at the college level, and those teachers who need to take courses for recertification. Undoubtedly, the reader will ask "why does this teacher persist year after year to fight what appear to be losing battles with administration after administration and even some fellow teachers?" The answer may lie in Helen Epstein's analysis of children of survivors of the Nazi holocaust. She argues that such children, of whom I am one, become martyrs as victims. This is because they subconsciously feel guilty for the suffering their parents experienced while they have been raised within an accepting environment in an affluent, relatively tolerant nation. She explains further that the Concentration Camp "became a badge of courage rather than a degradation. It became an untouchable standard of fortitude" (Epstein 1979, 11).

Like my parents, who felt like strangers in a new land, I felt isolated not only in Madison, but also while growing up in Brunswick, Maine. As my parents' only child and especially in elementary school, I felt no sense of belonging. Therefore, as a teacher in Madison, I believe it was easier for me than for my peers to become a controversial teacher, as I felt I was not an accepted part of the school community, the town, and the surrounding villages. It does remain true to this day in rural Maine, that if a person is not born here, and his or her ancestors are not White Anglo Saxon Protestants who had settled here several generations ago, he/she would still be considered a "flatlander" by many native Mainers. I subconsciously felt I had nothing to lose in being ostracized from a group to which I really didn't belong. At the same time I was driven by paranoia, constantly in fear of losing my job, and of being a victim of persecution. As readers examine my own experiences, they will see how I have lived out this pattern. Should Epstein be correct, which I believe she is, her analysis should not diminish the reality that the struggles to create more democratic schooling are both relevant and important. I hope this tidbit of information may help readers better understand my passion and struggle so that together we can actively work to build, foster, and support the kind of communities that make democratic schooling possible. I hope we can restrain those elements of the ravaging tide of corporate capitalism that I believe encroach upon democratic principles and diminish the quality of life each and every one of us deserves. This goal includes living a lifestyle and having a career that provides each person with optimal happiness. It encourages each of us to be spiritually uplifted by the many different people, ideas, cultures, beliefs, and lifestyles we encounter. At the same time, we are able to cherish and protect the natural environment in which we live.

As we progress on this journey together, we will examine the dire straits into which our public schools have fallen according to criticism from parents, legislators, and business and industry. We will look at the forces that have brought them into this predicament from an historical perspective that demonstrates the growing domination of capitalism over the principles and practices of democratic education. We will explore the relationship between democracy and the school, and, hence, what the role of the school and the purpose for teaching in a postmodern democratic society should be. We will have to inquire what the common needs of the community and its students may be and that our schools must address. Therefore, we will look as to how the so-called formal thinking reflecting a Cartesian-Newtonian mechanistic worldview, that emphasizes logic over experience, still all too prevalent today in our schools, is insensitive to human relations in an ever-shrinking and interdependent world and an endangered biosphere. Further, we shall look toward a postformal worldview that nurtures the wonderment of children and fosters human dignity, freedom, self-awareness and consciousness, and social responsibility. If we are able to begin to reach some agreement about these concerns, I hope we will be able to talk constructively together about ways how democratic schools can be structured to meet these collective requirements of the community and its students.

Project Limitations

Every book must have its limitations. This one, because of my career in secondary education, focuses upon reform at the high school level. There are at least two liabilities in concentrating on reform for secondary education. First of all, from the time children enter school in kindergarten, they are being thwarted from becoming independent, motivated, self-reliant learners. They are being conditioned to become passive receptacles of information dispensed by teachers, books, and computer programs that they feed back on tests. Should they fail, they are issued punishments that range from humiliation to poor grades to after-school detention. The older they grow, the more difficult it becomes for them to break from these patterns. For one teacher, or even a few teachers, in a traditional public high school, where emphasis is on control and accountability versus self-motivation and responsibility, it is difficult to change both student patterns and those of fellow teachers, administrators, and the locally elected school board. In addition, the increasing emphasis on national and statewide testing at designated grade levels, whose results are published in the press, only forces teachers to teach for this type of assessment.

Second, trying to bring about reform at the high school level appears analogous to integrating America's public schools in the late 1950s and 1960s. Instead of beginning school desegregation in kindergarten and in the early elementary grades, it was initiated originally in high schools. This seems to reflect a form of impatience that appears to be typical of American culture. The change must occur immediately, if not sooner. Therefore, the chance for a slow, but organic development does not take place. On the contrary, while superficial change takes place instantaneously at the higher level, chances are reduced to peacefully and permanently create meaningful reform in regards to emotional attitudes at the institutions and within the social order itself.

In spite of these limitations, I invite you, the reader, to experience together with me a roller-coaster ride of thirty years as a controversial teacher at Madison High School. I hope that together we can explore means by which, as a community, we can reform our public schools so students will want to attend them. I want to believe that we can work together to facilitate a process so that our students feel empowered to seek a gratifying lifestyle and to become active participants who uphold the democratic principles on which our country was founded. To accomplish these ends, our schools have to be egalitarian reflections of all aspects of the community, ranging from the white male power elite to the disenfranchised, including the poor as well as cultural, ethnic, racial, and sexual minorities. Through an educational system that is less hierarchical, it is possible to create democratic schooling that enhances humanity.

1

THE SETTING

Madison

Whizzing past the eroded slopes of the sandpits, with fallen trees and orange rust spotted machinery blending into the human created destruction of nature, my 1967 Volkswagen van sped steadily along route 201 A. Soon a sign, "Speed Limit 35," reminded me that the town of Madison was approaching. As I pressed on the brakes, I waved to Pinky, the thin, elderly police chief, who guarded the town limits from a cushioned seat in his pale green, unmarked Ford LTD cruiser, puffing contentedly on a cigar. From my side view mirror I could see him slowly raise his arm and faintly wave a return greeting.

Little has changed in this community of 4,900, nestled on the banks of the Kennebec River in rural central Maine since I arrived here in the fall of 1969. Sure the gravel pits have grown significantly larger. The community now has two white police cruisers, which bear the insignia of the town on their doors, and several new officers to provide added protection to the community. On both sides of Old Point Avenue are wooden frame houses, many with front porches, almost all with dormer windows, gables, and cornices. There are still some larger homes with stables attached, and a dilapidated duplex with gaudy yellow paint. Many of these homes were built in the early

1900s when Madison was experiencing its glory days as a prosperous textile and paper mill town. The little cash markets that extended from the porches of a couple of these homes have long since closed since Cumberland Farms and the Big Apple convenience store chains moved in during the mid-1970s and 1980s. Mobile homes have been hauled to vacant lots. In some cases parents have encouraged their children to place a house trailer directly on their land or on a neighboring plot. In one instance a mobile home for a widowed mother is located on the side lawn of a white clapboard house. In the front yards of many of these mobile homes and tar paper shacks are broken toys and one or more auto carcasses, a couple of snowmobiles, an ATV, and a "Chevy" 4 x 4. If a little satellite dish is not attached to the home, there is sure to be a big one in the yard. In a small, dilapidated, two-story green and black tarpaper house, Jim Brooks, a relic of the era of Madison's glory, lived alone.

In 1970 shortly before his death, this heavy-set man lay bedridden, wrapped in a wool blanket, next to his overheated wood stove. Then immobile because of age, fat, and arthritis, at the age of seventeen he had enlisted in World War I. He returned from Europe as a hero. Feeling a little threatened by the considerable influx of French Canadians and other immigrants from Italy, Eastern Europe, Russia, Armenia, and Lebanon, he became the leader of Madison's branch of the Ku Klux Klan. He felt this community belonged to the White Anglo Saxon Protestants (WASPs) whose ethic of hard work and thrift caused the community to prosper. At the height of the Klan's fervor in the late 1920s, all public offices, which included selectmen, policemen, volunteer firefighters, the superintendent of schools, all school principals and teachers, were held by White Anglo Saxon Protestants. The Klan regularly marched up Madison's main street turning right onto Weston Avenue and then onto Park Street until they reached the town's water reservoir atop a small hill.

I am aware of two acts of violence committed by the Klan. An elderly Franco-American citizen told of the time a stone was thrown through the plate glass window of his home. Around the stone a note was wrapped that said that he would be thrown into the Kennebec River later that evening. The threat was never carried out. On another occasion the Klan burned to the ground the sawmill of an Armenian immigrant.

Since many of my students were of French Canadian descent and others were of Eastern European origin, the target groups of the Klan, several of my students and I visited Jim Brooks. We wanted to learn more about the role the Klan played in Madison in the mid-1920s and early 1930s. However, he was very reluctant to talk about the Klan since its popularity had long since diminished.

In 1969 the population of Madison was 60% of French Catholic origin. Though the number of Catholics has remained about the same, fewer attend church regularly. Many church affiliated families are Baptist and Congregationalist. There are several nondenominational Christian churches in Madison and the outlying areas such as the Church of the Open Bible and the Church of the Lumberjacks.

Back in 1969, I stopped momentarily at the one blinking light in town to look both ways. At opposite corners, gas stations replaced prominent homes. A brick Congregational Church dominated the third corner, while a "superette" drew shoppers to the fourth. In 1999 when I left Madison the flashing light had been replaced by a full set of traffic signals. One gas station had been torn down so a drug store could be built on the site. The superette had just been transformed into a Chinese restaurant.

To the left the road descends a steep hill where businesses are located. At the bottom of the hill is the Kennebec River. In 1969 the river was filled with four-foot logs to feed the mill with pulp for paper production. The log drives came to an end in the mid-seventies when trucks were used to transport pulpwood to the paper mills. During the same period Madison's paper mill closed temporarily. After several difficult years a Finnish corporation together with the *New York Times* purchased it. After spending more than a third of a billion dollars to upgrade the mill, today one sees, from atop the hill, the blue and white Finnish flag graced by the American flag on the left and the state of Maine flag to its right. Because of its focus on upgrading its technology, the mill continues to boast the highest output of paper in the State. In 1998 a calcium carbonate precipitate facility was constructed to improve the paper quality. Whenever the mill decides to upgrade its facility, it successfully appeals to the board of selectmen for a tax break.

Upon turning right at the blinking traffic light, I headed up Upper Main Street for one-eighth of a mile to reach Madison Area Memorial High School. Within a few hundred yards of the traffic light, on the right-hand side, is the decade-old, modern, semicircular Catholic Church. Father Rancourt, who wore a black safari hat with his black clerical robe and who is now retired, successfully secured large sums of money from his dwindling parishioners to build this new memorial to God. The Turcottes, the LaRouches, the Dubois, the Ouelettes, and the Paquettes once again flock to this lavish House of the Lord. These were once the families whom Jim Brooks and his fellow Ku Klux Klan members successfully kept from holding any public office. By 1986 a new high school opened a mile and a half out of town.

One day in early October 1985, I received a phone call from the principal to tell me not to report to school because the building was on fire. Apparently, one of my sophomores, a quiet college preparatory student, who played in the school band but did not cherish academics, ignited the 1920s brick building. The fire was so hot that it completely gutted the inside of the structure, weakening it so much that the entire back wall fell in. The same boy had allegedly set a small fire at the junior high school as well as six houses on the street on which he lived including his own home. During the weeks preceding the inferno at the old high school, terrified residents of the community, especially those living on the street that had already experienced several fires, were ready to meet the arsonist head-on. They slept prepared with handguns and/or rifles by their beds. Following the fire, we held classes from 1:00 P.M. to 6:30 P.M. at a nearby regional high school. My student was finally caught during the school day igniting a fire there above the ceiling tiles in the boys' bathroom

Within a year the new school was completed at a cost of $4.3 million. It is a large rectangular box built to accommodate up to 400 Madison students. To the casual observer who drives by the building, it looks like another high-tech factory. Only the sign in front makes it clear that it is actually a school. True, the architect, Wilbur R. Ingalls, Jr., is a pure functionalist. He noted in a 1989 article in the *Maine Times* that it is "bad design to mix and match every kind of material and mix up all its historical periods and call it postmodern. If there's anything I hate, it's to take a building that has a heart and soul and wrap around it a lot of crap that doesn't have anything to do with it. If I'm a bear, I want to look like a bear" (*Maine Times*, 20 October 1989). The centerpiece of the school is the gymnasium. The central office is at the entrance to the academic wing. The school library, which I believe should be the focus of the school, is a small room located at the top of the stairs. Blue and white lockers, like tin soldiers at attention, line the corridors of the two-story academic wing. After all, the focus of the Madison community has been sports. When the state principals' association in the mid-1970s decided that Madison would be transferred to a sports class for schools smaller than its football rival, Skowhegan, the emotionally and sometimes physically heated football rivalry between the two communities ceased. Although Madison has continued to win football championships in the class C division, basketball has become popular. The girls' team has had several victorious seasons bringing the girls into the limelight as athletes. Cross country and track are now common. Naturally, baseball and softball remain spring sports. The school even has a tiny tennis team.

Madison is as much of a blue-collar community today as when I arrived there in 1969. For example, between 1995 and 2000, 36% of the new housing units have been mobile homes because they are the most affordable to the population at the lower end of the socioeconomic scale. The wage earners from these households have minimum-wage type jobs provided by either the wood processing/manufacturing industries or the textile/shoe manufacturing industries. Where there are two-parent households, both parents work. The managers of the mill live in Waterville, a city with a population of 18,000 twenty miles from Madison. Although the unemployment rate is

6.0% in Madison, it is higher for the outlying communities of Starks, population 500, Athens, with less than 1,000 residents, and the tiny hamlet of Brighton Plantation with no more than 100 folk.

The addition of the word "area" was added in the early 1960s to our little high school when it became the comprehensive high school for several area communities, Madison being the largest. Following are snapshots of the outlying communities.

Starks

Starks is a little village of fewer than 500 inhabitants on the other side of the Kennebec River toward the shiretown of Farmington. Nestled along Lemon Stream, it once had several gristmills and a canning factory. It was only in the early 1960s that the canning factory closed for good. Even gold was panned on Dyer Brook. However, when I once took a class gold panning, we were terribly disappointed to learn from the science teacher that all we brought home was fool's gold.

When driving into and immediately out of the village, one can make a right-hand turn onto Chicken Street. Following the street up the hill through fields and woods one will come upon the little home inhabited by witches, the last of a community of Wiccans who had settled there in the early 1970s. As the witches initially descended upon the community, wearing simple, dark robes and capes, the local townsfolk were sure that the Devil and his followers were taking over their little town. According to Wiccans Fred Griffith and his wife, Leigh, Wiccans do not worship Satan. Nor are they a cult that requires mindless obedience of its members. They don't sacrifice, torture, or kill animals or humans. Fred explained that, "Wiccans think for themselves with no central authority figure other than what's inside ourselves. That's one reason why Wicca can never become a cult. As one person, you are answerable to yourself. And that's sometimes your harshest critic" (*Morning Sentinel*, 10/29/90). Still the fundamental Christian groups of the area frown upon the Wiccans because they have their roots in beliefs of ancient pre-Christian Celts.

If the staid townspeople of Starks frown upon the Wiccans, they certainly hold animosity toward Harry Brown who opens up his vast field every August to the annual weekend celebration called Hempstock. The money raised during this three-day celebration of marijuana at which numerous bands perform is used to support the efforts of Maine Vocals, a Madison based organization that has been fighting for years for the legalization of pot. Its founder, who has been arrested on various occasions for smoking a joint on the steps of the county court house during protest demonstrations against police raids of local families at gun point, has recently completed a prison term for harboring marijuana and related paraphernalia.

Finally, the only black family, who lived in Starks, decided to open the little general store that had been closed for some years. Several months after opening for business, the store and later their home were destroyed by fire. To this day no conclusive evidence has been found to determine the cause of the fires nor what might have ignited them. With Yankee ingenuity the family rebuilt the store. After ugly battles with the village's planning board that felt the structure was too large for the plot, in a community that has no zoning ordinances, and after extensive court litigation, the store is now in operation.

Athens

The other major community in SAD #59 is Athens. It is divided into two parts, Athens proper and West Athens. In the early fall, during bear season, it is not uncommon to find bears hanging on the front porches of some homes. Because land was particularly inexpensive in West Athens, it became a haven for hippies in the late 1960s and 1970s. It also became the home, for nearly a year, of an Amish family.

I first encountered these folks on an early mid-September morning on my way to school. I spotted a black, covered buggy and horse grazing by the side of the road. Immediately upon arriving at school, I telephoned my wife, who was Swiss, to visit these people together with our three-year-old son and speak German with them before they moved on. She did. At the end of the school day she picked me up at work and we then traveled to their next night's campground just a few miles away. They had traveled to Maine all the way from Arkansas because they had heard that land was cheap and isolated. Here they hoped to draw more families, establish an Amish community where they could raise their children without the influence of the modern world. They found an abandoned farm house a mile off the main road. The trail to the farm was barely passable. Only under the driest conditions could it be maneuvered by a four-wheel drive pick-up truck. It was soggy and overgrown with brush and young trees.

Since our initial encounter, we on occasion in the fall and the following spring and summer visited them at their homestead. My wife became friendly with Lydia, the mother, who expressed regret that God will not allow her to have photographs of her children. In fact, when our three-year-old son gave them one of his picture books in German, the family refused because their children may not look at any pictures.

On our second visit to them in about two weeks' time during the summer of 1972, we were taken aback to find a sheriff's four-wheel drive truck and several officers there. We learned that their son had tripped while mowing the field with a horse drawn mowing machine. To regain his balance, he took a quick step forward with his foot landing in front of the cutting blade. Since his parents did not believe in antibiotics and other forms of modern medicine, Jeremiaha died of lockjaw after twenty days. His father buried him on the land.

I was asked to testify before the grand jury on the father's behalf. The court eventually ruled that if the family left, they would not press charges of manslaughter against the father nor charge him for illegally burying his son without a burial permit or in an unauthorized graveyard. When the court proceedings were over, we received a letter of thanks from the family, inviting us to join them. In the letter Eli, the father, wrote that we could join them in their wagon. He had a tent in which we could stay. Or he could fix us up with another wagon having gathered several over the past year. Later in the letter he wrote "To dress like us and such things seems to us a very small matter as we could soon help provide you in such lines."

On their journey to Pennsylvania, from where he and his family originally came, the family sent us several postcards. In late November, the wife wrote: "the family has kept in good health all the way except for one minor cold for a week. And the snow is keeping off so far here, but we know it may come soon and we hope to get to our home this week, Lord willing, and if all goes well. The horses have kept in very good shape, as their working days are short and we rest them during midday for two or more hours while they feed upon grass." The family made the *New York Times* when they were escorted by the New York State Police crossing the Hudson River over the Bear Mountain Bridge. New York law prohibits livestock crossing any bridge over the Hudson.

The hippies formed another element of the West Athens scene. Largely middle and upper middle class, college educated people in their early-to mid-twenties, they came from as far away as California in search of land where they hoped to establish a simple, back to the land lifestyle. Some already had experiences with a communal existence and were eager to start communes in Maine. Like the Amish they had heard that land was cheap in rural central Maine. Long cold winters with little money meant that people had to bring into their lives whatever was missing: art, theater, music, and dance. Each year, for instance, for thirty years and continuing, the hippies of west Athens put on an annual July 4th celebration produced by their own "In Spite of Life Players." The event begins with a parade in the tiny village center that includes outlandish floats, the local fire engine, and wild costumes. It follows the main drag, a dirt road, to the gravel pit. Here the players produce their annual "de resistance" play, a parody on political events be they local, state, or national.

The "In Spite of Life Players" theater group got its name because they thrived in spite of broken cars, freezing winters, having babies, and not having any money. They gathered pretty regularly to do theater. Because the hippies liked the arts, Anna, once a professional actress, mother of four, brought theater to the Athens Elementary School. When her kids were in high school, she directed plays at Madison High. I was able with the help of grants from the Maine Arts Commission to bring some of the "hippie" artists into the school. One outstanding artist, who had a great rapport with students, was Abby Shahn, the daughter of Ben Shahn. Other artists brought fiddling and dance to the school.

Besides being known for its hippies, West Athens was well known throughout Maine folklore as one of those tiny, poverty ridden, and isolated communities, in which inbreeding appeared to be the norm. Athens proper, on the other hand, population less than 1,000 including West Athens, is located on numbered highway 150. It has a couple of stores, a garage, even a post office, a grange hall, an elementary school that replaced the old academy when the town joined SAD #59, and a fairground. Two brothers, who own the community's largest business together with General Electric, a wood-chip electrical generating plant, have been outspoken members of the school board for several years. Their prime interest is to save tax dollars by cutting the school budget whenever and wherever they can. They want the schools to run like an efficient business of the industrial era where only the basics, like the 3Rs are taught, and students are all obedient to their teachers.

Brighton Plantation

The smallest of the communities is Brighton Plantation with a population of under 100. This little hamlet is surrounded by land belonging to South African Pulp and Paper that belonged to Scott Paper until recently. Little is heard of this quiet community, except when Michael Vernon makes the news for challenging the paper company's practice of clear cutting and spraying the forests with chemicals that harm the forest wildlife and pollute the waters of ponds and streams. He remains convinced that the Scott Paper Company was behind a plot to burn his isolated cabin in hope of extinguishing him as well.

Demographics Related to Madison High School

There is a strong relationship between the aspirations of youths and occupational outcomes. Both are based on the kinds of jobs their parents have and the socioeconomic class to which they belong. Therefore, the optimism and pessimism of the students depend on how open they see the society to be and to what extent socioeconomic barriers may hinder their upward mobility (Anyon, 1980). For example, Madison High School's graduating class of 1999 received high praise from school administrators because their class did especially well on the statewide eleventh grade Maine Education Assessment tests. Out of a senior class of 53, 48 graduated. Thirty-one graduates have enrolled in further education including two boys who enlisted in the Air Force and the Marines, respectively. An unusually high number of four students have been accepted at name colleges outside Maine, namely Brandeis University, Hofstra University, Rochester Institute of Technology, and Wesleyan College. In each instance these students' parents were college educated. Three of these families are from "out of state." The native Maine parents are both high school social studies teachers in a neighboring school system. The young woman, who was accepted at Wesleyan, the class valedictorian, will focus in her studies on balancing mind and body through the martial arts and meditation. She will be living and studying for a year at a residential, nature based foundation for the martial arts. It is an actual farm consisting of 200 acres of land.

Two young men were accepted at the Maine Maritime Academy. Six were accepted within the University of Maine system, which includes two-year associate programs. Three were admitted to two-year technical colleges in Maine.

Two students are enrolled either in the technical college system or in the state university system as part of an articulation agreement between these schools, Madison Paper Industries, and the high school. To be admitted to these schools the students had to take special courses in high school. These classes included calculus, physics, chemistry, and OSHA safety. Once they have completed their training successfully, these two young men will be placed on a waiting list for a job in the paper industry, not just in Maine, nor simply in the United States, but somewhere in the world where these multinational corporations have plants. This is a far cry from the mid-1980s when young men, whose parents were employed in the mill, automatically had a job there, even if they were in the lowest track group in high school.

Two students have been accepted at a small, environmentally oriented college in Maine. Three were accepted by Western New England College in Massachusetts to study business administration or sports management. The daughter of a local pastor will attend a religious college. The other students will attend small colleges outside of Maine focusing upon business management, sports, and computers. Those not going on to college will work in area shoe factories, while some will work in the woods-harvesting industry. Some will take seasonal jobs in construction. These range from working for a local contractor who builds homes or small earth moving firms to larger construction companies. In these instances, the workers will have to live away from home while on the job. Others will take minimum wage jobs at the Shop n' Save, a Maine based food store chain, and at a Wal-Mart store in nearby Skowhegan. Some will work in retail at small local businesses. A couple of boys will be auto mechanics. One girl has been trained to become a nurse's aid; another graduate plans to go to nursing school to become a registered nurse but, as of graduation, had not applied to any school.

Moving On

Arriving at Madison High School in September 1969, I departed forever in June of 1999. After thirty years I finally graduated with the class of 1999. Graduation in early June of 1970 was quite different from the almost flippant ceremony three decades later. In 1970 it was the culminating and most serious event of the year. The solemnity of the ceremony was in part reflected by the honor granted to a few selected girls to usher each guest to a specifically assigned seat. Each usher either purchased or had a beautiful, flowing gown made for the occasion. The school band ceremoniously played "Pomp and Circumstance" as the seniors, following days of after school marching practice, marched into the gymnasium. The ceremony that took place was dignified beginning with the invocation by the local Catholic priest and concluded by the benediction from a Protestant preacher representing one of the many denominations in the area. The graduating seniors filed out in solemn processional as the audience, remaining seated in their chairs, watched with joy and sorrow to see their now grown relatives move on toward the next stage in their lives. For many families, the graduating senior was the first in their family lineage to receive a high school diploma.

In the June 1999 commencement exercise, parents, relatives, and friends picked up programs from informally clad ushers at the door and grabbed a seat in the audience. A few men did wear jackets and ties; a number of women wore dresses. However, many men came in street clothes clad in blue jeans, casual-wear shirts, and even colorful T-shirts. Some women wore jeans as well. Many of the students in attendance wore their usual, informal school apparel. A brass quartet from neighboring Skowhegan, Madison's traditional football rival community, was hired to play the traditional "Pomp and Circumstance" since the school board, in its ultimate wisdom in budget cutting measures, decided to eliminate the position of band director.

Because of a relatively recent Supreme Court ruling prayer during such ceremonies has been forbidden. Church and state must remain separate. However, the state's independent Governor Angus King accepted the opportunity to give the commencement address. Although his speech was interrupted at the beginning by a drunken heckler, who was forcefully hauled out of the gymnasium by a police officer with the help of some other strong arms, the governor successfully connected with the entire crowd. He offered "a dozen things I wish somebody had told me when I was 18" combining humor, personal stories, and serious comments.

Throughout the ceremony it appeared that a restless, often inattentive audience was watching a television show to which they could not relate. Stodgy officials tried to carry out a traditional ceremony with the graduating class of 48 students clad in blue and white gowns. The students reluctantly sat through the rituals in which they were praised by the principal for their outstanding achievements in academics, athletics, and as model citizens.

However, just the day before the principal called a special faculty meeting because several seniors had made insulting comments to fellow classmates and underclassmen during the school's "final assembly" program. Over the years the faculty and administration had only taken mild steps to prevent such comments when seniors presented their class's history, its will, class gifts, and prophecy. This time official action had to be taken in response to parental complaints. Staff suggestions were made that ranged from public apology to removing students involved from the graduation exercise to taking away honors awarded and scholarships received. Apparently, the issue was resolved during a meeting between the principal and the students involved.

The audience seemed unable to sense the meaning of this ceremony. This was reflected when upon issuing diplomas, a boy, who had had confrontations with the school's administrators, slapped the principal on the buttocks.

In 1970 receiving a high school diploma was still considered a great accomplishment. At that time many students were first-time recipients of this honor in their families' history. In those days no further education was needed to get a well-paying job at the local paper mill. Today, just to even get a minimum wage job, it is necessary to have that certificate. For most students it is imperative to seek further education that translates into, at least, another two years at a technical or a community college.

Although the class president opened the evening ceremony with a typically sentimental speech, the program concluded with nontraditional remarks by the class valedictorian. This extraordinarily intelligent young lady from Starks was the daughter of two hippies who had escaped the urban sprawl of Connecticut. She was the student who postponed her acceptance to Wesleyan College to study martial arts intensely. I was delighted that at my graduation from Madison High School, Ayanna explicitly exposed the nature of public schools to prepare students for traditional careers in business and industry that uphold the capitalist tradition. I felt encouraged and honored as she lamented the reality that school generally does not encourage youths to become inquisitive, independent thinkers in search of life's meaning. In her address she said:

. . . I hope that each of us leaves here feeling freedom in our hearts. After all, this is the first time we truly have the choice to make our lives what we want. Since we entered school in kindergarten, we were expected to learn the same curriculum as every other student in the same manner. We were rarely encouraged to explore the world of ideas, to utilize our own experiences to gain wisdom, or to seek a path in life that may be different from the norm. Although we approached school and life individually, school has, in a way, limited our choices because we have never been expected to be truly independent thinkers. Nevertheless, we must take what knowledge and insights we have gained through school and grow from them as we advance through life.

Now that our high school years are over, it is completely our own choice to decide what each of us wants to do. Hopefully, each and every one of us will take whatever path we feel is right for us, socially and environmentally responsible, and makes each of us, and even others happy. By happiness I mean inner contentment. It is never too late, for that matter, to begin anew, to make a change that will bring fulfillment to each of our lives. There is never one path that is more acceptable than any other if it brings satisfaction.

All too often we have been conditioned by school, by society, by our family and friends to believe that everyone needs to follow a similar path.... Do not feel limited, because, I believe, there are no limits in this world. The limits that we imagine exist have only been conditioned in our minds by our culture.

I hope that each and every one of you does what makes you happy in your search for the truth. There will be countless challenges but commitment and perseverance have rewards. This, I believe, is the only way in which each of us will find contentment in our lives.... (Booth-Athenian, June 1999)

It is within this setting that I have observed and confronted for thirty years the role Madison High School has played in trying to accommodate the opposing forces of capitalist-economic domination and the impact and essence of democratic egalitarianism. To understand why I place great emphasis on the egalitarian imperative, the reader needs to comprehend some of the factors in my life that have contributed to my becoming a critical pedagogue. The subsequent snapshots from my life lay out my philosophic background to become a controversial teacher, a martyr as victim, as Helen Epstein would say, at Madison High School.

2

LEARNING TO ASK QUESTIONS AND SEEK ANSWERS

To understand my approach to teaching, as well as the conflict of values that I experienced while teaching at Madison High School, the reader should know a little about my own background and the factors that influenced me. My father, a German-Jewish refugee who became a college professor in my hometown of Brunswick, Maine, had a profound effect upon me especially in respect to the development of my values. In addition, my values were rooted in nineteenth century American transcendental philosophers, as well as other books I read while in high school. Since my father was a philosopher, whom I saw more as a visionary than a pragmatic, I tried to put into practice at the community level the ideals for humanity to which he strongly adhered.

My Father's Sensitivity toward Others

My parents were refugees from Hitler's Germany. In fact, on Crystal Night, 9 November 1938, my father was arrested and incarcerated at the

Nazi concentration camp at Dachau. Upon accompanying my father to the initial detention center in Munich, my mother encountered a kindhearted officer. With her persistence and his help she was able to secure the necessary documents for their departure to the United States. Since the Second World War would only begin nine months later, the Nazis still let some prisoners out if they were able to leave Germany immediately. Luckily my father had close friends in England and relatives in the United States. In January 1939 they boarded a plane for England and waited there for a year until their quota number to the United States had been reached. Since the age of three, I grew up in Brunswick, Maine, where my father first taught German and then his great love, philosophy, at Bowdoin College.

My father, Walter Solmitz, was a distinct figure in Brunswick, Maine. Anyhow, that is the way he appeared to me as a child growing up close to sixty years ago in this provincial Maine college community of about 8,000 people. He was a tall man, balding, with short black hair. His dark brown eyes reflected the wisdom of a sage, of one whose search for the truth was never ending. He also appeared different from the common man. During the warm months he rode a bicycle to the college. In winter he wore a black, great coat and a Basque beret as he walked to and from the college.

As an avid student of Plato's *Republic* and his ability to read and even write ancient Greek, he used the Socratic method with his students to challenge their thinking and bring them to deeper levels of understanding.

My father *lived* the motto, penned by the Greek philosopher Pindar: "become who you are." It suggests a never ending, lifelong search. It represents the noble goal of education itself: to propel humanity to new heights. It allows its adherents to find an inner peace. These concepts radiate appreciation for the great diversity that exists within humankind and the natural world. In turn my father instilled that same maxim in me. It has become not only the cornerstone of my own teaching career, but also the very core of my quest for truth. Whenever I struggled, for example, with mathematics, he would quote Nietzsche to me: "Was mich nicht umbringt, macht mich stärker." (What does not kill me, makes me stronger.)

As a child and teenager I felt intimidated by my father. I felt that he had very high expectations of me, expectations that I believed I would not be able to fulfill. He was eager that I have some of the classical background in which his own life was deeply rooted. I did not relish taking four years of high school Latin, going to his office at the college to conjugate verbs and decline nouns. Instead, I would have much preferred taking four years of French with a lively, exciting teacher, who had studied in France. My father was also determined that I learn math, a subject with which I had difficulty. I remember many a frustrating session in his smoke filled study at home or at his college office belaboring arithmetic and beginning algebra. While I was impatient just to get the answer, he wanted me to understand the concepts and the logic of mathematics. Even while he was a patient at a mental institution, he created and sent me little math books, the *If-Then* series.

My father was not the stereotypical college professor who associated largely with his colleagues and their families. He made it a point to reach out toward people of varied backgrounds. He was revered by the less educated people in the college community. Since he worked deep into the night at his office, the college night watchman would visit him on his rounds to talk personally with him. The janitors appreciated his friendliness and warmth. This was always evident as he would inevitably stop and chat with them, even when he and I were together. He reached out to the common laborers throughout the community. For example, on a hot sunny day, as a small crew from the town's highway department patched holes with tar in front of our home, he invited them into our home for coffee and cigarettes. I clearly recall, as a small child, riding on the cross bar of his bicycle making the six-mile round trip to a saltwater bay. He would regularly stop to chat with a clam digger in front of the little, tarpaper shack in which the man lived with his large family. There were other people we encountered on these bicycle trips, who lived in abject poverty, with whom he would stop and talk.

My father was always sensitive to the suffering of other people. On one occasion he saw me together with my neighbor throwing pebbles at a mentally disabled boy in our neighborhood. For this he promptly sent me to my room. He said he would return in half an hour. During that time I would have to think about and explain to him what I had done wrong. My father did not yell at me then or ever, nor did he even once spank me. Seeing the disappointment in his eyes toward me hurt. Having to explain to him why I picked upon a helpless person caused me to feel remorse.

While reading and then translating a report he had written in March 1939 in London following his incarceration at Dachau, I was deeply impressed by my father's acute insight into human behavior. At the same time, I was struck by his empathy for all of his fellow human beings. I was amazed that he could write with great feeling yet without anger about the suffering of others at the abusive hands of those who held power in the camps:

> During marching and especially at roll call the four rooms of the barrack came together. Immediately, in front of us stood the smallest from the neighboring rooms, the very young and the very old. One of these small people from the neighboring section could not go any further on the way to the roll call square. We supported him and massaged him as best as we could during roll call. Afterwards, two young men from our group, who always energetically seized the opportunity to help, brought him to the infirmary. He was not admitted and sent back to the barrack. For days he

had not been able to eat and the episodes of weakness occurred again and again. He was again brought back to the infirmary. Again he was kicked out. The capo in charge was a baker from Mainz, a powerful, huge man. He had a sly face, but also a humorous as well as an indifferent good-natured expression and a furiously brutal chin. (He was in the camp because his wife had denounced him). This capo could be quite pleasant and cheerful. However, this totally inconspicuous little man became the target of his scorn. The third time that he was brought back to the infirmary, he was literally kicked out with actual blows and kicks. He was brought back to the barrack and kicked out from there by the room leader. That evening money was distributed. Therefore, we had to stand in the cold after the evening roll call. We wanted to put this man in the lobby at least until our turn came. This would occur late since his name started with "S." Comrades brought him into the lobby. After a while the room leader noticed him and kicked him out again. He had to stand with us. He died during the following night. In view of these cases one can presume that the room leaders were given a quota by their higher officials demanding that a certain number of people die. Although this cannot be confirmed, it is not improbable. (Solmitz, 1939, 65)

From this quotation, among many others in this report, I gained a sense of urgency. As a social studies teacher, I achieved significant understanding as to how such events as the Nazi Holocaust came about that are particularly relevant to events evolving in our own so-called democratic society. It encouraged me to cause my students to become socially responsible and active citizens to uphold the principles of a democratic society. I learned that people who are unfulfilled in their life, unhappy in their personal relationships and their economic situation, and often angry, will take their frustration out on those who appear different from and weaker than they. The perpetrators feel ever safer as the government and the society at large sanction violence toward such people. Therefore, the crimes they commit become increasingly less secretive, more open, and more horrific. With such an understanding of human behavior in the following passage, my father intuitively predicted the atrocities that occurred in the early to mid-1940s in death camps like Auschwitz and Bergen-Belsen.

When we were brought by truck to Dachau, the truck ran out of gas [Dachau is only about 20 minutes from Munich where my father was arrested]. The young, smart aleck, SS officer, who drove the truck, got a can of gas from a nearby gas station and poured it into the tank. Next to him stood one of the repulsive men in civilian dress, smoking a cigarette. He was one of those who had been busily occupied with us during the night. The SS officer said to him, so that all could hear: "Stand back with your cigarette or else the whole caboodle will go up in flames. That wouldn't be a shame at all, but I can't take responsibility for it." I asked myself: "would it really be a pity? Would it really be a shame if this little heap of Jews would no longer exist? No! If that's the case, maybe it wouldn't be so bad if that SS officer, himself, were no longer either." If one begins to think in this way, that is, what would be a shame, what would not, then there is very little left that would truly be a shame. The National Socialists think that way. In regard to the Jews it would not be a shame. On the contrary, it would be their good fortune if there weren't anymore Jews left. They are bad luck! They are responsible for all the misfortunes in the world. They alone are the blight, the vermin that spoils everything. They must be destroyed. But why don't they exterminate us like rats and mice are exterminated? They could line us Jews up and shoot us? Why don't they do that? Why can't they take the responsibility? Is it the rest of humanity that prevents them from doing it? (Solmitz, 1939, 52)

My father also realized that Nazism represented the need for power and the compulsion to release hostility onto those who until this time were disadvantaged. Their anger, he wrote, "was in essence directed against capitalism and against the capitalists and their money" (Solmitz, 1939, 47). The government used this disparity between the rich, the capitalists, and the poor to target the Jews. My father even perceived that "if the capitalists had introduced at the right time possibilities for social reform, the present conditions in Germany would never have become possible" (Solmitz, 1939, 48).

As horrible as his experiences were in Germany at the hands of the Nazis during the 1930s, he never gave up his idealism for a world without war. While a student and teaching fellow at Harvard University during World War II, he prepared a "Declaration of Intention" for a world of lasting peace. He proposed a world court that would resolve problems through law and justice. He wrote:

> We want to achieve a state of affairs such that all conflicts between individual men or between groups of men or between groups and individuals are settled by means of negotiations, and if this cannot be done, by arbitration, and if this cannot be done by the appeal to and the decision of an independent court. Such an independent court is to have at its disposal the means to enforce its decisions, if necessary, by sanctions or armed force. Thus, we want to prevent wars and to replace them by the methods of law and justice.

In order to bring such a society about all people need "to work with passion and patience towards the lawful achievement of a social and economic order within which the happiness and wealth of the one is never acquired through the aggression and want of the other."

Therefore, he promoted a society in which everybody would live by a decent minimum standard. Everybody would be provided with sufficient medical care regardless as to whether they were employed or not. However, for the common good, legal provisions need to be made that require those able to work but unwilling to do so be gainfully employed. Distribution of goods must be equal. Under no circumstances may a surplus of food in one area be thrown into the sea while people in another part of the world are going hungry.

In order for such a society to exist, people must be trustworthy and capable of trusting other trustworthy people. "Mutual trust is the necessary condition for every covenant and lawful order. Mutual trust and lawful order are to protect from the uncanny the peace in which we want to work out and live and enjoy our life." As a parent and educator my father believed that he, and all people who hold similar views, must educate to foster trustworthiness.

He continued to model his ideals in a mildly politically active manner. During the mid-1950s he promoted Adlai Stevenson's bid for the U.S. presidency against incumbent General Dwight D. Eisenhower. Locally, at the annual March town meeting in Brunswick, he spoke up in favor of a salary increase for poorly paid public-school teachers.

My Father's Influence upon Me: I Become a Social Activist

It was my father's influence that caused me, since my early childhood, to become an advocate for the poor and abused people in our society. During the Vietnam War, it was not enough for me to be philosophically against it, I felt I had to take a strong stand against it by declaring myself a conscientious objector. I also developed a lasting commitment to promote greater understanding between people of different ethnic and religious backgrounds, whose cultures and nationalities were foreign, and those whose lifestyles and sexual orientations digressed from mainstream American society.

During my high school years four authors had a significant influence on me: Ralph Waldo Emerson, Henry David Thoreau, Mahatma Gandhi, and Fydor Dostoyevsky. Emerson taught me to become self-reliant. His famous dictate: "Trust thyself, every heart vibrates to that iron string" along with his saying "whoso would be a man must be a nonconformist" suggested that I must stand up for the principles in which I believed. I certainly was encouraged by his quip: "To be great is to be misunderstood." Therefore, it became a little easier when I met defeat with some students and was frequently devalued by my administrators at Madison High School to try to pass these off as being misunderstood. Of course, I was impressed by Henry David Thoreau, who stood up for his beliefs as reflected in his essay "On Civil Disobedience." "For it matters not," he wrote in that essay, " how small the beginning may seem to be, what is once well done, is done forever." If I had not often reminded myself of this dictum, I doubt I would have been able to survive the many years I did at Madison High.

Thoreau's desire to "live deep and to suck out all the marrow of life" appealed to my youthful spirit. I really wanted to experience what life had to offer and in Thoreau's words: "If it proved to be mean, why then to get the whole and genuine meanness of it, and publish its meanness to the world, or if it were sublime, to know it by experience, and be able to give a true account of it in my next excursion." I hoped to get to know people from different cultures and to explore them. At the same time, I tried to develop the courage to bring about positive changes in the world. I wanted each and every one of us to be able to appreciate each other regardless of our cultural, ethnic, and racial backgrounds. In addition, I also wanted to try to preserve the natural environment.

As a high school junior I initiated the creation of "The Political Discussion Group," a rather formidable title for an informal group that met regularly to discuss a variety of world issues. Our first discussion was: "Should Red China be admitted to the United Nations?" Frequently, we invited foreign students who were studying at Bowdoin College just a block from the high school. With a Swede we discussed the advantages and disadvantages of socialism. A student from Kenya, who also had an Asian Indian background, explored the impact of British culture on his country. A white student from South Africa exposed us to the system of apartheid in his nation. Together with our advisor, a history teacher at the school, we embarked upon a discussion of freedom versus responsibility with regards to the democratic framework of this country.

Therefore, it was not out of character as a high school senior that I wrote a letter to the town's newspaper *The Brunswick Record* in January of 1961.

> Brunswick is said to have the widest main street in the State of Maine. There are no more streetcars running down the middle of our Maine Street. There is only a long black strip of asphalt with yellow lines painted on it. Why don't we have a green isle of grass in place of that ugly black strip, an isle of rich green lawn with flowering shrubbery and beautiful trees. Imagine how much more beautiful our Maine street would look.
>
> Soon a new highway will be completed which will lessen traffic on Maine Street. After the new sewer pipes are finished being laid this year, the state will repave Maine Street. During this period of construction, why not put in a green center isle which will brighten up our town and make it even more pleasant. (*Brunswick Record*, 8 January 1961)

Several traffic islands were constructed during the following year. In June of 1962, I approached the town's Board of Selectmen:

> Town selectmen went along with their "expert" on petunias Monday night.
> They voted unanimously to authorize the planting of petunias in one of the traffic islands along Maine Street. The cost will be approximately $7.50, since the work will be done free of charge.

Solmitz claimed that people would show far more respect for the flowers than they now do for grass. "The grass all but disappeared," selectman Charles Rogers explained. "I believe we should go along with the suggestion to plant petunias. People won't walk all over them. They'll think twice before they'll step on a petunia."

The argument appeared sound. The board voted unanimously to furnish 10 boxes of petunias for Solmitz to plant. (*Portland Press Herald*, 6 June 1962)

As I was to be away during the summer, I approached the local fire department requesting that they water the petunias. They agreed to take on the task, purchased a special nozzle for the fire hose, and around nine in the evening Tank Engine #1 drove out of the fire station to the traffic island. A fire fighter diligently watered the flowers. As I write this 37 years later, petunias are still planted annually on this island.

I had dreams of returning to my hometown to plant flowers in the town park bordering the center of town. I felt that, like an artist creating colorful collages with flowers, the people's spirits, who came to the downtown area, would be uplifted. In that sense I reflected the ideals of Thoreau who had a deep appreciation for nature and felt the beneficial effects of nature by living in harmony with it.

As I read more about Thoreau as well as Gandhi's autobiography, I discovered that Gandhi got his idea of nonviolent resistance from Thoreau. Gandhi's gentleness and his courageous ability to stand up for principles impressed me deeply. I recall an incident from his autobiography that occurred in Durban, South Africa. Not only, as an Indian lawyer was he referred to with humiliation as a "coolie barrister," but also he was forced to take off his turban in court because if he did not wear it, he would be insulted. By wearing a hat he felt he would avoid insult and unpleasant controversy. When he wrote to the press about the incident in defense of wearing the turban in court, he gained recognition both in the form of criticism as well as praise.

Although Thoreau and Emerson influenced me, Roskolnikov in Dostoyevsky's *Crime and Punishment* was an inspiration. He was distressed by the vast amount of suffering in his country. Knowing a greedy and wealthy pawnbroker, he murdered her so that with her money he could devote himself to serve humanity. "Hundreds of thousands, perhaps, might be set on the right path, dozens of families saved from destitution, from their own ruin, from vice, from the lack hospitals, and all with her money," as he put it (Dostoyevsky, 1950, 67). Later Raskolnikov noted that all men of greatness, i.e., Lycurgus, Solon, Mohammed, Napoleon, and others, transgressed the law. There are two categories of men, "the first are men conservative in temperament and law abiding; they live under control and love to be controlled.

The second category all transgress the law; they are destroyers or disposed to destruction according to their capacities. The crimes of these men are, of course, relative and varied; for the most part they seek the destruction of the present for the sake of the better" (Dostoyevsky, 1950, 255).

To save the destitute, though, I did not find it necessary to commit murder. Rather as a Bowdoin College senior, in the fall of 1964 I returned to my high school to embark on what today would be termed a community service project. This was the time when President Lyndon Johnson's war on poverty was well underway. Michael Harringtron's book *The Other America* had become mandatory reading for socially conscious students.

Having befriended children from the town's most blighted poverty pocket while in elementary school, I was very much aware of what poverty was about. I recall being surprised, upon visiting one of my friends, that the floor of his "home" was dirt. Many of these families lived in tiny, one-room shacks that had no running water. I wanted to get college and high school students with the support of well-to-do merchants in the community to work together with low-income folk to winterize their homes. By doing so, I hoped to generate greater awareness of poverty. To alleviate these dismal conditions, it would, I believed, be necessary for the different socioeconomic groups in the community to work together. Full of idealism, I believed that this project would be the cornerstone by which the community could demonstrate that townspeople could handle, without federal help, one of the most pressing aspects of poverty. It could be conducted not as a charity but in the spirit of neighbors helping each other. When the community understands the reasons for poverty, they would become more active in seeking means to abate it. Knowing that the American Friends Service Committee had conducted similar projects throughout the nation, it seemed relevant to seek their support in an advisory category.

However, from where would I gain initial support for a Community Work Day? How would I enlist the aid of merchants to supply materials free of cost and organizations and individuals to contribute funds? I turned toward the newly formed chapter of "Turn Toward Peace." As a college student I was one of the founders of this local chapter. By 1964 this national organization had already brought together more than thirty national peace, labor, religious, veterans, and public affairs organizations "who seek to build major public support throughout the country for a disarmed world under law, safe for free societies and democratic values" (Turn Toward Peace brochure). Since the members of this local branch consisted of influential and concerned citizens in the community, it seemed the support for an anti-poverty project would be found here. The membership included the liberal editor of the local newspaper, a prominent local merchant in the oil and lumber business, a politically active Unitarian minister, and a college professor who was a strident peace activist. Initially, a steering committee was formed that consisted of the president of the Bowdoin College Student Council, an exchange student from Morehouse College, several other college students, various high school students, and members of the peace organization.

Following the donation of materials, i.e., paint, lumber, and plastic, and financial support from local businesses and organizations, as well as the donated use of trucks for the day, student and adult teams visited families. They explained the project and sought their participation as well as learned what needed to be done. A local carpenter offered his service as advisor to the construction type projects. One of those tasks was to build and install an outhouse door. Other less complicated projects included installation of plastic storm windows, painting indoors, and outside.

Finally, the Saturday in mid-November arrived when 60 volunteers, half of whom were Bowdoin College students and the other thirty were Brunswick High School students, came together to renovate eight homes. Members of the participating families, including young children and the students worked together.

At the first home whose owner was unemployable because of illness, students painted the walls, the woodwork, and the ceilings of two bedrooms. They corrected draftiness, cleaned up, and painted a back wall, and repaired the front porch. At the second house, occupied by a fatherless family, they whitewashed a kitchen and the only bedroom. In another single-parent home, four children helped four students paint the living room. At a fourth home, the students found a living room thoroughly cleaned and emptied of furniture. Wall decorations had also been removed so that the students could get to work at painting. At the fifth house, occupied by a large family, whose father had just returned from a long hospital stay due to tuberculosis, the students completely painted the outside of the house and removed two junked auto carcasses. Two elderly residents of another home did advance preparations and brought out a radio to entertain the young workers as they painted the walls and floor, and installed plastic storm windows and installed a new outhouse door built by the carpenter who was advising the project. Similar improvements took place at the seventh house. The owner, who worked along with the students, promised to finish the cleanup himself. At the eighth house, the volunteers repaired the roof, put up plastic storm windows, painted the kitchen, and cleaned up the yard. Here children of the family assisted the workers by washing windows.

At the spaghetti supper, prepared by adults, plans were being made to continue the effort that had just begun. People from the low-income neighborhoods were actively involved on the planning committee. Bordering the town's most obvious poverty pocket was a large tract of land, abandoned for many years, the Town Commons. It was decided to invite an American

Friends Service Committee (AFSC) summer project to build a playground on a five-acre corner of this wooded land for the children from this neighborhood. A group of about twenty high school students from all over the United States and Canada plus counselors converged onto this section of Brunswick. Children from the area helped the AFSC volunteers clear brush, build picnic tables, a basketball court, and playground equipment. They cleared trails through the woods and built fireplaces to accompany the picnic tables. The AFSC workers created a summer program for the children with whom they did arts and crafts and read stories. An editorial in the *Brunswick Record* of 20 July 1965, highlighted the success of this venture and raised important questions for the future. It made it very clear that teenagers were capable of doing great works together in an organized, thoughtful, and harmonious manner.

> There were many reasons why the project could have failed. None of the 20 young persons who came to Brunswick had ever been here before, none of them had ever met each other before. Nor had they met their leaders. None of these people is over 22. None under 16; most are in the 18 to 20 year bracket. None of them is experienced in the ways of the world, and much less in the professional techniques which many might insist their project demands. And, as if inexperience and unfamiliarity were not enough, their organization is run by consensus of their group opinion. This means not one action can be taken until it is fully discussed before the entire body approves it. And this with teenagers! [Visitors who enter a small building near the Common] will see preschool children being read to, being made enthusiastic about the act of learning, being encouraged, being shown, being taken to places they have never before visited. The young persons doing the reading and showing and teaching are AFSC teenagers, but they are doing what few adults in the community have had the time or inclination to do before.

The article concluded that the work that had begun must be continued. Brunswick High School students who volunteered for the summer project indicated they would continue their efforts in the fall. However, the same editorial noted that "they need leadership, organization, and, most of all the support from the town, the same sort of support which has been given to the AFSC project, and more." The article concluded by stating: "the people of Brunswick have been shown what it takes to change a community. Now they must keep up the good work."

I left Brunswick before the AFSC project had begun to teach in Switzerland. After two years of teaching at a progressive boarding school in the heart of the Swiss Alps, I returned to Brunswick to be a community worker for a federally funded "Community Action Agency" (CAP) that had evolved from the anti-poverty project I had started three years earlier.

In the meantime the Town Commons project had fallen to disrepair. It had been severely vandalized and never rebuilt. The community's recreation department never fulfilled its promise to carry on the work that had been started there.

Instead, the Brunswick Area Coordinating Committee was formed under the leadership of a local psychologist and others who had been involved with the AFSC summer project. This committee became the catalyst to prepare a lengthy application to the Office of Economic Opportunity for federal funds to establish a CAP agency. However, no low-income families were members of this committee. Only upon receipt of the grant were low-income people contacted to try to get them actively involved. This federal agency, instead of focusing upon one community, handled eight towns in the region.

Although the project appeared to begin with the philosophy that the poor and the well-to-do work together to improve the living conditions and opportunities for low-income families, the concept was eventually lost. In February 1968 I resigned because I lamented the lack of a sense of community, which I felt would be the eventual demise of the project. Sadly, my idealistic hope that the community would resolve the war on poverty without turning to a federal agency to do the work for them was not to be realized. For example, the president of the organization, who represented low-income families, became merely a figure head. The first executive director, a Maine native, was fired for one from the Midwest who mistakenly believed that Saul Alinsky's approach to organize the poor against the rich would succeed in small Maine communities. Within a year a young bureaucrat took the helm. The center of operation moved to a neighboring town. The position of community worker, a job held largely by low-income individuals, was soon eliminated for a more efficient but less personal bureaucratic operation. The agency essentially wrote grants to seek available federal funding, i.e., for low-income housing. The employees from amongst the "poor" were replaced by college educated professionals since they could handle the vast amounts of paper work, grant writing, and finances required by the agency.

This Community Action Program grew through a variety of transformations. At the end of the twentieth century it had become the Coastal Economic Development Center (CED). It now serves seven counties. It still "helps low-income families and individuals by providing support and new opportunities necessary for their self-sufficiency and well being. Each year our agency helps over 11,000 individuals in the mid-coast area by providing affordable housing, fuel assistance, nutritional assistance, Head Start, job training, and housing repair. We also have a successful youth community service program which allows us to assist many in the community using the volunteer services of the area youth" (letter from the executive director,

1994). On the board of directors, consisting largely of professional people, there are few token representatives of low-income families.

It was during these years that I began to realize when "good" ideas become institutionalized they lose their admirable spirit. Since institutionalization requires standardization, bureaucratization, and regulation, the natural flow that allows all sorts of people from different economic classes to spontaneously work together for the common good is lost. As I became a teacher I carried this lesson with me. I realized that, if public schools were to work effectively, students, teachers, and administrators must work as partners for the common good. Since this appeared unrealistic, at least I could try to create an environment in my classroom in which students and teachers worked together. Just as I had listened to and learned from the low-income families with whom I had worked about community, I realized that I had a lot to learn from my students. With such an attitude I believed that together we would reach new horizons. Of course, as the reader will discover, it took thirty years of practice and patience intertwined with frustration to pursue this ideal with gradual success.

Political Activism: Crusading for World Peace

My interest in international relations and different cultures motivated me to join the International Club at college. By working together with the Brunswick Area Peace Center, we were able to bring in 1965 Arthur Waskow as a guest lecturer. A Research Fellow at the Institute for Policy Studies, he elaborated upon his just completed book *From Race Riot to Sit-In: 1919 and the 1960s*. It provided a fascinating comparison between the riots of 1919, which were effectively crushed by the government, and the race riots of the 1960s. In exploring the riots of the 1960s, Waskow focused on the underlying nonviolent philosophy of the protest movement, i.e., the boycotts, the marches, and the sit-ins. He wanted to demonstrate that racial justice could be established without a national disaster taking place.

Also, together with the Brunswick Area Peace Center the International Club was one of the sponsors of a lecture at the college by the well-known physicist, Dr. Linus Pauling. In 1960 he received the Nobel Peace Prize for his persistent struggle to generate public awareness of the genetic dangers of nuclear fallout.

With the war in Vietnam escalating, I tried to find out more why the United States became involved. The more I read up on the war in newspapers and periodicals, the more I became convinced of its immorality. As a college student and active member of Turn Toward Peace, I helped draft a petition to President Lyndon Johnson for which I gathered many signatures. It was printed as a nearly full-page advertisement in the local newspaper. Quoting from a policy speech that President Johnson had made at Johns Hopkins University in April 1965, we expressed support for "his fine words." We urged him "in earnest hope that you will try to turn this nation's course from cruelty to compassion, from destruction to healing, from retaliation to negotiation, from war to peace" (*Brunswick Record*, 5 May 1965).

As I had graduated from college, not knowing what I would be doing in life, but all too well aware that chances of being drafted into that war were unacceptable to me, I sought employment at the progressive, international school, the Ecole d'Humanite, in Switzerland, the German/Swiss equivalent of A.S. Neill's Summerhill. My father had attended this school in the early 1920s near Heidelberg, Germany. It was founded about 1910 by the philosopher and theologian Paulus Geheeb as the Odenwald Schule. During the Second World War the school fled Nazi rule for Switzerland. I was accepted to teach a few American high school students American history so that they could pass the SATs and enter an American college. For Paulus Geheeb's 80th birthday, my father wrote numerous letters urging the Nobel Committee to nominate him for their annual peace award.

Paulus Geheeb's philosophy of the school was based upon a sense of cooperation among people, a need to seek harmony with people of all sorts of different ethnic, racial, and cultural backgrounds, and with nature itself. He worked to achieve an all-sided, balanced development of the human personality.

Geheeb's interests in theology and philosophy drew him into a lifelong friendship with the Indian philosopher, educator, playwright, and poet Rabindranath Tagore. Both Geheeb and Tagore believed that education must allow the child to develop in the context of nature. Just as there is harmony in nature, there must be harmony within the child's inner nature. Both taught that the intellect should be developed along with the emotions and the will. All of these aspects should grow harmoniously through many kinds of activities. Therefore, at the Odenwald Schule and later at the Ecole d'Humanite the arts were equally as important as the study of mathematics and science.

Much attention was paid to the outdoors. Each day began with the ringing of a gong when all students and staff were required to take an ice cold shower. Throughout the spring, summer, and fall students tended the school's gardens. During both the spring and fall all students and staff participated in weeklong hikes in the Swiss Alps. They brought a week's supply of food with them that they communally prepared daily. Usually, they slept in farmers' hay barns. Only on occasion did they spend a night at a youth hostel. In the winter all took part in day hikes on cross-country skis.

At Christmas time the students would trek through the snow into the forest to decorate a fir tree with natural berries and other foods for the birds to eat. A little celebration would be held at that time.

Geheeb challenged the entire, rigid German education system. This challenge ranged from his firm belief in co-education, nearly considered a crime in Germany at that time, to awaken and develop a sense of responsibility in his children. To this end, he replaced the inflexible German syllabus of German public schools allowing each student to study what he liked. Girls could study carpentry, boys dressmaking if they so desired.

He believed each student would learn to develop his or her own personality that is always inherently good.

Actual courses were offered. However, these were intense five-week classes. A student might simultaneously study French, math, and literature during one five-week term. During the following period the same students could drop literature and French and study science and English. Then during the following session, the student could return to math or take another subject. Students were taught how to learn and think independently, do research using the school's extensive library, and form their own opinions. Academic courses were offered in the morning, the arts were studied in the afternoon. Drawing, painting, sculpture, pottery, bookbinding, dance, and music were all part of the curriculum. The school had its own orchestra, formed exclusively by the students.

Attendance at classes was never compulsory. Students, however, were made to feel it was a privilege to attend. Absenteeism was therefore rare. School's rules, and all decisions affecting the school, major and minor, were made at the *Schulgemeinde*. This school gathering was presided over by Geheeb and included all students and all teachers. It met once weekly. Each member of the *Schulgmeinde* had one vote no matter whether it was Geheeb or the youngest child in Kindergarten. It voted on all issues that required a decision and even allotted punishments. To avoid vengeance and to develop responsibility of justice, those students who were most friendly with the culprit proposed punishments.

The Ecole d'Humanite was truly a school for humanity. It was an international school with children representing many different countries where the guiding philosophy abhorred violence, intolerance, and arrogance. When I taught at the school, there were several students from India, many from Europe, and some from the United States. The wife of the school's director at that time was an American who was able to draw students of means to this international boarding school. In fact she operated an international camp in Freedom, New Hampshire. Geheeb also had become personally acquainted with Mahatma Gandhi. His daughter, Indira, and her two children attended his school in Switzerland.

If my father was any example of the graduates of Paulus Geheeb's School, he certainly reflected Geheeb's ideals throughout his life. He was a gentle man, a lover of nature, concerned about the poor, an ardent advocate for world peace, and a philosopher in the Socratic tradition.

In order to teach at the Ecole'd'Humanite I needed a waiver from my military status because the draft for soldiers to fight in the Vietnam War had been initiated. I asked Maine's Senator Edmund Muskie to write to my draft board in support of my request to teach at this school. Being granted the necessary waiver toward the end of the summer of 1965, I headed for Switzerland. Teaching at the Ecole d'Humanite certainly bolstered my decision to become a conscientious objector to war.

My parents never spoke to me about their experiences in Germany at the hands of the Nazis before the onset of the Second World War. I never did ask about their lives in Germany. Subconsciously, I must have felt that they had experienced something terrible. For instance, often on Sunday mornings my father and I walked the mile downtown to pick up the Sunday New York Times at Morton's newsstand. One bright Sunday, as we were walking home, a convoy of army tanks passed us by. I recall being frightened. I had no idea why these threatening machines were moving past. My father looked at me and clearly said that they were going to the local armory. Once when I was a teenager he took me to see a documentary film on the Holocaust being shown at the local movie theater. We both watched in silence; we never talked about it. His pain was visible but unspoken. In August of 1962 he took his own life. Having in recent years worked with veterans from the Vietnam War, it has become obvious to me that he demonstrated many of the symptoms of those who suffered from posttraumatic stress disorder.

I officially applied for the status of conscientious objector in early 1967. I was influenced by the legacy of Paul Geheeb, his impact upon my father, and therefore onto me. Thoreau, Emerson, Dostoyevsky, Gandhi and later William James, author of The Will to Believe, helped me realize the need to have faith in searching for the truth in approaching the difficult and often unknown ways of life. Although one of the stipulations for applying for the status of conscientious objector at that time was belief in a Supreme Being, the influence of these people comes through clearly in my application. I wrote:

> God exists often hidden in every living person as "the Inner Light." The Deistic view that god created the world and has left it up to mankind to make of it what he can has been expressed by Thomas Jefferson, third president of the United States. Ralph Waldo Emerson, also, spoke similarly in that each person must rely upon his strengths to stand upright for what the inner voice has bade him to seek: justice, peace, righteousness. "Nothing

can bring you peace but the triumph of principles," wrote Emerson in his essay "Self Reliance." Each must rely upon himself to "become," in the words of Pindar, "what he is!" This means that each person must develop his individuality. Each must continuously strive to develop his own abilities (mechanic, teacher, architect, musician, artist, doctor, etc.) to his fullest. Sometimes his artistic talents are herein included. A person must learn to fulfill these strengths as playing a musical instrument, painting, partaking in a non-competitive sport, caring for plants and many others, because he, spiritually inspired, will become a more complete and sensitive individual. Furthermore, by means of these experiences, his ability to love, the highest capability man has above animals, becomes greater. Love is to help another "become what he is!" As he develops this ability, he will be able to help others in the worst of distress. I further believe that love includes everybody's equal right to live and develop his abilities. Nobody has the right to end by his own hand the life of another. Man will thus become better capable of performing his duties to God and society.

The rearing of children in the home, and ideally at school, a difficult question which is much discussed, shall help to clarify my opposition to the use of force between individual persons on account of personal reasons and prejudices. Professor Rudolph Dreikurs in his book *Children: The Challenge* spoke of democracy not autocracy in the family. The parent by treating the child with love and rationality should try to win its cooperation and should allow it to learn from its own experiences. Corporal punishment should under no circumstances be used. This method is not force; it is careful guidance with foresight on the part of the parents. It is my belief that the child should have the opportunity to discover his own way in life and develop social and human duties which are to respect the equal rights of each person, the individuality, and above all the Supreme Being which exists however hidden in every human being.

The draft board never officially acted on my status as conscientious objector. During the two years I taught at the Ecole d'Humanite I met and married a fellow teacher, Esther Bircher. Upon returning to the United States during the summer of 1967 our first son was born. Esther was both a talented artist and pianist who warmly cultivated the arts with small children while exploring literature through pantomime and other forms of movement. She came from a family that was devoted to human fulfillment and improved interpersonal and international relations through natural foods and good health

By the time I taught at the Ecole d'Humanite it had lost its pioneer spirit. Like so many private schools in order to survive it had become more of a conventional international school. However, my experience at this school influenced my teaching philosophy. I was impressed by the mutual respect that existed between staff and students as it fostered appreciation for one another and a sense of community. Emphasis upon the arts that ranged from a variety of studio projects to integration in both the humanities and science courses appeared to make them more meaningful and enjoyable. Students and teachers were actively involved in music, dance, and theater discovering new ways of self-expression. The biannual hikes that lasted an average of five days through the Swiss Alps were an incredible bonding experience for teachers and students as well as a breathtaking experience of nature. All of these events seemed to help students discover their path in life that would bring fulfillment. Therefore, as an educator for more than a-third of a century, I have introduced students to all sorts of different experiences and encouraged them to make their own in search of life's meaning. These included meeting all sorts of people representing a wide variety of viewpoints in the classroom or on field trips. Students have been exposed to world literature and film. They have learned many different forms of self-expression such as writing prose and poetry, movement and dance, painting and sculpture, and different genres of music.

Living Up to My Father's Expectations

I like to remember my father as a philosopher and as a great teacher. He did not preach, and he did not "just lecture." Often by using stories and even fairy tales, he tried to open the minds of his students onto a never-ending search for answers to questions that they, sometimes with his help, would raise. One such example was a morning talk he delivered in December of 1961 at the Bowdoin College chapel.

He titled it "The Frog King" based upon a fairy tale by that name. Through the metaphor of Iron Henry, who had iron bands placed around his heart after his master was changed into a frog, my father wanted his listeners to understand the impact of oppression and the concept of freedom. In the same vein, he was asking his audience to look beyond the superficial appearance of people, to search for and appreciate the humanity in each. It is this ability to search, to allow ourselves to make new realizations, to discard those that we found to be inappropriate that lead us to new appreciation and understanding, to self-realization, self-confidence, and thus to freedom itself.

My father's pedagogical approach was effective. The fairy tale became a nonthreatening way for him to cause his students to gain new insights. They could not rely for answers on familiar conventions. Rather they were encouraged to use their imagination, to be creative, in order to seek fresh insight and gain new understanding.

Although my father experienced the horrors of the Nazi regime, he was both a philosopher and an idealist. He was a holistic thinker who in contrast to the dominant theory of positivism was able to free himself from dogma and opinions to actively search for truth and justice. According to the Pennsylvania State Universities education professor, Henry Giroux, positivism denies the reality that knowledge is biased by the values of the status quo. Because it is based upon objective, experimental, and statistical testing called research, in reality it is based upon the normative criteria established by scholars in their specific field of study. According to Giroux, "the notion that theory, facts, and inquiry can be objectively determined and used falls prey to a set of values that are both conservative and mystifying in their political orientation" (Giroux, 1997, 12). Such a theory is void of a holistic outlook that embraces a comprehensive view of humankind and its ability to nurture humanity. Rather it is caught up with the moment, that truth can only be verified by the scientific, in other words, the empirical, tradition. In fact, Giroux contends "since there is no room for human vision in this perspective, historical consciousness is stripped of its crucial function and progress is limited to terms acceptable to the status quo" (Giroux, 1997, 13). In today's terminology, my father would be considered a postmodern thinker because he never objectified the world in search for knowledge and control. Instead, he developed his insights by acting upon his beliefs and observing the consequences. He was always open to new ways of looking and perceiving. His struggle was to advance the cause of humanity in a generally chaotic, insensitive, and violent world.

With a sense of urgency and the zeal of a missionary, I felt I had to put into practice the ideals for which he strove. Therefore, as an educator, over the years, I have incorporated my commitment to social activism within my teaching. More than anything I wanted to foster among my students a sense of and commitment to humanity. Recalling feelings of intimidation and rebelliousness toward my father's high expectations of me, I knew that I could not impose my views on others. I could not be frustrated and angry if my students didn't immediately buy into my wisdom. I had to learn to listen to them and learn from them. In this way we could develop a partnership to search for life's meaning together.

I found myself facing a dilemma. How could I balance traditional expectations of excellence that I wanted to receive from students with the debilitating societal trend toward instantaneous gratification and sensual titillation, accompanied by a growing sense of alienation and despair among many youths? I have been trying to face this dilemma on the one hand by going with the flow of the class while at the same time demanding thorough in-depth work from my students. By running the class democratically, I encountered traditional control problems yet, I was empowering at least some students on their paths to finding a niche in life that was spiritually fulfilling to them. I had to learn not to take personally their misbehaviors in my classroom.

Subsequently, we will examine the reasons for and the development of universal public education in the United States. As we see schools catering to the needs of business and industry since the First Industrial Revolution, we will observe how the democratic imperative has lost balance with capitalist domination. With the rapid growth of the corporate elite and transnational corporate expansion, the concept of an egalitarian society of, by, and for the people appears to be fading.

3

PURPOSES OF
AMERICAN PUBLIC EDUCATION:
THE HISTORICAL CONFLICT BETWEEN
DEMOCRATIC PEDAGOGY AND CAPITALIST
DOMINATION IN PUBLIC EDUCATION

Democracy's Success Requires
Universal Public Education

Thomas Jefferson's famous words in the Declaration of Independence that "all men are created equal" suggest that democracy's success relies upon an educated citizenry. This concept is further supported when he wrote: "To secure these rights [life, liberty, and the pursuit of happiness], Governments are instituted among Men, deriving their just powers from the consent of the governed; That whenever any Form of government becomes destructive of these ends it is the Right of the People to alter or abolish it, and to institute new Government, laying its foundation on such principles and organizing its powers in such form, as to them shall seem most likely to effect their Safety and Happiness." Therefore, if a people wants such rights as Jefferson suggested, they must not only be willing to establish their own government, but also must have the knowledge and skills by which to create such a government. Furthermore, they have to be able to develop the safeguards by which to make sure that the people remained involved so that their rights are not eroded. This demands not only the ability to read and write, but also to gain insight by studying, understanding, interpreting, and dialoguing about historical events and literary works.

Jefferson believed in the rule by wise people. This "educated aristocracy" was necessary to nurture and maintain the ideal of democracy. In 1779, he proposed a "Bill for the More General Diffusion of Knowledge." However, free education was for only three years and just for all nonslave children. Frequently, only those who demonstrated the most talent were selected at taxpayers' expense to attend regional grammar schools. The bill mandated that all children be fluent in reading, writing, and arithmetic. They would receive a classic education in Greek and Roman history as well as learn about English and American history.

Jefferson believed that language, the ability to read, write, and speak effectively were the basic tools of the intelligent citizen. He believed in and actively promoted a free press by which citizens would be able to make up their minds based on opposing points of view expressed in newspapers and judge politicians by "arraigning them at the tribunal of public opinion" (Lee, 1961, 17). He also believed in a person's natural ability to reason and therefore arrive at correct political decisions. Furthermore, only a free press could bring about reform peacefully that would otherwise happen by revolution.

As much as Jefferson believed in an educated citizenry, he particularly lacked faith in the ordinary citizens. Since he seemed to fear that the citizens may not know exactly what a correct political decision might be, he advocated censorship of political texts at the University of Virginia. In chapter VI the reader will observe that censorship remains alive and well in our little high school in Madison, Maine.

Jefferson, as both a philosopher and a pragmatic exponent of the American Revolution, appeared cautious in his vision for the education of youths. He believed that youths needed to be taught to become good citizens. Through the process of academic selection, the ideal citizen, the political leader would evolve as a member of an "educated aristocracy." That notion still seems to resonate today. Today, though, the politician generally belongs and adheres to the wealthy, corporate elite rather than to an "educated aristocracy." The concept of the ideal citizen seems to have become replaced by the notion of the corrupt, all-powerful politician.

Thirty-eight years later, while serving on the Massachusetts Board of Education, Horace Mann took a much broader view of universal education. He possessed a great deal more faith in the average citizen than did Jefferson.

Mann believed that in order to achieve social and political stability, all citizens must accept a common set of political values. This could only be accomplished if all children attended the same type of school, namely the common school. No matter whether they were rich or poor, or what their religious or cultural backgrounds might be, all children would receive the same common education. Thus, Mann's primary goal for education was to create a sense of social harmony out of the diverse and often conflicting cultural traditions in this country.

Mann's concept of universal education meant that public schools must be of equal quality to the best private schools. He saw the public school as the "great equalizer" of human conditions, "balance wheel of the social machinery" and the "creator of wealth undreamed of" (Cremin, 1957, 6). He imagined that as the result of a common education, poverty would disappear. The knowledge provided and equal opportunity offered meant that new possibilities to create material wealth would arise. With the abolition of poverty, he believed, the age-old conflict between social classes would disappear, and so crime would decline sharply as well. Such moral vices as "intemperance, cupidity, licentiousness, violence, and fraud" (Cremin, 1957, 9) would diminish.

As a strong believer in a democratic society, Mann argued for universal, public education. In his Twelfth Annual Report (1848) he emphasized that a republican form of government cannot exist without an intelligent citizenry. Without universal education the result could easily be "the despotism of a few succeeded by universal anarchy, and anarchy by despotism, with no change but from bad to worse" (Cremin, 1957, 90). He also noted in the same report that "in a republican government, legislators are a mirror reflecting the moral countenance of their constituents. And hence it is that the establishment of a republican government, without well-appointed and efficient means for the universal education of the people, is the most rash and foolhardy experiment ever tried by man" (Cremin, 1957, 90).

As idealistic as Mann appeared to be in the accomplishments of public education, as a pedagogue he was more realistic. He realized that children cannot be forced to learn. Rather their desire and excitement for learning must be stimulated, for instance, by reading stories that are interesting to them. He suggested, too, that students learn more rapidly if they focus on words before they are taught letters. In his Second Annual Report as Massachusetts Commissioner of Education he wrote, "To learn the words, signifying objects, qualities, actions, with which the child is familiar, turns his attention to those objects, if present, or revives the idea of them, if absent, and thus they may be made the source of great interest and pleasure" (Cremin, 1957, 39).

Almost as in the ancient Greek tradition, Mann added both physiology and vocal music to the academic curriculum. He realized the benefits of health education affected the community as a whole physically and emotionally. He was one of the first to call for school buildings that were both roomy and airy. In the same vein, he felt that vocal music would promote health. It would strengthen the lungs, stimulate circulation, purify the blood, and speed up digestion. Therefore, he believed the death rate, at least from tuberculosis, would decrease. Vocal music would also stimulate the intellect since all musical tones have mathematical relations. Mann even went so far as to believe that vocal music had such a strong moral influence that it could "curb youthful passions and enhance classroom discipline; it could serve as the great tranquilizer of the young and the grand mediator or peace-keeper between men" (Cremin, 1957, 11).

There is a certain degree of what I would term "classical idealism" in the thinking of Jefferson and Mann. Both appeared to see the roots of democratic thought and process in ancient Greece. Although their difference lies in the approach as to how to achieve and uphold the democratic ideals for which they fought, both relied heavily upon the Western tradition in terms of the ideal democratic society they wanted to achieve.

Therefore, it is understandable that until the early 1930s the architecture of school buildings, especially high schools, reflected elements of the classical tradition. Some adorned their portals with Greek columns. Some even had the phrase "I light the flame" and other inscriptions in Latin imprinted above an arched doorway decorated with the flame of learning and other classical images.

It is the great story of democracy, to which Neil Postman in his book *The End of Education* refers, that gave purpose to schooling at least to Jefferson and Mann. The political artist of the 1930s, Ben Shahn, he recalled, referred to it as "the most appealing idea that the world has yet known," while Alexis de Tocqueville called it "the principle of civic participation" (Postman, 1996, 13). In a similar vein Emma Lazarus, like Horace Mann, talked of America as the place in which numerous different peoples, many of whom were oppressed in their native lands, came together to start a new life and were able to breathe freely. Based upon these narratives, Postman sees the purpose of schools

> to fashion Americans out of the wretched refuse of teeming shores. Schools are to provide the lost and lonely with a common attachment to America's history and future, to America's sacred symbols, to its promise of freedom. The schools are, in a word, the affirmative answer to the question: Can a coherent, stable, unified culture be created out of a people of diverse traditions, languages, and religions? (Postman, 1996, 14)

Although the democratic imperative has been lost to capitalist domination, universal public education has become engrained into the fabric of American life. The emphasis of our schools, both public and many of the private schools, as well as that of our political and economic leaders is to increase the economic productivity of the students and the profits of U.S. corporations.

My principal, who learned that he had become a dispensable object in April 1999, repeatedly reminded his staff as well as parents at meetings and through letters sent home: "Our job is to create marketable products out of the raw material, our students, for business and industry." This process to which he referred didn't take place overnight. It gradually took hold with the victory and expanding conquest of the First Industrial Revolution.

Although Horace Mann did not predict the domination of capitalism as an agent of greed for profit at the expense of the employees and the natural environment, he believed that intelligence, as a result of effective schooling, would bring about a wealthy nation and a wealthy people. In other words, he wanted to create a level playing field that would decrease the disparity between social classes: rich and poor. In his Twelfth Annual Report to the Massachusetts Board of Education he wrote:

> That Political Economy, therefore, which busies itself about capital and labor, supply and demand, interest and rents, favorable and unfavorable balances of trade; but leaves out of account the element of a wide-spread mental development, is nought but stupendous folly. The greatest of all the arts in political economy is, to change a consumer into a producer; and the next greatest is to increase the producer's producing power; — an end to be directly attained, by increasing his intelligence. (Cremin, 89).

During the nineteenth century, as the First Industrial Revolution gained a stronghold over the United States, the ideals of which Mann spoke were ignored by the industrialists. The fact that the nineteenth and early twentieth century factory worker was unhappy was of little concern to the employer. After all the employer's prime interest was to meet his manufacturing quota, to achieve maximum profit for the company. Milton Meltzer in his book *Bread and Roses: The Struggle of American Labor* described the debilitating effect of the factory system upon the once skilled crafts person. He quoted from an 1883 report of a U.S. Senate committee describing the effects on a young machinist: "It has very demoralizing effect upon the mind throughout. The man thinks of nothing else but that particular branch; he has got no chance whatever to learn anything also because he is kept steadily and constantly at that particular thing" (Meltzer 1967, 7).

Quoting from a report by the Boot and Shoe Workers Union to a congressional committee in 1899, Meltzer effectively demonstrated that the workers lost a sense of curiosity and interest in the world of ideas. As Mr. Eaton spoke:

In those old shops, years ago, one man owned the shop; he took in work and three, four, five or six others, neighbors, came in there and sat down and made shoes right in their laps, and there was no machinery. *Everybody was at liberty to talk; they were all politicians, of course, under these conditions, there was absolute freedom and exchange of ideas; they naturally would become more intelligent than shoe workers can at the present time, when they are driving each man to see how many shoes he can handle, and where he is surrounded by noisy machinery.* And another thing, this nervous strain on a man doing just one thing over and over again must necessarily have a wearing effect on him; and his ideals, I believe, must be lowered. (Meltzer 1967, 9, emphasis added)

Meltzer also reported about a factory in Massachusetts in 1879 in which a young machinist described young men being hired to patrol the shop. He was ordered to instantly fire those employees who were caught talking to each other.

Thomas L. Livermore, manager of the Amoskeag mills in Manchester, New Hampshire, felt "there is such a thing as too much education for working people sometimes. I have seen cases where young people were spoiled for labor by being educated to a little too much refinement" (Meltzer 1967, 33). Of course, if they were to be educated, they would realize the horrific conditions under which they work. God forbid, should they learn about unions and fight for better working conditions and wages.

The Progressive Era Adds a New Urgency to Education Reform

The early twentieth century, a period known as the Progressive Era, offered a new sense of zeal to the education reform movement. It was similar to the kind of religious fervor and faith typical of Horace Mann's approach to education reform.

This new movement discovered that "science" possessed the precise tools needed to guide the course of social evolution. In fact the leaders of the movement were referred to as "administrative progressives" according to Tyack and Cuban in their book *Tinkering Toward Utopia*. These primarily white males were career educators: city school superintendents, education professors, leaders of professional education organizations like the National Education Association (NEA), and foundation officials. They adopted what is commonly referred to today as modernist thought — the seventeenth-century Cartesian and Newtonian philosophy that extends the mathematical method of human knowledge to all fields of human knowledge. This way of thinking is commonly referred to as *modernism*. They believed that science could lift education above politics so that educational professionals could make the crucial decisions that shape education.

They believed they had found the key to educational efficiency through their own, inner circle, elite management system. In order to gain greater control of education, they wanted to eliminate local control of schooling as much as possible. Therefore, they succeeded in giving power to individual states to certify professional educators. In that way "standards in professional qualifications, staff, administrative procedures, social and health services and regulations, and other educational practices" (Tyack and Cuban, 1995, 17) could be accomplished. These administrative types succeeded in securing legislation in several states that in order for local school systems to receive state aid, minimum requirements had to be met.

They argued that school curricula should be differentiated to prepare students for different professions based upon their socioeconomic backgrounds as well as their abilities and interests. Thus, a national trend toward tracking and the use of intelligence tests as a form of social engineering was established, a pattern that is still with us today. This system modeled after the natural sciences classified students similarly as biology has classified species of plants. They considered this to be egalitarian, as students of all abilities would find their niche in public education. The trend toward tracking intensified in the 1940s. Since boys seemed to be slower learners, had more discipline problems, and dropped out of school in larger numbers than girls, sex-segregated vocational courses that would appeal to boys were created. Competition among male-only athletic teams was stressed.

Tyack and Cuban observed that this so-called scientific approach, which appeared to be objective, in reality was insensitive toward ethnic differences as well as those of race and gender. It had a debilitating effect upon public high schools. They wrote:

> Through all this planning for a socially engineered new society [that added numerous tracks and watered down the curriculum to keep adolescents in school] educational leaders showed little appreciation of ethnic differences, for they were convinced of the appropriateness of their middle-class 'American' values and unconscious of the bias in their supposedly universal science of education. Their confidence about that science, their optimism about the power of education to correct social ills, and their search for professional autonomy, led them to intervene, with an arrogance that was typically unwitting, in the lives of people different from themselves. The facts of racism, of poverty, of gender bias, of alienating relationships in the new mass-production industries — these realities undermined the aspiration of making the high school an efficient engine of social progress" (Tyack and Cuban, 1995, 52)

In 1940 the National Education Association (NEA) together with the American Association of School Administrators (AASA) wrote a book for the Educational Policies Commission entitled *Learning the Ways of Democracy: A Case Book of Civic Education*. This book was given to me by Eva, the alienated student about whom you will read in chapter 3, with the inscription: "I wanted to give this book as a gift for being such a wonderful teacher and then going beyond what most teachers are expected to do. I thought you might be able to use this book in any studies you may pursue in the future. Continue to open minds, Eva." She was absolutely correct.

This book is most useful to document continuing adherence of "administrative progressives" to the concept that efficiency is an important aspect of the democratic school. It did adhere to a rather hierarchical structure at which the principal remained the head of the high school, and the superintendent was an efficient manager of the school board. However, it did encourage teachers to have a stronger say in school policy than they do in the school district in which I have taught. It encouraged student participation in policy formation based upon their level of maturity. It welcomed communitywide participation in curriculum development and other aspects of school programming. Finally, it suggested components of school curricula that advocate student involvement to understand and help bring about the process of social change.

There were strong reasons for compiling this book in 1940. Hitler threatened democracy worldwide. World War II was raging, even though it was still a year away before the United States became fully entangled in the war. In the foreword it is stated: "At a time, when the development of an active and intelligent loyalty to democracy is clearly the nation's supreme problem in education and defenses, the Commission is glad to be able to give this account of what good schools are doing to develop good American citizens and to present recommendations concerning the further improvement of citizenship education" (NEA and AASA, 1940, 3).

The authors observed the *teaching* of citizenship in several schools. Teaching as opposed to actual practice restricts student empowerment as active, socially responsible citizens. Student, teacher, and citizen critique followed the authors' descriptions.

One account characterized a principal who hand selected the majority of teachers on his staff because they supported the principles upon which his school operated. He promptly got rid of those teachers who disagreed with his approach because "it is hard enough to teach democracy under the best of conditions, without being troubled with disloyal or insubordinate teachers" (NEA and AASA, 1940, 2). The teacher had high praise for this school because he simply had to do what he was told to do. "Democracy? We practice it instead of talking about it" (NEA and AASA, 1940, 2). The student liked the school because it had a student council. Even so, the principal must approve all decisions. The council couldn't even propose a solution until it had consulted with the principal to see whether he found it acceptable. The citizens from the community liked the efficient manner in which the school was run; both teachers and students knew exactly what was expected of them at all times. Since democracy is very difficult to define, the citizen added, "why should we start children going in fuzzy-minded circles trying to do it?" (NEA and AASA, 1940, 3).

This description written in 1940 is identical to Madison High School in 1999. For example, the school does have a student council. Their classes elect students to this governing body. Elections are held in homerooms. No platform speeches are made. No debates between candidates are held. It is simply a popularity contest among the college prep. students. The president, for instance, runs every year on the same issue, namely, to raise money for senior graduation activities. A major endeavor of the student council is to crown the king and queen, prince and princess, duke and duchess at the annual homecoming football game. The council also organizes student dress-up days during Halloween week and hosts two blood drives for the general public including students 17 years of age and older at the high school.

Attempts to control the schools by those in authority continued to become tighter in the light of school violence that made news headlines in the spring of 1999. Soon after school commenced in the fall, the principal at Madison High, just like other headmasters at so many other high schools nationwide, responded to parental and school board "concerns" about students wearing chains. He threatened to suspend students who didn't remove such attire promptly. He also requested that the school board draw up a policy that would forbid students wearing chains. One student pasted some photocopied sheets on the walls explaining why such a ban was a violation of a student's right to freedom of expression. Another student wrote in defense of this policy not only on grounds of safety, but that schools had an obligation to prepare students for the proper attire for the workforce. Having removed the first statement, the principal obviously felt it appropriate to remove the others as well.

Students in my so-called "low-level" group, described by more than one teacher as low lifes and wastes, were upset by this action. They felt it was the right of students to express their opinions, especially opposing points of view. Therefore, two boys approached the student council with a proposal that a bulletin board be set up so that a proper forum for opposing points of view could be held. The student council ignored their request. Finally, they drafted and signed the following petition to the principal:

> Students should have a board in which to express him or herself [sic] on any subject so long as it is appropriate and signed by the author. As far as being able to go to the principal's office with anything, students are intimidated

by the office and relate it to an authority figure. This is not what the idea of an opinion board is all about. It is to create dialogue between students, faculty, etc. In addition, many subjects may not have anything to do with the principal. Also, the board should be subject to school policy regarding defacing property. We, the students, feel this could create a more positive environment in Madison High School.

The students requested that the principal come to their class to discuss this issue with them. When he appeared, they gave him the signed petition. He said he would not approve such a bulletin board because his office door is always wide open for all students to come to him to discuss their concerns. However, he did admit that he was a benevolent dictator, and he told the students that he had their best interests at heart. He was, therefore, obligated to make sure that each succeeded in school and left with an education well qualified for a job.

Even the NEA in 1940 concluded that "the treatment of students as individuals worthy of respect should be at the very heart of teaching and of the school administration. The student spoke truly who replied, when asked how her school helped her to understand democracy, 'The teachers here treat us students like real people'" (NEA and AASA, 1940, 69).

The NEA report observed more democratic schools as well. At one high school they found satisfaction within the staff but not among all students. Here, a democratic system of student-teacher cooperation in planning units of work was established. At the beginning of each unit in each course, all teachers and students worked together to establish goals, determined how these goals would be reached, and selected the materials needed. They argued that ready made programs handed down from the top were undemocratic.

The teacher felt that such a plan was truly democratic. Students are motivated and this plan is *efficient*. "You would be surprised to find how carefully and intelligently the students plan our work with us. I am convinced by this experience that a democratic method of this kind is just as efficient as the traditional pattern of teacher domination and of course it is far better for the students. It gives them the feel that they have a say in their own affairs" (NEA and AASA, 1940, 7). Some students and community members were less positive. The students did admit that some students felt they were learning how to use freedom and weren't simply memorizing lots of information.

One student felt that all of this democratic effort still resulted in students having to come up with the proposals that the teacher wanted: "I think we're just wasting our time. Why? We really don't learn to plan our work, for we always have to come out where the teacher wants us to come out. If we don't come out there, the teacher keeps the discussion going on and on, with everyone in the class trying his very hardest to hit upon the suggestion the teacher wants. And when some someone hits it, you can hear the whole class sigh with relief. Yes, I suppose it's part of being democratic. But sometimes I get sick of that word" (NEA and AASA, 1940, 7).

As much as I want to frown upon the student who does not trust the teacher, who believes teachers are manipulative in trying to get students to see everything their way, and adopts their suggestions, I can empathize with the critical student. After all, it certainly is possible that this student sees right through the teacher's manipulative approach. On the other hand, I would want to believe, probably naively, that back in the late 1930s there were fewer exploitive teachers than we find today.

Still the criticism of the community members must be heard. They felt that such methods of teaching are wasting taxpayers' money. Since teachers are supposed to be experts at what they teach, they should be teaching it, not spending their time discussing with the students what they want to study.

Having been conditioned to the need to learn the three Rs plus basic knowledge in history and science taught from books and disseminated by teachers, it is understandable that such taxpayers would be upset with a school in which students may have some say as to how the curriculum is taught. Therefore, those people who are practicing a more democratic approach to schooling need to explain to the community at large why this approach is more effective than the traditional method. Parents and other community members should be invited to attend classes that are conducted more democratically. With some broader understanding of this approach, at least some skeptics might become supporters.

The authors of *Learning the Ways of Democracy* were weary of a school that gives the students considerable freedom in creating and developing the curriculum. This was especially evident as they honed into the criticism of one student who seemed to support their need to hold onto a more hierarchical and authoritarian approach to schooling.

The greatest concern of the administration was to make sure that the individual liberties of students and teachers were protected at all times, and that there were as few rules as possible. "We do not try to impose our notions upon teachers. We give them academic freedom to the fullest extent" (NEA and AASA, 1940, 5). This they considered to be the essence of democracy.

Some teachers complained that the staff members were never able to agree. Groups of like-minded teachers seemed to work together, but were unwilling to compromise on their ideas, i.e., regarding the curriculum. Some students felt that the school lacked energy compared to other high schools. I assume this means the kind of rah-rah spirit that exists in many high schools as the staff and students rally behind a successful athletic team.

Since both students and teachers have been conditioned to a hierarchical structure, in which commands are given and fulfilled, it is hard for many of them to deal with freedom. Such freedom encourages them to take initiative, to make decisions about the curriculum and how to teach and study it. Instead of focusing on achieving high grades, students become motivated to learn and master concepts more easily. Teachers become excited about exploring ways to facilitate the learning process for their students instead of concentrating on rising to the next step on the hierarchical ladder.

A parent of one of the students at this liberal school the NEA observed before 1940 said the principal was one of the finest men he knew, but felt that students and staff took advantage of his benevolence and ideals. Therefore, teachers failed to work to their limit and students sluffed off. "We all have a real affection for him, but when he retires, I hope we can get someone in his place who will have a firmer hand on the school. Of course, we must have freedom in a democracy, but freedom must be limited by considerations of public welfare" (NEA and AASA, 1940, 11).

It is obvious that the authors of this book believed in the concept of the philosopher king. Only their philosopher king is manager but not necessarily an educator. Only this "expert" is more of a policy maker who guarantees that the school is run efficiently:

> In a democracy, the expert is responsible in the long run to the entire society that he serves. The people, either directly or through their representatives, decide when the expert is needed and what his duties are to be. If the people call upon the expert to lead them in policy-making, it is to the people that he supplies the information which is the product of his experience and research, as data which the people may employ in choosing their purposes more intelligently. (NEA and AASA, 1940, 25)

This statement clearly supports the system by which our public schools are still largely run. A school board elected by the citizens continues to establish the curriculum based on a combination of the wishes of the majority of the community and the state and national mandates. It hires the staff: superintendent of the school system, building principals and teachers to carry out these wishes. The attitude that schools can *teach* democracy as opposed to *practicing* it is explicitly expressed by the authors in the following lines:

> A school, therefore, can be an effective teacher of democracy only to the extent that it recognizes for each member of the school community his right, within the limits fixed by the nature of legal requirements and by the maturity of students to share in determining school purpose. (NEA and AASA, 1940, 28)

In other words, students are conditioned to be submissive to school authorities. This authority is sanctioned by the conventional practice of *in loco parentis*. Therefore, school administrators and teachers acting in place of parents while students are under their jurisdiction have more authority over students than do police officers in the community at large. By taking the place of parents school officials control every aspect of the students' lives from their clothes to what they say, read, and write. By deciding for children to what we have been conditioned to believe is best for them, many educators and parents stifle children's curiosity to make new experiences that broaden their horizons, develop their self-confidence, and enhance their maturity.

Some thirty years later John Holt in his book *Escape from Childhood: The Needs and Rights of Children* would rather that we, parents and schools, allow youths the widest possible range of experience (except those that hurt others) and allow them to choose those they like best. He added:

> If we want the child to grow not just in age, size, and strength, but in understanding, awareness, kindness, confidence, competence, and joy, then he needs not time as such but access to experiences that will build these qualities. And he needs the right to shun and flee experiences all too common in the lives of most children, the experiences of terror, of humiliation, of contempt, of endless anxiety, of deception, of lack of trust, of being denied choice, of being pushed around, of having his life filled with dull and pointless and repeated drudgery. (Holt, 1974, 108)

Even though many adults use the time-honored approach to direct students in a nontrusting manner, we wonder why so many youths today lack initiative and a sense of social responsibility. Maybe, just maybe, more educators and many parents need to show some faith in children. Teachers should provide stimulating experiences that motivate their charges' curiosity. Students should be involved in all aspects of program development and the management of the school. They should be encouraged to take responsibility for the daily maintenance of the building and grounds. In this way our children will grow up becoming ever more mature. Maturity then might refer to socially responsible, caring, and active citizens, whose yearning for knowledge and search for answers persists throughout their entire lives.

Decision making by consensus is often an arduous process, but it is important for teachers and students to understand and practice this process because it affords the learning and mastery of listening skills and the ability to reach what I refer to as "principled compromise."

This means, for example, that there is plenty of room for accepting different points of view while at the same time arriving at some common ground. For instance, should condom machines be installed in the school's bathrooms? This is clearly a controversial issue, where some parents with strong Christian fundamentalist views would be in rigid opposition.

Initially the reality must be acknowledged that a large number of students do indulge in teenage, premarital sex. At the same time couldn't world literature, e.g., short stories, be provided that address these issues or have guest speakers who have experienced the beauty of a truly loving relationship without immediately indulging in sexual intercourse? Specifically, topics that are of interest need to be presented to the students for open and honest discussion. Isn't this part of an important process by which young people develop self-confidence so that they are able to reach their full potential as individuals? The teacher's role would be to facilitate the discussion. As the students learn this process, they can share the facilitator's role throughout the year.

None of the above discussion negates the need to study academically and explore the democratic process. *Learning the Ways of Democracy* presented, for instance, a unit from a ninth-grade class in Cleveland, Ohio, that was entitled "The Struggle for Personal Liberty." Clearly, this unit, developed in 1936, was created because of the dangers that appeared to be threatening democracy in the late 1930s. The subsequent questions were raised in this course:

- What is Liberty?
- What is the difference between personal and political liberty?
- Do we have more or less personal liberty than our grandparents had?
- Consider restrictions on liberty imposed by laws about health and sanitation, building inspection, fire prevention, hunting and fishing, speed and traffic regulations, fireworks, etc.
- Why are such restrictions of personal liberty imposed?
- Do we have more political liberty than our ancestors had?
- Are the liberties provided in the Constitution threatened today?
  Do dangers to our liberties come from the same sources that they did in Colonial times?
- Are the constitutional guarantees of certain liberties ever used to secure unfair advantages?
- Why are amendments to the Constitution sometimes needed?
- Are the people who demand personal liberties for themselves always willing to extend the same liberties to others?
- Have we arrived at a condition of religious toleration in our times? (NEA and AASA, 1940, 66)

One of the inappropriate features of *Learning the Ways of Democracy*, was that it did reflect racism in America at that time. Although it acknowledged its existence, it told how Blacks, referred to then as "Negroes," "until existing legislation and social practices are radically changed, few of their graduates (referring to two southern high schools emphasizing skills in the 'manual occupations') are likely to know the dignifying experience of the full exercise of the franchise. Unless they can look upon manual labor as honorable and socially useful, these Negro youth will enter life handicapped in their effort to achieve self-respect" (NEA and AASA, 1940, 78) However encouraging, a unit was developed for junior high students of the Des

Moines, Iowa, public schools dealing with minorities. Among the purposes the teacher should have in planning a unit on minorities are:

To help boys and girls recognize the rights of other people who may be different from themselves

To help pupils develop a growing consciousness of the problems faced by minorities

To develop an appreciation for the contributions of various groups of people to our civilization

To help children learn to value opposing opinions as an aid to finding democratic solutions for problems vital to their living. (NEA and ASSA, 1940, 76)

The minority groups to be studied included racial, political, religious and economic groups, as well as school minorities, e.g., transient students, as well as neighborhood minorities. At that time, alternative lifestyles that included communal living, homosexuality, and single-parent families were not considered.

Competition with the Soviet Union Sparked Education Reform

In 1957 the real shocker came when the USSR launched Sputnik. The worst American fear had become a reality. The Russians were ahead of the U.S. technologically. This fact created a crisis in American public education. The reason for America losing its position as the number one global power was blamed on public schools. Therefore, they had to be revamped, first among them the high schools because these students were the closest to going on to college to become the next generation of scientists, who could once again put the United States back into the lead.

Within two years former Harvard President James Conant, who during World War II had served as advisor to the Manhattan Project, compiled what was to be commonly known as the *Conant Report*. This "first report to interested citizens," *The American High School*, was the culmination of a two-year study under a grant from the Carnegie corporation administered by the Educational Testing Service of Princeton, New Jersey. In this report Conant noted that academically talented girls had not studied as much mathematics and science as the boys.

For reasons demanded by corporate America and tied closely to the nation's military security, Dr. Conant became a strong proponent of the consolidated, comprehensive high school. Comprehensive refers to the notion that the public school is expected to provide education to all youths living in a town, city, or district. This large school was to offer a broader range of subjects than was possible in the small community high school. Because there were more students, the schools could afford to hire specialists and purchase the materials and equipment necessary to teach the sciences, foreign languages, and vocational skills. These large schools were supposed to assure our government that American scientists and industrialists would quickly cause America to catch up with the Russians.

The recommendations Dr. Conant made were simply well established features of the traditional high school. Although he recommended that experimentation and innovation in all phases of the curriculum should be explored, his emphasis was on using new technology, such as television.

Among his suggestions for reform were some that were emphasized by those who wanted to restructure high schools in the 1990s. He proposed a strong counseling system whereby the counselor would provide advice to students while staying in close touch with parents. He proposed a gifted and talented program as well as individualized programs for each student ranging from college preparatory to vocational. He hoped in this way to push the concept of the comprehensive high school to meet the needs of all students. However, he remained a strong proponent of tracking and grouping students according to ability: advanced, average, and slow learner. He even urged the formation of homerooms "for the purpose of developing an understanding between students of different levels of academic ability and vocational goals....to make them significant social units in the school" (Conant, 1959, 74). Although Conant appeared to show some interest in guidance counselors for them to create accord among students of different tracks, the counselors' primary job was to guide students to an appropriate career using intelligence testing as a major determining factor.

In order to achieve his goal of ascertaining that the United States would continue its position as the number one world power, he still adhered to the Cartesian tradition, extending the mathematical method to all fields of human knowledge. He continued to ignore the impact of human relations, the relationship between students' daily experiences and knowledge, as well as introducing students to new ways of looking and perceiving the world. He seemed to ignore the stifling impact of authoritarian rule, and the gradual repositioning of relationships between dominant and subordinate cultural groups. He failed to consider that the education he proposed was limited to training students for a career. Therefore, he continued to emphasize the cultivation and measurement of formal operational thought as the most efficient and cost-effective way to achieve his goal.

Unfortunately, Dr. Conant did not foresee the loss of community spirit as the small-town high school closed its doors, and as teenagers were bussed for miles throughout rural areas to the regional high school. He failed to anticipate the problems created by uprooting children from their communities and placing all of them within the same age range into large, impersonal schools, gathered into big classes lacking close student/teacher relationships. In the State of Maine comprehensive high schools appropriately have the acronym SAD (School Administrative District).

Madison Area Memorial High School became the centerpiece of an SAD in the mid-1960s. When I arrived, the school had over 400 students. Some of the students were members of the district while others, who came from small, neighboring communities without high schools, had the choice of attending our school. Madison High now has a population of only 300 for several reasons. The town of Norridgewock, which allowed their students to attend Madison High School, was required by the state to send their high school students to SAD #54 in Skowhegan. As a result Skowhegan built a new high school that incorporated a separate vocational school. Anson and North Anson became member communities of a new SAD located in North Anson. Therefore, the newly formed SAD #74 had to build its own new high school. Ironically, communities that comprise one SAD often have to bus their students through parts of towns that belong to others SADs. Finally, the populations not only of the Madison SAD, but also of neighboring school systems have been dwindling because of a lack of employment opportunities.

One of the sad realities of the SAD is that students from the outlying small communities have difficulty in being accepted by the kids in the town that already has a high school, the one that they must attend. This has been and continues to be a particularly painful experience for the kids from West Athens. This tiny, isolated, community is ridiculed for its reputation of poverty, inbreeding, and low intelligence. Students from this area attending Madison High School are still ostracized. In the mid-to late 1960s this little community became the haven for the "back to the landers" as property here was quite inexpensive. Seeking to escape the domination of Madison Avenue materialism and feeling a new urgency to preserve the environment, young people flocked to this area as well as to rural, central Maine in general.

The Alternative School Movement

As more and more pressure was placed on student academic achievement in math and science, and the arts and humanities seemed to be delegated to the back burner, in the late 1960s and early 1970s some Maine middle-class parents, including myself, reflected upon our own meaningless public education. We were eager to nurture the wonderment of our children that so often was destroyed when they entered public schools. We opposed teachers who primarily dispensed information to their students and judged them as to how well they could feed the material back on tests. We objected that students were labeled as good or bad individuals by the grades they received from their teachers. We wanted them to be forever curious, to ask questions, to seek answers that led to more questions and more answers. We were enthusiastic for them to become sensitive and responsive to the needs of others and the endangered natural environment we all inhabit. Inspired by such educators as A.S. Neill and John Holt, among others, we took the education for our children into our own hands by forming cooperative, alternative schools.

The sense of a community school that allowed all to be helpful to one another — parents, teachers, and students — became the basis of our small, ungraded school in which students learned at their own pace and were provided with a lot of individual attention from their teacher. As in the home, relations between student and teacher were informal yet respectful. Children were encouraged to release their creative energies through art, music, and dance, and together share their knowledge of science and history through these forms of artistic expression. Frequent field trips ranging from a study of a tidal saltwater marsh to visiting science and art museums in Boston and culminating with a meal in an ethnic neighborhood, were one of the cornerstones of these experimental schools.

The New Day School, of which I was a founding parent and parent director until its demise twenty-two years later, was a prime example of these experimental ventures. Initially, we started our school as a K-12 venture. However, we soon discovered that high school kids with nine or more years of traditional public schooling were unable to adapt to the lack of structure at the free school. Therefore, the school eventually focused upon preschool through grade six. It came to an end as more and more parents sought an alternative to the public schools, which had been gaining a bad reputation for discipline problems, substance abuse, and an overall unsafe environment. Under such circumstances ambitious middle-class parents looked to the alternative schools as the place that would provide their children with the education necessary to get into colleges that had notably fine reputations. As our little school, with the standing as the longest, continually running free school in Maine, was losing its creative spirit, myself, and other old guard members of the school felt it best to close its doors permanently. The decision-making process of consensus was diverted to majority rule; the need for a professional director was advocated, and the voices of the children were listened and adhered to less and less.

The New Day School, like other alternative schools, flourished because parents were deeply committed to creative community education. They had faith that their children would learn best at their own speed, that, with coaching from the teacher, they would tackle challenging subject matters. They had the courage to relinquish their fear that without a traditional academic schooling their children would be rejected by colleges. In fact, the great majority of children who attended the New Day School and other alternative schools excelled both academically and socially in comparison to their counterparts in public schools. These schools also succeeded because parents were directly involved in their children's education. They actively volunteered on a regular basis in offering a wide variety of learning experiences for their children from teaching math to dance to cooking to carpentry to taking children on field trips. Students together with their teachers created school rules and developed the curriculum. Each person, including students and teachers, had one voice at school meetings. Here decisions affecting the entire school were made, and problems were brought forth and resolved by students and teachers together. Every month a general meeting for the entire school community was held. Decisions were reached primarily through consensus. Sometimes the process of reaching and adhering consistently to these decisions turned out to be quite painful as in enforcing tuition agreements.

Students together with their teachers created the curriculum. Often students worked on hands-on projects together. For example, as part of their study of the solar system, they created a musical together with a parent volunteer, who was a professional actress. Math and problem solving skills were developed as students built tree houses on the school's three acres of land.

The alternative school movement has evolved into the home schooling venture. It is currently gaining rapid momentum. Here parents have the right to control and direct the learning of their children. Many parents with strong, fundamentalist Christian beliefs feel that public schools are breaking away from the tradition of simply teaching the basics. They are critical of what has been labeled as "outcome based education," which we shall see later is simply the manner in which public schools are meeting the new paradigm of business and industry.

Even though during the 1960s, 1970s, and 1980s greater emphasis was placed upon academic achievement, business and industry remained unhappy because students entering the job market did not possess the skills that would cause American corporations to recapture their status as world leaders in business and industry. Furthermore, with the rapid advancement of technological developments, the nature of work changed from primarily blue-collar assembly line workers to skilled problem solvers for multinational corporations to expand their markets. Actual manufacturing jobs decreased in the United States as they were transferred to developing countries where labor remains cheap, unfettered by laws that protect both the employee and the environment. In the following chapter we will examine the cries by corporate America to reform America's schools to meet the needs of their newest paradigm to make profits. We will also see how corporate America and public education are utilizing many of the methods that alternative schools used, only for a very different purpose.

4

TRANSNATIONAL CORPORATIONS AND GLOBAL ECONOMICS DOMINATE AMERICAN EDUCATION

With the appearance in 1983 of "A Nation at Risk" school administrators and teachers were once again targeted for national economic decline and cultural deterioration. Instead of acknowledging that more students were completing high school from among the poor and disenfranchised, corporatists and politicians tried to demonstrate through statistics that students were doing academically more poorly in the 1980s and 1990s than they had in the 1960s and 1970s. Therefore, it was easy for them to demand education reform to meet the new needs of business and industry. Already in 1972 when George Gallup asked parents why they wanted their children to be educated, the number one response was to get better jobs while the third-ranked response was to make more money.

Although the noted historian of American education, Lawrence Cremin observed that to blame educational decline for the nation's woes was irresponsible, government officials, politicians, and corporate leaders took advantage of the new scare. They demanded that schools be reformed and that statewide and national standards be established to bring education in line with the new basic skills demanded by corporate America. They failed to understand the erroneous argument that poor schools produce poor workers, while improved schools solve economic ills. According to Cremin, this argument "scapegoats educators; and it blurs understanding of a labor market in which the largest proportion of new jobs are relatively unskilled and millions of skilled workers are jobless" (Tyack and Cuban, 1995, 39).

Therefore, the effects of the education reform effort do nothing to reclaim the wonderment of learning that children so often lose when they enter school. The focus remains on amassing as much knowledge and developing as many skills as possible to meet the current demands of business and industry as opposed to encouraging young people to explore the purpose of life, to foster human dignity, freedom, and social responsibility.

Economic Woes and Social Anguish Intensify in the 1970s

With the collapse of the economy in the early 1970s, following the oil shortage crisis, material uncertainty became real. Technology displacement, a rapid rise in unemployment, and increasing stress levels on the job led to a dramatic rise in crime and random violence. Women and Blacks, in particular, became the targets of scapegoating, a vicious phenomenon that always seems to occur when hard times strike. In order to try to maintain a consumptive lifestyle, it became ever more necessary for both parents to work. In addition single parents needed employment to support their families.

American society appeared to remain in the throes of cultural decay represented by the social breakdown of the nurturing system for children. It meant, according to Cornell West "the inability to transmit meaning, value, purpose, dignity, decency to children" (West, 1991, 17).

Jeremy Rifkin in his book *The End of Work* pointed out that with the majority of women in the work force, children were becoming increasingly unattended at home. The increase of work has created what he calls an "abandonment syndrome." The effects of this appear to be childhood depression, delinquency, violent crime, alcohol and drug use, and teen suicide.

West continued to reflect that he was not simply referring to those children living in poverty, but about the

deracinated state of their souls. By deracinated I mean rootless. The denuded state of their souls. By denuded, I mean culturally naked. Not to have what is requisite in order to make it through life. Missing what's needed to navigate through the terrors and traumas of death and disease and despair and dread and disappointment. And thereby falling prey to a culture of consumption. A culture that promotes addiction to stimulation. A culture obsessed with bodily stimulation. A culture obsessed with consuming as the only way of preserving some vitality of a self. (West, 1991, 17)

The effects of a culture of consumption are readily evident in rural, central Maine. To escape from burdens of everyday life, parents and students often succumb to an addiction to stimulation. When both parents work or in the case of a single parent, it is easier, though more expensive, to spend money on "ordering out" pizza and collapsing exhausted on the sofa in front of the big home entertainment center than to prepare a home-cooked meal. The corporate advertisements on TV whet the appetites of both parents and their children for the newest fads: in winter snowmobiles and elaborate skiing gear; in summer all terrain vehicles (ATVs) and jet skis. Naturally, with working parents and the complete absence of public transportation, it is imperative for teenagers to have their own cars. Since it is always possible to get what they want instantaneously through credit cards and bank loans, paying off the escalating monthly bills only intensifies parent and student desires for more instant gratification.

Kids are always the next generation of victims of our consumption based, corporate society whose profits feed off kids' needs for addiction to stimulation. Many become passive spectators glued to the TV and computer screens. Professional sports entertainment and graphically violent and explicit sexual material titillate their sensations. They are inundated with massive amounts of unrelated information that they are unable to digest.

More and more students are less inclined to read a book, digest a story and allow their imagination to flow from the printed page, creating new and beautiful images. Rather, many seek to escape by numbing themselves listening to music with the highest decibel rating, releasing their frustrations out in such video games, as for example, the one in which they play the cops who beat Rodney King.

Maybe, because corporate power is so eager for profit at any expense, it is not at all surprising to read a news brief in the regional paper that noted that Japanese youths are becoming more violent:

TOKYO – Violence among Japanese schoolchildren increased over the past year, the government announced Friday in a further indication of growing youth malaise.

Education Ministry official Akira Kusume blamed the rise in serious acts of violence on deteriorating student teacher ties and strains in family life.

The increase was 24 percent over the previous year, according to an Education Ministry survey. However, a portion of the rise was the result of

new guidelines that explicitly asked schools to report minor cases of violence.

    Nevertheless, experts said violence was increasing, a cause for partic-
ular concern in a nation that has long prided itself on one of the most effective educational systems in the world. (*Morning Sentinel*, 14 August 1999,
B8)

Insensitive to the growing economic and social decay, power remained
at mid-century in the hands of a white-male elite. Tyack and Cuban accurately observed that "a system of governance and finance rooted in local
school boards and state legislatures and professionally guided by the administrative progressives placed most power in the hands of prosperous, white
male leaders born in the United States who tended to assume the correct-
ness of their own culture and policies" (Tyack and Cuban, 1995, 22). The
effect was that the poor Blacks, the working class, immigrants, the disabled,
and women had little influence over educational policy. Even so, there
seems to be little evidence that this state of affairs has changed significantly
at the beginning of the twenty-first century.

    The decline of American business, its increasing difficulty in competing
in the international markets, and cultural decay were blamed on schools. If
only schools had been preparing students with the skills needed by business
and industry to compete successfully in the world market, the social and cultural problems with which America is faced wouldn't have happened—at
least not so easily. Therefore, today, school administrators and teachers are
held accountable through all sorts of local, statewide, and national standardized testing. Because of the changing demand upon the workforce for a
broader knowledge and skills based education, a high school education is
mandated for almost all forms of employment. As a result public schools are
supposed to be trying to retain and graduate students who previously would
have dropped out: the disenfranchised poor and minorities.

"A Nation at Risk": Reform in the 1980s

    It was not surprising that in early 1983 the National Commission on
Excellence in Education, an eighteen-member panel appointed by Secretary
of Education Terrel H. Bell, prepared a scathing report entitled: "*A Nation
at Risk: The Imperative for Education Reform.*" The reason for education
reform, purely economic, is succinctly stated in the very first sentence: "Our
nation is at risk. Our once challenged preeminence in commerce, industry,
science and technological innovation is being overtaken by competition
throughout the world" ("A Nation at Risk," 1983, 13). The report continued on with its harsh attack on American education:

History is not kind to idlers. The time is long past when America's destiny was assured simply by abundance of natural resources and inexhaustible human enthusiasm, and by our relative isolation from the malignant problems of older civilizations. The risk is not only that the Japanese make automobiles more efficiently than Americans do and have government subsidies for development and export. It is not just that the South Koreans recently built the world's most efficient steel mill, or that American machine tools, once the pride of the world, are being displaced by German products. It is also that these developments signify a redistribution of trained capability throughout the world. Knowledge, learning, information and skilled intelligence are the new raw materials of international commerce and are today spreading throughout the world as vigorously as miracle drugs, synthetic fertilizers, and blue jeans did earlier. If only to keep and improve on the slim competitive edge we will retain the world markets, we must rededicate ourselves to the reform of our educational system for the benefit of all, old and young alike, affluent and poor, majority and minority. Learning is the indispensable investment required for success in the 'information age' we are entering. ("A Nation at Risk," 1983, 23)

The report even quoted Thomas Jefferson on education not for fostering his democratic ideals, but in order to strengthen the nation's economic prosperity. "I know no safe depository of the ultimate powers of the society but the people themselves; and if we think them not enlightened enough to exercise their control with a wholesome discretion, the remedy is not to take it from them but to inform their discretion" ("A Nation at Risk," 1983, 13).

The report promptly listed statistics, which it referred to as "indicators of risk." For instance, in comparing 19 different nations with which the United States competed in business and industry, American students never ranked higher than 7th place. It noted that 23 million American adults are functionally illiterate and that the same were held true for 13% of all seventeen-year-olds. It expressed dismay that the average achievement of high school students was lower than it was 26 years before when Sputnik was launched.

Of course, it did not mention that more minority students were attending school and that the level of poverty was on the rise. Nor did it take into account that inner-city schools and low-income, rural community public schools never receive the same amount of state and federal subsidies that are allotted to middle-and upper-middle class suburban communities. Nor did the report acknowledge that more minority students and those attending poor quality inner-city schools were reflected in the decline in the College Board's Scholastic Aptitude Test (S.A.T.).

The report expressed concern that many seventeen-year-olds did not possess the "higher order" of intellectual skills necessary for the contemporary world of business and industry which include drawing inferences from

written material, writing persuasive essays, and solving mathematical problems that require several steps. Of course, the report reflected the complaints
from business and the military that they "are required to spend millions of
dollars on costly remedial programs in such basic skills as reading, writing,
spelling, and computation" ("A Nation at Risk," 1983, 13).

Since school administrators and teachers traditionally adhere to the status quo, they all too easily and passively accept the blame for the failure of
public schools by those who hold power: business and industry, state and
national legislators, and frightened, vocal members of the general public. By
fearing to become involved in an active and constructive dialogue with
these forces, school administrators blame teachers, and teachers blame students for the problems with which schools seem burdened. In this way, they
aid and abet the problems that our schools currently face.

New, rigorous, and measurable statewide and national learning standards which assess students' abilities across the board at designated benchmarks, i.e., grades 4, 8, and 11 arose from the recommendations outlined in
this report. Even so, the report's recommendations, typical of an impatient
society that wants results instantaneously, focused upon secondary education. In addition to the three "Rs" (reading, writing, and arithmetic) three
years of science, three years of social studies, and six months of computer science were mandated. Two years of foreign language were only strongly recommended. The fine and performing arts were later lumped together with
foreign language to "constitute the mind and spirit of our culture" ("A
Nation at Risk," 1983, 15). Other mandates included a fine arts credit for
high school graduation, a secondary developmental guidance program,
extending the gifted and talented program for grades 9 through 12.

Although the recommendations that noted that lifelong learning should
be a goal appear noble, the intent, clearly, was to accept the reality that
youths will have to change jobs and even careers at least eight times throughout their lives as new technologies replace present jobs they currently hold.
Emphasis on problem solving, the ability to write well, and critical thinking
were considered important skills for the success of any business or industry.

Realizing that youths in countries that are America's strongest competitors in business and industry attend a longer school day and year, the report,
needless to say, recommended not only better management and organization
of time, but also a longer school day and academic year. Although the
authors preferred to extend the school year to 220 days, they realistically
suggested a minimum of 200. Madison's school system still abides by the
state minimum of 175 student days plus five teacher workshop days.

Besides recommending stricter attendance policies and more consistent
discipline procedures, the report did admit that alternative classrooms, programs, and schools should be established to meet the needs of continually

disruptive students. The intent of these schools was also to try to reduce the high dropout rate. When students compete with one another, there are always winners and losers. Therefore, many students give up. Among the teaching methods that work well is cooperative learning that emphasizes the quality of scholarship as opposed to grades. As students learn to help each other out, a sense of community evolves.

This approach differs from the team approach where students learn critical thinking and problem solving skills that they may eventually use when they work for business and industry. Peter McLaren observed that the expressions "cooperative learning" and "communities of learners" "promote a convenient alliance between new fast capitalism and conventional cognitive science" (McLaren, 1998, 441). In other words, these terms hypocritically represent the concept of democracy, namely, the will of the people versus the privatization of democracy characterized by the will of the dominant power, i.e., the corporate elite.

In spite of alternative programs the average dropout rate of a graduating class in Maine in 1999 was 5%. It is predicted that the dropout rate will continue to escalate as the statewide Maine Educational Assessment administered to all students in grades 4, 8, and 11 become tougher, and students, at least initially, do more poorly on these.

The rise in the dropout rate has much to do with students feeling that they are personal failures. This perception is related to both the purpose of schooling to prepare students with marketable skills for economic survival and success and to their background. Students have been socially conditioned. For instance, if they fail at school, "they are incapable or undeserving of economic well-being, a state that destines one to live a life of cultural, material, and social subordination" (Shapiro, 2000, 105). Since their families are poor, jobless, and sometimes homeless, they are seen as personal failures and as morally deficient by middle- and upper-class people. They appear to lack the traditional protestant work ethic — that passageway to salvation. The reality is that all of these factors are due to structural inequities of a class-divided society that includes racism and sexism. Shapiro correctly states that, "poverty is the product of policies promulgated by economic and political elites that have produced urban disintegration, 'capital flight,' 'redlining,' and discrimination against women and people of color" (p. 105).

Certainly, there are students in the middle class who drop out of school because they find it meaningless. It does not relate to their daily life and interests. With little communication and nurturance at home other than parental pressure to succeed in school, they drop out feeling lost and frustrated.

I am troubled by the idea of establishing alternative programs and schools just for "disruptive" and "at-risk" students. Attaching negative labels to young people antagonizes and alienates them more. Instead, I would like to see the alternative school model adopted by mainstream schools since the majority of high school students undoubtedly would fare better in such programs. By examining the reasons why students fail and why their behavior patterns are sometimes not compliant with the status quo, innovative programs are created that make for more successful schools.

Just as students are under increasing pressure to survive within the system so are teachers. Teachers according to "A Nation at Risk" would be required to pass statewide and even national exams to prove that they meet new, high standards required to become competent in their field of study and within the classroom. The report even suggested they should take charge of their own certification process as do other professionals such as doctors and lawyers by designing teacher preparation programs and supervising probationary teachers.

In Maine new mandates were established by the state whereby teachers created their own professional development plans. Once a team of peers approved these detailed action plans, credit would be awarded after the applicants not only completed their projects, but also documented in detail their individual portfolio each step including the time spent. The intent was to hold each teacher accountable and make sure that none of them "cheats" the system. Teacher teams were also responsible for developing in-service education for their colleagues.

Instead of applauding teachers for their unique and creative ways of inspiring students in their search for life's meaning, teachers are now evaluated by how well their students do on standard achievement tests. To make sure that teachers adhere to the norm in order to be granted tenure, they are evaluated by their own peers. On the surface these approaches appear to be egalitarian. However, those teachers who agreed to be part of the peer review in many instances compete among themselves to be selected as master teachers. Just as in the world of business the master teacher achieves a higher salary resulting from professional competition that is market sensitive and performance based.

In this way, local school boards, school administrators, teachers, and students are held accountable to the social hierarchy beginning with the local school boards, the state legislators, the national legislators, and business and industry. In other words, according to Bruce Beezer, "The teacher is legally the agent of the state and, therefore, the state has a legitimate interest as in how the teacher exercises that authority" (Beezer, 1991, 118).

There is a significant difference between accountability and responsibility. Accountability refers to documenting tasks accomplished for higher officials, a process that is based upon fear, mistrust, and even paranoia. It fosters the negative concepts of blaming, scapegoating, and punishing. Responsibility, on the other hand, suggests taking the initiative to be trustworthy, to be conscious of and responding to the needs of others, even to take risks out of moral conscience. Responsibility nurtures the idea of creating a situation that is better than one that already exists.

According to David Gabbard, "The message of accountability is clear. Teachers' work must help the state achieve the ends of government (increased wealth and increased strength), or they must look for other work. Or, again they can refuse and resist" (Gabbard, 2000, 61)! I would only reinforce the idea that as corporations gain more and more power, they support representatives to the government and lobbyists who advocate and ascertain that their interests are met. Therefore, the reform effort in education exemplifies the corporate stake enforced by the government. To these teachers are held accountable. Big Brother is watching!

The Purpose of Schooling Will Not Change, Only the Methods

The nature of our schools will not change as long as our schools continue to focus primarily on preparing students to become economically viable. As long as educators are held accountable to the standards demanded by corporate America to produce marketable assets so that these corporations can make vast profits, the emotional health and well-being of our students will continue to be of secondary importance.

That schools are geared to meet the needs of business and industry is nothing new. Back in 1939 John Studebaker in an essay entitled "Education Moves Democracy Forward" expressed this concept. He quoted the United States Commissioner of Education of that time:

> Education will not move democracy forward by merely teaching courses of study concerned with the democratic philosophy and principles. Self-government is being undermined by its failure to solve the crucial problems of the technological age. Education for democracy, therefore, is basically concerned with the social and economic issues, which have been put up to us by the machine empire. Unemployment, surpluses, foreign trade, social security, housing, money and credit, wages and hours, conservation of natural resources, taxation and purchasing power, these are the fundamental matters requiring the constant attention of the schools and colleges and adult groups. (Studebaker, 1939, 354)

Even in 1939 reference to the technological age sounded as if it were written in the 1980s and 1990s.

However, with the rapidly increasing corporatism of America and trend toward global capitalism, the emphasis upon education for economics as opposed to education for democracy continues to rage ahead. In their book *The New Basic Skills*, Richard Murnane, a professor at Harvard Graduate School of Education and Frank Levy, a professor of urban economics at MIT, wrote that "the economy is changing much faster than schools have improved. Many people, including roughly half of recent graduates, have an education that is no longer in demand" (Murnane and Levy, 1996, 4).

The need to reform our schools to meet the new corporate paradigm is also expressed by Phillip Schlechty. In fact Bill Clinton wrote the foreword to his book *Schools for the 21st Century: Leadership Imperatives for Education Reform*. Mr. Clinton wrote: "Schlechty offers no quick fixes, nor does he recommend steps prescribed by outsiders. Rather, he works closely with business and community leaders, as well as school boards and personnel, in making real changes" (Clinton, 1990, 3). Schlechty politely notes that business and labor leaders, as well, support reform initiatives in the schools because they see this as the only way for America to compete in a global economy and maintain its present standard of living.

Unless the citizens, and I am sure Schlechty refers not just to training youths but also to retraining adults, are prepared for what he calls knowledge work ("putting to use ideas and symbols to produce some purposeful results") (Schlechty, 1990, 35), economic problems will increase dramatically. Jobs that are too labor intensive and do not require a significant amount of knowledge will be exported to countries where labor is less expensive. He also predicts American wages will be depressed to the global rate.

Like the 1940 Educational Policies Commission report, Schlechty believes that capitalism can only function effectively in a democratic state. He seems to oppose political dictators if they interfere with the growth, global spread, and profit of multinational corporations.

The reality is that global capitalism is a new form of dictatorship that is both predatory and parasitic. According to William Robinson, already in 1996 "some 400 transnational corporations owned two-thirds of the planet's fixed assets and control 70 percent of the world trade. With the world's resources controlled by a few hundred global corporations, the life blood and the very fate of humanity is in the hands of transnational capital, which holds the power to make life and death decisions for millions of human beings" (Robinson, 1996 20).

The term *democracy* originated in ancient Greece, and it means reign of the people. It has become a euphemism for a worldwide trend of multinational corporations to create a global economy. Although multinational corporations like to talk about democracy, they are what Robinson calls a "polyarchy": a system that "is neither dictatorship nor democracy. It refers to a system in which a small group actually rules, on behalf of capital, and participation in decision-making by the majority is confined to choosing among competing elites in tightly controlled electoral processes. This 'low-intensity democracy' is a form of consensual domination" (Robinson, 1996, 21).

These corporations espouse the concept of democracy; in reality, though, it is synonymous with economic freedom in a free-market economy. Corporations cannot function effectively under political dictatorships unless they have the support of the dictator as they had formerly in El Salvador, Nicaragua, and the Philippines. For instance, when Iraq's Saddam Hussein wanted to nationalize the entire oil industry at a terrible loss to such multinationals as Exxon and Texaco, these corporations pressured the United States government to abandon weapons sales to Iraq and eventually considered him an enemy.

For similar reasons, the executive of Madison Paper Industries, whose firm is a joint venture between a Finnish firm and the *New York Times*, spoke with my government and economics class. He supported President Clinton's military involvement in the Serbian province of Kosovo. He believed the United States had an obligation to protect human rights and to do what it could to halt genocide that was occurring there. This was necessary in order to establish political stability vital to economic expansion in that part of Europe. To maintain stability, a democratic form of government is essential, he explained.

The trend toward globalization was well expressed when the same executive of Madison Paper Industries spoke with my students. He noted that Indonesia was America's biggest competitor in the paper business. They could make paper from bamboo and eucalyptus, which are much faster growing woods than spruce and fir that are used in this country. The only way his company can survive is through global competition. This is tough. In the 1990s several paper mills in Maine have shut down partly because the machinery was outdated. When Madison Paper Industries wanted to expand again by building a new paper machine at the cost of three quarters of a billion dollars, a company in New Brunswick, Canada, got a head start. The Madison expansion was placed on hold.

The executive frightened the students when he said that there is no guarantee to find work in paper companies in Maine. Expansion doesn't necessarily mean many more new jobs. What jobs will be available will demand a considerable amount of technical training, he explained. Since the company has several factories in Germany and Switzerland, ten percent of the Madison workforce is learning German. It is possible some Madison employees might have to work in those countries — at least for a time.

More evidence toward capitalist globalization occurred when a student asked why the company doesn't expand its plants in Finland. The answer: Finland is a socialist country. It is less competitive because management cannot properly manage because the unions there are very powerful.

Because multinational corporations advocate democracy, they disguise their hierarchical structure by espousing the concept of cooperation for the common good. After all, when employees feel they can take ownership for their accomplishments, their productivity increases and the corporation's profits often skyrocket. When companies employ this new paradigm, the traditional antagonism between management and employees is reduced. Labor agreements between corporate management and the union are now negotiated utilizing interest bargaining principles. The result is supposed to be a win-win situation, i.e., both sides are mutually satisfied with the results.

Madison Paper Industries is one multinational corporation that uses interest bargaining. It turns face-to-face confrontation into side-by-side problem solving. There is no doubt that a nonconfrontational approach is more effective. After all the company realizes that if the workers are content, they will work harder for the company and the firm will gain greater profits. In its labor agreement with the United Paperworkers International Union, Local #36, the company specifically stated, "the intent of this Model and Guideline is to actively contribute toward the long-term growth of M.P.I. as a place of secure employment and increased profits for all."

As ideal as this form of bargaining appears, the Madison mill is male dominated. According to one girl, who participated in a class discussion, this imbalance weakens the effect of process. When she asked the executive, how many women worked at the Madison mill, he answered 13.5% of the workforce. When he added that this figure was better than at most paper mills in Maine, she was infuriated. Already frustrated by his arrogance, she told him that he had to change his attitude especially towards women. He responded that her attitude wouldn't be accepted at his mill.

Another weakness in this agreement is the hypocrisy between reaching decisions by consensus while the management has the final say. The agreement specifically states that management and employees agreed, "to use consensus decision-making principles in arriving at recommendations in areas where we have mutually agreed to work." Nevertheless, a few sentences later it reads, "This Model and Guideline does not remove Management's responsibility to manage the business."

Although the new knowledge workers will continuously have to gain more knowledge, by which I assume Schlechty means information, they will, according to him, reflect characteristics of the ideal democratic citizen about which he learned in his high school civics course. They will have to be able to "function well in groups, exercise considerable self-discipline, exhibit loyalty while maintaining critical faculties, respect the rights of others, and in turn expect to be respected" (Schlechty, 1990, 39).

I do wonder what loyalty to a company means, when corporations continue to downsize, laying off the knowledge workers whose ingenuity, team work, and critical thinking made the advancements possible for firms to be run more efficiently? It seems obvious that by critical thinking Schlechty means solving problems for the firm but in no way being critical of its purposes and policies.

If I am correct, this is by no stretch of the imagination close to the democracy the founders of our nation had in mind. Jefferson, Franklin, Adams, and others were genuinely interested in promoting a democratic society that relied upon critical thinking to prevent dictatorships. They tried to create a society that encouraged learning and upheld freedom of expression. They believed that only through the tolerance and acceptance of different ideas could the principles of a democracy be upheld.

Schlechty simply fails to acknowledge that human beings are dispensable objects to corporations unless they help and continue to bring enormous profits to their companies. As Charles Kettering of General Motors in the 1940s put it: "the key to economic prosperity is organized dissatisfaction" (Rifkin, 1995, 20). Therefore, General Motors took the lead in introducing annual model changes in its cars and launched a spirited advertising campaign to cause customers to be dissatisfied with the model they owned so they would desire to purchase a new one.

Schlechty doesn't seem to realize that the American government aids and abets employee downsizing. The Clinton administration, whose economic and educational policies he seem to support, like others previously, continued to uphold the trickle-down technology theory. Rifkin argues that there is overwhelming evidence that "technological innovations, advances in productivity, and falling prices will not generate sufficient demand and lead to the creation of more new jobs than are lost" (Rifkin, 1995, 40). In fact, the instantaneous movement of information, owing to new technologies, permits these corporations to savagely take on more and more power as they rapidly gain ever more control of the global market by overtaking or merging with their competitors.

It sounds beautiful when Schlechty speaks of cooperative learning. However, his definition represents "a technique of putting children in work groups and assuring that children with different backgrounds and differing abilities have experience in working together in productive ways" (Schlechty, 1990, 41). Of course, this will best serve the purpose of corporate success in an information-based society: "develop students as thinkers, problem solvers, and creators" (Schlechty, 1990, 41). Particularly frightening are the noble words of caring and humanity that many corporations use to sway leaders in the educational field to adopt these methods to meet their own business needs: to improve quality and productivity.

The British educationalist, Andy Green, observed that the language of the new capitalism is identical to that of those humanists who are concerned about appreciating diversity and empowering minorities. He concluded that "what we are left with at the end is a 'free market' in classroom cultural politics where the powerful dominant discourses will continue to subordinate other voices and where equality in education will become an ever-more chimerical prospect" (Green, 1997, 80). The new capitalists use language that champions cultural diversity and repudiates hierarchical control because business emphasizes the inclusion of everyone from workers to CEOs in making meaningful business decisions. Therefore, according to Peter McLaren, the boundaries between life inside and outside the workplace are blurred.

Schools and Social Class

Education has become a commodity like a car, brand-name clothing, a computer, and all other consumer products. Therefore, many people who become educated, can either afford the high cost of being a consumer or want the social status of middle-class in order to have the income to be consumers. Furthermore, it is wealth that generally determines educational achievement. Certainly demeaning attitudes of the white majority toward race and ethnicity have contributed to this problem. Blacks and Hispanics, for instance, have been relegated to substandard jobs and living conditions. Children in the ghettos and slums, regardless of their racial or cultural background, have lower academic scores on standardized tests. This poor performance can almost be expected primarily because inner-city urban schools are large, overcrowded, and drastically underfunded. Steve Tozier observed, "Taking all ethnic groups and both genders together, low social economic status (SES) students drop out *six times as often* as high SES students. Similarly, Whites are more than twice as likely to complete college as Blacks, but high-SES students, regardless of ethnicity, are more than six times as likely to complete college as low-SES students and more than twice as likely as middle SES students" (Tozier, 2000, 154). Therefore, children from high social economic status have a much greater chance to secure a good education culminating at least with a college degree, while those with lower social economic status have much less of a chance.

Low-skill jobs with reasonable pay have disappeared. Therefore, schools try to keep students in school who had previously done fine when they dropped out in past eras. At the same time schools are expecting all kids to perform at a much higher level to meet the needs of corporate America. Prior to the mid-eighties schools were still preparing only a fraction of their students for a high level of skills.

With so much pressure placed upon both students and teachers, more children will slip through the cracks. Many children, ranging from those whose learning style is more hands-on to those from lower economic strata, the disenfranchised, and those for whom English is not their native language, will have a hard time to meet these standards. They will experience stress, low self-esteem, and lose motivation to learn. The result already is showing up: more frustrated and angry students, violence in middle-class schools like Columbine, zero tolerance policies that control students more tightly resulting in increased anger among many youths, and a higher dropout rate at the high school level.

Legislators and leaders of the business community do not address the economic inequalities that underlie our educational shortcomings. They appear to singularly demand that schools meet their immediate needs to train students in the new basic skills. In other words, they believe the nation as a whole will benefit if schools produce marketable products by which they can garner greater profit and secure a lead in global competition. By failing to address the socioeconomic issues that create unequal educational and professional opportunities and disenfranchisement among an ever larger disproportionate division of wealth in America, education reform can only be of little and only temporary benefit to the economic well-being of the United States.

The concept of diversity is important to multinational corporations' success since they are intricately involved not only with different nations, but also with different cultures. In order to make a profit, American multinationals are realizing their representatives must get along with those peoples with whom they do business.

According to Harry C. Triandis in his book *Culture and Social Behavior,* many Americans are arrogant and look down upon foreign cultures as less advanced as the United States. This is detrimental to their motive for profit. Triandis writes: "Some American managers seem to be more arrogant than their counterparts in other industrial countries because they feel they have little to learn from their competitors, while the Europeans and Japanese think they have a lot to learn from theirs" (Triandis, 1995, 275). He went on to point out that only one-third of U.S. multinational corporations offer some formal cross-cultural training while two-thirds of European and Japanese multinationals offer such training.

The arrogance of American corporatists appears to be symptomatic of power since English is the international language favored worldwide for business. In other words, the English language has become synonymous with capitalist expansion. English has also made it easier for these corporations to establish bases in foreign countries. For example, a Maine leather tanning company, which has offices worldwide, recently built a second factory in Guangzhou, China. Not only are two-thirds of the world's shoes made there, the Asian rim hosts the majority of the world's population providing an excellent market for the shoe industry.

The company is welcomed as it helps boost the Chinese economy which is growing at an annual rate of 10% to 12% in comparison to the American economy of 2% to 3%. Even so, the company's president and CEO, Dick LaRochelle, who spoke recently to my government and economics class, speaks no Chinese. He doesn't even have an idea as to how much his employees are paid there.

As much as America has been regarded as a world leader economically, considers itself policeman of the world, and is looked upon with admiration by people in countries that are not as technically advanced as this country, does not mean America is the greatest in every respect. America's cultural tradition is the shortest of any of the world's cultures. America is a country that places emphasis more on the practical rather than on the heart and soul. Material needs and pleasures appear more important than aesthetic and spiritual life for the great majority of Americans. For these reasons its culture remains rather superficial.

Operating Schools Like a Business and for Business

Since the purpose of schools is to create human capital for business and industry, it is no wonder that Schlechty envisions operating the schools like a business. For example, he actually says:

> Automobile companies are in the business of producing automobiles that satisfy customer needs at a price customers will pay and from which a decent return to investors can be derived. Schools are in the knowledge-work business (that is, the schoolwork business). What school is about, its reason for being, is to invent forms of schoolwork that will engage the young and cause them to invest their talents and resources (energy, enthusiasm, wits) in doing the work (purposeful activity) in ways that satisfy the students themselves and from which results flow that satisfy the adult community as well. (Schlechty, 1995, 55)

What more evidence is needed to prove that schools' prime purpose is to provide the most suitable workers for corporate America? The hidden curriculum is no different from the one during earlier phases of industrial capitalism according to Peter McLaren. It is only expressed in a more sophisticated, more manipulative manner so that people can "buy" into it more easily. Its function, argues McLaren, continues to "attempt to de-form knowledge into discrete and decontexualized sets of technical skills packaged to serve big business interests, cheap labor, and ideological conformity" (McLaren, 1998, 441). Of course, if students are going to learn, they must find their schoolwork interesting.

However, Schlechty hints that the motivation has been preestablished because the investment that students are going to make not only will please themselves, but also the adults in the community. Those adults are the very people representing the dominant culture, the status quo, who are addicted to the consumptive nature of American society promoted through the brainwashing techniques of advertising and the mass media. Therefore, the purpose of education to empower all students to find their path in seeking life's meaning seems to have been lost. For teachers to make possible the process for students to become active and socially responsible citizens, who uphold the democratic principles upon which this country was founded, seems like a distant cry in the wilderness.

Authors Murnane and Levy in *Teaching the New Basic Skills* specifically put into practice the concepts about education for business that Schlechty discussed in his book. They adopted Five Principles used by Honda and Motorola, as well as other successful industries to greatly improve quality, productivity, and profits. These principles are:

1. Ensure that all front line workers understand the problem.
2. Design jobs so that all front line workers have both incentives and opportunities to contribute solutions.
3. Provide all frontline workers with the training needed to pursue solutions effectively.
4. Measure progress on a regular basis.
5. Persevere and learn from mistakes; there are no magic bullets. (Murnane and Levy, 1996, 63)

Murnane and Levy even state that there is a compelling reason to use these five principles to improve schools. "In management terms, fostering the motivation and development of frontline workers in businesses is similar to fostering the motivation and development of teachers and students and parents in schools. Thus, the five principles provide an action plan for schools as they reorganize to teach the new basic skills" (Murnane and Levy, 1996, 53). In other words, they have adopted outcome-based education to foster problem solving and critical thinking skills. National and state standards are created to assess student achievement.

In business, goals are established and monitored to make sure that they are achieved. To ascertain that the ultimate end is achieved on schedule, progress is measured at several stages along the way. These points are called benchmarks. This means that the workers, who are assigned to meet these goals, are evaluated according to their performance. Honda of America (HAM) demonstrates this concept. According to Murnane and Levy, "HAM does not wait for media reports to provide feedback on the firm's success. It monitors operations closely, checking continually that goals for costs and defect rates are on target and that training investments are resulting in payoffs. Much of this information is displayed on computer monitors located throughout the plant and on the walls of the Quality Communications Plan" (Murnane and Levy, 1996, 73).

The same concept holds true for education. The standards, in Maine referred to as the Learning Results, establish the requirements (goals) that students must complete in order to graduate from high school. In order to meet these goals benchmarks are established at grades four, eight, and eleven. Just as in the world of business, students and teachers are held accountable to reach these goals. The results of each state mandated benchmark for every school system throughout the state of Maine are published in the press. This method creates competition among school systems to try to achieve the best results.

The reader might ask, "Is this so bad? After all our own democracy is based on competition. In an election supposedly the best qualified candidate is the winner because she or he was elected by the majority." This is true. However, the concept of majority rule came about in part because of the inequality established in Europe, i.e., in mid-eighteenth century France, when a small group of people, the King, the nobility, and the clergy controlled the majority of the citizenry. This Fourth Estate had no say in the government. Of course, included among the members of the Fourth Estate was the rising merchant class. At a time when an agricultural based economy was dying, it is clear that this new class came to power because of its economic strength.

In the United States it seems that Thomas Jefferson wanted to propel the more ideal concept of democracy, which included the exploration of ideas. Only in this way, by educating people so that they will be able to make wise decisions, and educating a particular group of wise people, from whom the representatives of government would be elected, certainly a more humane government and society could be established.

The economic emphasis of American education to prepare students to become productive workers and insatiable consumers to sustain the economy hasn't changed, even though the new paradigm in education is touted as developmental education. Educators using the new approach are supposed to prepare an Independent Education Plan (IEP) for all students as they enter kindergarten. In fact it is a euphemism for proliferating the competitive system that produces the best workers who will be most profitable for the firms for whom they work. Therefore, teachers are required by the Learning Standards to achieve certain results at each grade level. Both students and teachers are considered failures if they do not produce the required outcomes.

Much pressure is placed on teachers and students to meet the standards. In many schools teachers must indicate on their daily and weekly lesson plans the standards that they are teaching and exactly what they are doing to meet each performance indicator along the way. Numerous high school faculties meet weekly to talk about teaching to the standards. Some schools dispense with teaching the curriculum for a whole week in order to prepare students for the statewide tests given in grades 4, 8, and 11. This approach is analogous as in past generations of teaching to the test.

In their book Murnane and Levy encouraged school systems nationwide to implement the five principles to enhance student achievement so that students will be prepared to become qualified employees in successful, modern businesses and industries. This concept was confirmed and even applauded by Thomas W. Payzant, Superintendent of Boston's public schools. He wrote in the foreword of this book:

> They describe them (the new basic skills) as the "hard skills" of basic mathematics, problem solving and reading at higher levels and the "soft skills" of working effectively in groups, making effective oral and written presentations and using computers well. From best business practice, the authors found that skilled employees and good management produce outstanding results. Their studies of schools demonstrate that the management principles used by the firms also work in schools. (Payzant, 1996, ix)

I doubt Superintendent Payzant's assertion that it is possible to train youths to become both productive members for corporate America while at the same time educating them for responsible citizenship in our democracy. He wrote, "Use of the five management principles can help schools improve what they do to enable students to become responsible adults who will keep the economy strong and democracy vibrant. What is at stake is the quality of life for everyone" (Payzant, 1996, xii).

It may be because our values are different that he does not see a discrepancy. I imagine that the emphasis of his definition of the *quality of life* stresses more a materialistic rather than a spiritual lifestyle. He appears to be more concerned about preparing youths to become energizers of the economy than to engage in each individual's search for a lifestyle and career that nurture self-actualization and happiness. He clearly represents the mainstream purpose of education to prepare youths for sustainable jobs.

Holding these values, I believe it is very difficult if not nearly impossible to foster Jeffersonian ideals that enhance students' ability to question and think independently in order to be able to preserve the liberties expressed in his writing. It becomes even more difficult when school boards and administrators try to conduct their institutions as a business based on the Japanese model of lean production.

Clearly, Payzant would agree with Levy and Murnane that the way schools train students for the workforce today, only ten percent of entry-level candidates who apply for employment in the United States operations can be hired:

This dismal statistic has forced us to examine the situation with our "supply base" for human resources, the education system. The question that this book presents, and that we must all answer, is 'Is the pre-kindergarten through university system in this country developing students who have the skills necessary to be successful in a workplace driven by continuous change in a global, competitive environment?' (Payzant, 1996, xv)

Because education is changing very slowly in an environment that is developing at an exponential rate, fewer and fewer people are being prepared for a global economy. Therefore, Murnane and Levy argue that it is necessary to look at companies like Motorola that have moved from a focus on building the best hardware and software in the world to one based on the realization that it is "world-class mindware" which determines the competitiveness of their firm. In fact, the chairmen of Motorola's executive committee and its director of education-external systems wrote in another foreword to this book that "in our view, the mission of the education system has three components: to develop socially responsible, employable young people with lifelong learning skills" (Galvin and Bales, 1996, xvii).

At least Murnane and Levy are straightforward in stating that the purpose of schooling is to prepare students for the workplace. But to say, as they do, toward the end of this passage that "education must adapt to meet the need of the child rather than forcing the child to meet the needs of the system" (Murnane and Levy, 1996 xvii) appears hypocritical unless one accepts Schlechty's point of view. Remember, he had said that if students are motivated to invest in their learning, they will not only please themselves but the adults as well.

Basically, Murnane and Levy advocate casting away the old assembly line paradigm where students sat in rows of desks and took different, not necessarily related courses every forty-three to fifty minutes. They support longer classes, cooperative and interdisciplinary learning, and teaming because the workplace today is driven by problem solving teams. They even adopt John Dewey's concept that the best learning comes from direct experience because in the current corporate paradigm students need to develop multiple solutions to real-world situations of the business community.

Unfortunately, Murnane and Levy seem to misunderstand or at least misuse the ideas of John Dewey. For example, Dewey is a strong supporter of interdisciplinary learning to advance human intelligence in order to create a balance between people and nature. He states in *The School and Society* that "the great advances in civilization have come through those manifestations of intelligence which have lifted man from his precarious subjection to nature and revealed to him how he may make its forces co-operate with his own purposes" (Dewey, 1963, 152). While Murnane and Levy appear to believe that the sustainability of humans upon the material benefits provid-

ed by corporate profit, Dewey is interested in working towards a natural harmony that arises out of an understanding of people, cultures, and their biosphere. This integrative approach, as Dewey wrote, incorporates the concept
of interdisciplinary learning:

> The child who is interested in the way in which men lived, the tools they
> had to do with, the new inventions they made; the transformations of life
> that arose from the power and leisure thus gained, is eager to repeat like
> processes in his own action, to remake utensils, to reproduce processes, to
> rehandle materials. Since he understands their problems and their success-
> es only by seeing what obstacles and what resources they had from nature,
> the child is interested in field and forest, ocean and mountain, plant and
> animal. By building up a conception of the natural environment in which
> lived the people he is studying, he gets his hold upon their lives. This
> reproduction he cannot make excepting as he gains acquaintances with the
> natural forces and forms with which he is himself surrounded. The interest
> in history gives a more human coloring, a wider significance, to his own
> study of nature. His knowledge of nature lends point and accuracy to his
> study of history. This is the natural "correlation" of history and science.
> (Dewey, 1963, 15)

In *Teaching the New Basic Skills* the authors document how successful
businesses have adopted these principles and how some schools have
embraced their own versions of these principles to teach students the new
basic skills. By documenting what transpired in each of the schools observed,
Murnane and Levy demonstrated that other schools should be able to do
likewise.

Madison High School has effectively embraced the bandwagon of
preparing youths for careers in the world of business. The school takes great
pride that it has pioneered an articulation agreement with the paper mill
located in the town, with the regional two-year technical college, until
recently called a technical school, and the state's university system.

Junior students may enroll in this demanding program that includes
such subjects as physics and calculus, as well as a course held at the mill dealing with OSHA (Occupational Safety and Health Administration). If they
do well, they can get scholarship assistance to go to the technical college.
From there, if they so desire, they can continue their studies at the state university to complete a degree in engineering for the paper industry. Once they
have completed the program and received their degree, they will be placed
on a waiting list for a job in the paper industry that will open up somewhere
in the world. After all, Madison Paper Industries' parent company in Finland
has mills in Germany and Switzerland. A similar program is currently being
developed between the high school, the technical college, and a regional
hospital for careers in the health occupations.

These programs still represent tracking students. Tracking was initially instituted during the early part of the twentieth century to make sure that all students would stay in school. To reduce the dropout rate David Tyack and Larry Cuban in their book *Tinkering toward Utopia* referred to a report by a group of education reformers entitled *Cardinal Principles of Education*. The report suggested that different training programs be offered to students of "widely varying capacities, attitudes, social heredity, and destinies in life" (Tyack and Cuban, 1998, 51). This was part of a movement to socially engineer students for a peacefully stratified society. Since tracking is now considered a politically incorrect term, the euphemism "paths of preparation" is used. The students in the lowest track are still considered losers and wastes.

For those who haven't been kicked out of school or dropped out, some school systems have developed alternative programs for them. However, Madison, which tried such a program for a few years, decided to drop it because the teachers didn't maintain the kind of discipline the administration desired, and many teachers felt that these kids were not learning the same material that was being taught in "regular" classes. These kids, they argued, found an easy way out.

Education Reform Movement in Maine in the 1980s

It was a conservative governor who in 1989 commissioned the creation of *Maine's Common Core of Learning: An Investment in Maine's Future.* Just as "reinvention" was at the heart of President Bush's "America 2000" proposal, "restructuring" was the cornerstone of Maine's. This proposition did question traditional beliefs about schooling. It tried to cause educators to rethink the way they teach. It looked at education holistically, encouraging students to experience common strands between the subjects they study: math, science, language arts, the fine and performing arts, music, social studies, and the humanities. Environmental issues with which children will be faced, such as solid waste disposal, acid rain, air and water pollution, and depletion of the ozone layer were stressed. It reflected on the ethical and moral questions posed by developments in medicine and biotechnology, i.e., the right to die, frozen embryos, and the enormous cost of national health care. It appeared that youths are to be taught with compassion so that they would become self-actualized individuals.

Unfortunately, I believe the report was largely responding to the alarm Maine businesses pulled "at the lack of competency in reading and writing, and mathematics of entry level workers" (*Maine's Common Core of Learning*, Maine Department of Education, 1990). The document spoke of youths as "Maine's most precious resource," conjuring up the image that children are just another product, a renewable resource like trees. Since the reason for reforming the public schools is primarily to meet the needs of corporate America, to make our community, state, and national economy competitive and militarily superior, I contend the very foundation of reshaping Maine's public schools is flawed.

Those involved in the restructuring effort are a business unto themselves. University professors sell their consulting services at the tune of at least $700 a day to public schools. They are careful to inform those schools that have jumped on their bandwagons to carefully document every step of their efforts. By building a base of support, they are able to secure federal grants that perpetuate their livelihood. They often lack the very vision they claim is deficient among traditional administrators and teachers. This information is used in their research to chronicle the validity of the theories they are developing. A prime example is former Brown University's Ted Sizer who wrote such books as *Horace's Compromise: The Dilemma of the American High School* and *Horace's School: Redesigning the American High School.* These address nine common principles that guide his Coalition of Essential Schools.

The reason that Sizer has gained such widespread recognition is that he has piggybacked his school reform proposals upon the demands of corporate America. His recommendations follow the current corporate paradigm for successful business. They help schools prepare students for the qualifications these businesses and industries demand from successful employees. Like the authors of *Teaching the New Basic Skills* who adopted five principles of corporate management to education, Sizer came up with his own nine principles by which to make America's schools more marketable to corporate demands. They are:

1. The school should focus on helping adolescents learn to use their minds well. Schools should not attempt to be "comprehensive" if such a claim is made at the expense of the school's central intellectual purpose.

2. The school's goals should be simple: that each student master a limited number of essential skills and the areas of knowledge. [Doesn't this sound like Schlechty as well as Murnane and Levy?] While these skills and areas will, to varying degrees, reflect the traditional academic disciplines, the program's design should be shaped by the intellectual imaginative powers and competencies that students need, rather than necessarily by "subjects" as conventionally defined. The aphorism "Less is More" should dominate: curricular decisions should be guided by the aim of thorough student mastery and achievement rather than by an effort merely to cover content.

3. The school's goals should apply to all students, while the means to these goals will vary as those students themselves vary. School practice should be tailor-made to meet the needs of every group or class of adolescents.

4. Teaching and learning should be personalized to the maximum feasible extent. Efforts should be directed toward a goal that no teacher have direct responsibility for more than 80 students. To capitalize on this personalization, decisions about the details of the course of study, the use of students' and teachers' time and the choice of teaching materials and specific pedagogies must be unreservedly placed in the hands of the principal and staff.

5. The governing practical metaphor of the school should be student-as-worker rather than the more familiar metaphor of teacher-as-deliverer-of-instructional-services. Accordingly, a prominent pedagogy will be coaching, to provide students to learn how to learn and thus teach themselves.

6. Students entering secondary school studies are those who can show competence in language and elementary mathematics. Students of traditional high school age but not yet at appropriate levels of competence to enter secondary studies will be provided intensive remedial work to assist them quickly to meet these standards. [Very obviously Sizer is an adherent to the national movement toward competency standards]. The diploma should be awarded upon a successful final demonstration of mastery for graduation—an "exhibition." This Exhibition by the student of his/her grasp of the central skills and knowledge of the school's program may be jointly administered by the faculty and by higher authorities. As the diploma is awarded when earned, the school's program proceeds with no strict age grading and with no system of "credits earned" by "time spent" in class. The emphasis is on the students' demonstration that they can do important things. [This ability resembles critical thinking skills as a team member to problem solve for their corporate employer.]

7. The tone of the school should explicitly and self-consciously stress values of unanxious expectation ("I won't threaten you but I expect much of you"), of trust (until abused) and of decency (the values of fairness, generosity and tolerance). Incentives appropriate to the school's particular students and teachers should be emphasized, and parents should be treated as essential collaborators.

8. The principal and teacher should perceive themselves as generalists first (teachers and scholars in general education) and specialists second (experts in but one particular discipline). Staff should expect

multiple obligations (teachers-counselor-manager) and a sense of commitment to the entire school.

9. Ultimate administrative and budget targets should include, in addition to total student loads per teacher of 80 or fewer pupils, substantial time for collective planning by teachers, competitive salaries for staff and an ultimate per pupil cost not to exceed that at traditional schools by more than 10 percent. To accomplish this, administrative plans may have to show the phased reduction or elimination of some services now provided students in many traditional comprehensive secondary schools. (Sizer, 1992, 207–209) [My comments are addressed in brackets]

On the whole I like his principles. My only regret is that he doesn't address the underlying reasons as to why corporate America, some colleges and universities, and public school systems buy into these principles. For instance as a teacher, I whole-heartedly support goal number four that includes the suggestion, "efforts should be directed toward a goal that no teacher have direct responsibility for more than 80 students. To capitalize on this personalization, decisions about the details of the course of study, the use of students' and teachers' time and the choice of teaching materials and specific pedagogies must be unreservedly placed in the hands of the principal and staff" (Sizer, 1985, 227). I certainly also agree with goal number five that supports the concept of a "student-as-worker rather than the more familiar metaphor of teacher-as-deliverer-of-instructional services. Accordingly, a prominent pedagogy will be coaching, to provoke students to learn how to learn and thus teach themselves" (Sizer, 1985, 227). As a result of Sizer's efforts, a number of universities and public high schools are associated with his Coalition of Essential Schools to carry forth with his suggestions for educational reforms. Still, Sizer seems to feel that his suggestions are being adopted too slowly.

The superintendent and school board of S.A.D. #59 hired consultants to teach them management skills used so successfully by Japanese corporations. According to this model, school boards, management, and teachers, even students, are components of one *family*. Teachers represent subcontractors on the Japanese model who are considered a permanent component in creating the desired product. They work as a team. Administrators trained on this model give their teachers a feeling of empowerment. That is, teachers are told that they are taking ownership of the restructuring effort. This is what was supposed to have happened in the Madison school system.

Under leadership of an English teacher, eager to become an administrator, a position he now holds in another school district, Madison High School was awarded a grant from the state's department of education for a two-day retreat for the entire high school staff. At a large ski resort, teachers and the new high school principal were to create a reform package for our school based upon Sizer's works. This endeavor, in which students missed two full days of classes, was sanctioned by the school board.

We were trained in the process of reaching decisions by consensus. It didn't take long to discover that this form of decision making did not require that all persons involved must be in unanimous agreement. The large group was broken up into smaller groups. Each group was given the same problem to resolve. Each had to select its three best suggestions before presenting these to the staff as a whole. Then the staff selected the top three suggestions from those listed by each group. Finally, a vote was taken. Thumbs up meant those in favor. Thumbs sideways represented those who didn't care either way. Thumbs down designated disapproval of the measure. However, those with thumbs down had to come up with a proposal that the group would accept by the same voting procedure. I cannot recall one incident in which this happened.

When we, the teachers, requested remuneration for the many hours we dedicated to this process, a request not unheard of in a capitalist society, we were informed by the superintendent that we had volunteered because "we care so much about children." The administrators were quick to point out how rewarding our team effort has been as both students and teachers demonstrated more enthusiasm and productivity than before.

When the plan to establish committees to carry out the proposals developed at the Sugarloaf ski resort were presented to the school board, it promised that no teacher would have more than a total of 80 students. We were also assured we would have cooperative planning time. We were even told that we would be in charge of developing our curriculum. However, the actual result was that a block schedule of 80-minute classes was administratively imposed upon our school because surrounding high schools had already implemented 80-minute classes. Our input, which had been requested by the administration, was ignored. Flexible scheduling appeared to be too much of a headache for the administrators to carry out. In addition, we were suddenly required to teach six classes. The school board created a student teacher ratio of 19:1 meaning that each teacher would have a class load of about 120 students. This was a money saving device. Several teachers were pink-slipped. At the same time the Board, by adding new courses to the program, smelled like artificial roses.

This management style, always conducted with a friendly smile, does not defuse employee (teacher) and employer (school board and administration) tensions. It simply is a less direct, more subtle, manipulative, and deceitful approach to goal achievement. As former President George Bush would say, it is a "kinder and gentler" way to resolve differences and accomplish meaningful objectives for all concerned.

At the same time many teachers are utilizing an analogous approach with their students. To illustrate, team building begins on the first day in late August when a new freshman class enters the high school. These ninth-graders and their parents meet together with teachers and school administrators. The students participate in a mini "ropes course." This is an exercise to build mutual trust by walking on tight ropes. All share food and entertainment together. Each student will be issued a T-shirt sporting such mottos as "we deserve the best" to motivate them and boost their self-esteem.

Other methods are developed by which students imagine that they are taking ownership of their learning. For example, a team of ninth grade English and social studies teachers, with the help of their highly paid consultant, selected the theme "what it is to be human." In order to make the curriculum meaningful to these freshmen, they began the year by asking: "What does it mean to be a freshman? What do I have to do to become accepted? What does it mean to be human as a ninth-grader at this high school? What is acceptable behavior to this group, in this classroom?"

Since the students were actively involved in the process of establishing rules of acceptable behavior, it supposedly would be a lot easier for them to buy into these rules as opposed to those the teachers laid down. In other words, by giving students the feeling that they have had a say in establishing the rules, they are manipulated into the behavior the teachers desire. The reader must by now realize that this method is very similar to the one reported earlier from the 1940s NEA in which students may have been astute enough to realize that their teacher is manipulative. A similar approach is used in business.

The new corporate methods of management replace the traditional concept of authority. Murnane and Levy (1996) point out that corporate America uses workers in very different ways from the ones employed today in the not too distant past. Until recently, workers were hidden amidst the cacophony of heavy machines deep inside factory walls. Blue-collar workers knew their place; they submitted to the demands of their supervisors: their bosses, who instilled the fear of God in them. Today "frontline workers are no longer do- as-you-are-told warm bodies, but people with the skills and incentives to constantly improve their performance. The challenge is to select employees who could live up to this code" (Murnane and Levy, 1996, 20). In modern manufacturing, the blue-collar worker, now euphemistically called a production associate, must take charge of quality control. When problems arise in regard to the quality of the product being produced, this manager must work together with his associates as a team to seek solutions. Production associates work together with their managers who mingle freely among the workers promoting a sense of team and family spirit. To accomplish this sense of family, the managers even dress informally like their production associates. Employees are given a false sense of empowerment. They have been flattered into compliance and can easily be manipulated by those in charge.

Similarly, the traditional schoolteacher may no longer use the threat of physical assault to assure student submission. Now, people's rights of self-determination and freedom from abuse, physical and verbal, are protected by the courts. Since teachers do not want to be fired and possibly incarcerated for assaulting a student, they are learning to use new techniques of behavior modification disguised in the cloak of school restructuring. Like their counterpart in business, in some schools, teachers dress informally like their students, wearing jeans and running shoes, giving kids the impression that they are their friends and equals. By utilizing these methods, which develop skills in interpersonal relationships and enhance team building, schools are preparing students for participation in today's corporate world.

The corporatism of education in Maine picked up momentum as the state department of education with the backing of the state's legislature established and then mandated learning standards called *The State of Maine Learning Results* (Maine Department of Education, 1990) based upon the initial document *Maine's Common Core of Learning* (Maine Department of Education, 1997). The preface of this 1997 document clearly suggests that the emphasis for these standards is upon preparing students for work and for higher education, which implies employment at a "professional level." Furthermore, it underlines the need to "develop consensus on common goals for Maine education" (*Learning Results*, 1997, ii). Even so, it cleverly states that these "do not represent a curriculum nor do they reduce the school's responsibility for curriculum planning or determining instructional approaches" (*Learning Results*, 1997, ii). This expression is simply a framework for state legislated mandates disguised in the euphemism that "communities, schools and teachers work together in implementing effective instructional strategies to achieve high expectations for all students" (*Learning Results*, 1997, ii).

Not surprisingly, when the state's house of representatives and the senate legislated these mandates, they failed to provide the funding necessary to carry them out. In fact, for a student to succeed, each must take more courses, accomplish over 1120 competencies from grades K to 12, get high grades and do well on statewide, high stakes, assessment tests in grades 4, 8, and 11. Therefore, school systems have been put in a bind. They have to abide by the new law or else some of their limited state subsidies might be discontinued. In addition the teachers' union had for several years an agreement with the Madison school board that teachers who serve on board appointed committees would be paid an hourly wage of $12.50. The school board must make sure that these mandates are being carried out, but it also has to deal with communities in which the unemployment rate is high and the average wage is low.

When the SAD #59 school board tried to appease angry taxpayers, like so many others throughout the state, by increasing class size and laying off teachers, it sent an ugly, subliminal message to the students: "we don't care about you." Therefore, many feel that their parents, their community, their school board, and even their teachers do not care about them. Similarly to children of divorcing parents who feel they are at fault for their parents fighting, students are caught in the middle of this dilemma. All this puts additional stress on the students and their families. It dramatizes a conflict of values that involves each of us.

Maine's Learning Results *Feed the Very Problems They Were Created to Alleviate*

As serious as the socioeconomic problems of our society are, and as beautifully as the *Maine Learning Results* portray goals for "citizenship and personal fulfillment" (*Learning Results*, 1997, ii), they aid and abet the very problems they proclaim they are trying to alleviate. They establish what appear to be noble goals for education, e.g., as integrative and informed thinking, open-ended questioning, self-directed and lifelong learning, and responsible and involved citizenship. However, each of these ideals is not only geared to the newest paradigm of business and industry, but students are rigidly and routinely assessed to make sure they have achieved each standard's performance indicator. As a result the creativity of teachers is stifled and their ability to meet the needs of their students is curtailed by bureaucratic technicalization.

As a social studies teacher, for instance, I was required to sit on the committee to revise the social studies curriculum for grades K through 12 for my school district. Although the committee chairperson assured us that we would write our own curricula, we, in fact, simply copied the format of a neighboring school district that had already completed the process. On the surface it might appear that we did create our own curricula. However, the *Learning Standards* specify for each area what is to be covered: i.e., a topic: civics and government—fundamental principles of government and constitution. It also specifies the learning standard: "Students will understand the constitutional principles and the democratic foundations of the political institutions of the United States" (*Learning Results*, 1997, 84). It even tells the teachers in pre-kindergarten, kindergarten through grade two "the students will understand that the United States has a Constitution" (*Learning Results*, 1997, 84). The elementary teachers, however, determine the resources. They include a copy of the Constitution, a copy of the classroom Constitution, *Weekly Reader*, *Scholastic Magazine*, software, and field trips. Among the learning activities students will read and discuss the Constitution of the United States and create their own classroom constitution.

I feel sure that the reader needs to be reminded again that this course work is for pre-kindergarten, kindergarten, and grades one and two. Sure, as a dad, I like to brag that as I write this, my daughter, who is barely five years old, is already reading simple books. She takes piano lessons and plays a simplified version of Beethoven's "Fuer Elise" from memory. However, does she know what a constitution is and that the United States has such a document? No. As a teacher and parent I do not feel that this is important knowledge for her age. Should her pre-kindergarten class or even her kindergarten class have an actual classroom constitution? Certainly not in the formal sense. Should the teacher together with the children work out rules by which all can live comfortably and harmoniously? By all means, yes.

Just this year the Waterville public schools initiated an all-day kindergarten program for all children. This is very practical for single-parent families and those in which both parents work as these families have fewer day care hurdles to overcome. However, small children have less opportunity simply to be playful children. The main reason for implementing a full-day kindergarten program is to assure that students start at an early age to achieve the competencies required by the Learning Results. In fact, all kindergarten teachers as well as those in grades 1 through 12 are required to teach a standard curriculum. Although teachers were on committees to revise the curriculum, they had little say in the changes that were made.

By the time that students complete their high school requirements, they will have to demonstrate competency based upon the Learning Results. The "Learning Results" specify the criteria that must be covered for elementary grades 3 and 4, for middle grades 5 to 8, and secondary grades 9 to 12. Since I teach government and economics, I must fulfill this same performance standard as all previous grades. I am required to:

1. Explain the historical foundations of constitutional government in the United States (e.g., Magna Carta, Roman Republic, Declaration of Independence, Articles of Confederation, Constitution of the United States).
2. Evaluate the Constitution as a vehicle for change.
3. Demonstrate an understanding of the meaning and importance of traditional democratic assumptions such as individual rights, the common good, self-government, justice, equality, and patriotism.

4. Demonstrate the United States Constitution uses checks and balances in order to prevent the abuse of power (e.g., Marbury vs. Madison, Gulf of Tonkin Resolution, Watergate).
5. Evaluate, take, and defend positions on current issues regarding judicial protection and individual rights.
6. Evaluate civil rights issues related to well known Supreme Court decisions. (*Learning Results,* 1997, 84).

For each of the six listed areas that the student WILL master, teachers must fill in the resources they will use, the learning activities he/she will apply, and the means of assessment they will employ. Since my approach is to use a variety of resources and learning activities and my method of assessment has never been multiple guess or fill-in-the blank type tests, I fit right in line with the new paradigm. For instance, for resources I have included articles, video, the Internet, guest speakers, newspapers, and primary and secondary readings. Since a textbook is required, it simply becomes a reference tool. Incorporated in the learning activities are small group discussion, debate, speaker analyses, cause and effect essays, comparative essays, and research. Assessment consisting of essays, identifying events in which students explain their significance, and oral presentations by students are listed.

Even though I am severely curtailed by the *Maine Learning Results* and the Maine Educational Assessment, the statewide benchmarks, i.e., tests, that all students are expected to achieve in grades 3, 8, and 11, as a teacher I still can, do, and must continue to incorporate critical literacy as a daily ingredient in my classroom practice. Critical literacy refers to the method of teaching that causes students to raise questions and seek answers. It particularly encourages students to examine the cultural context in which they have been immersed since birth. These include the values, history, behaviors, symbols, and truths that have shaped their very being. The task of critical literacy in the words of Kathleen S. Berry is "to shape a child's oppositional readings of the world" (Berry, 1998, 21).

For example, our institutions—schools, churches, business and government—are entrenched in traditional thinking, even though they are currently being restructured. With the advent of the Industrial Revolution, the traditional extended family was reduced to a two-parent nuclear family with the father being the primary breadwinner. Today many people appear to be coming to terms with the fact that the nuclear family now includes large numbers of single-parent families who are both breadwinners and domestic caregivers. Still, in spite of the reality that there are numerous homosexual families, homosexuality remains primarily taboo. The theory and practice of critical literacy motivates students to become researchers, seeking answers to their own questions. They are encouraged to explore the cultural constructions of any text that they encounter, in this example, the changes within the extended and nuclear families. In other words, the teachings are challenged with which our children and we have been brought up in the West and that have shaped our attitudes and outlooks for the past several centuries. By learning to look at traditions and patterns differently, students have the opportunity to become more appreciative and accepting of others within the context of fostering a broader sense of community on an ever shrinking planet.

As a result of Cartesian thought, much emphasis has been laid upon what is objective and subjective. Therefore, with emphasis upon science, logic, and technology, the importance of human consciousness has been ignored. According to a practioner of critical literacy, Kathleen Berry:

> Technology or techniques (and education is filled with techniques of 'how to' on teaching, learning, behavior management) become the major way in which the world is constructed. Problematic to our interest here is that the world can be constructed in such a way that human values, histories, truths, knowledge, gender, class, and so forth are excluded or dominated by one particular cultural construct such as male over female, European white race over other races, or ruling and working classes. Consequently, modern constructs that are dominant, privileged, powerful, and mainstream can rule out any cultural, social, constructs that do not fit within the frameworks or borders of these dominant groups. (Berry, 1998, 22)

The role of the teacher, who practices critical literacy, is to help students understand and question the context of the society in which they currently live with the hope that together they can explore means by which to create theories and practices that do not exclude, misrepresent, or oppress.

Although the learning methods supported by the Maine Learning Results appear to use an open-ended approach, students are not encouraged to ask questions and seek knowledge beyond the parameters established within the learning standards. Since they are tested regularly by their teachers and by the state, teachers are obligated to teach to the test.

God forbid I use the word *testing*. It is now an outdated expression and has been replaced by the term *assessment*, which doesn't bear the stigma attached to tests as limited devices by which to determine how much information students have compiled in their brains. Of course, accountability is still the name of the game. According to Jerome Murphy, dean of the Faculty of Education at Harvard University, even the new forms of assessment, i.e., portfolios and exhibits, "fall short as an accountability device" (Jerome, 1999, 65). He noted that even in Vermont, known for innovative education, these methods are unreliable because the people who score these are subjective. No matter what kinds of testing are developed, the measurement techniques used are always norm referenced. Therefore, there will always be a bell curve with a top and bottom group.

The changes in assessing student learning are adapted from the new methods of evaluating workers under the current corporate paradigm. According to Murnane and Levy,

> a supervisor at a Honda plant today finds it much harder to rate workers than did a supervisor in a traditional Ford plant. Many of the most important activities are now products of group interactions, not of repetitive actions by individuals. The group activities depend on taking initiative and applying skills . . . . Because initiative and the application of skills are not easily measured, supervisors cannot use the threat of frequent checks to guarantee worker performance. Rather, they have to rely on employee initiative and knowledge, and they have to think very hard about how these qualities can be fostered. (Murnane and Levy, 1996, 13)

Murnane and Levy go so far as to say "a school that would teach the New Basic Skills faces a similar management problem. It must help teachers to learn to teach the new material. It must devise different kinds of tests that better assess what students actually understand . . . ." (Murnane and Levy, 1996, 13).

It is so obvious that both the Learning Results and the assessment methods are geared foremost to the demands of the new paradigm for business and industry. Therefore, it is hypocritical that Thomas Jefferson is quoted on the cover of the *The State of Maine Learning Results*. He wanted, ". . .to provide an education adapted to the years, to the capacity: and the condition of every one, and directed to their freedom and happiness." Every student should ask what does happiness and freedom have to do with the learning results if their prime purpose is to make students into marketable products to be consumed by business and industry so they can accumulate even greater profits.

I find the *Learning Results* misleading and hypocritical in their intent. For example, a guiding principle says that each Maine student must leave school as "a self-directed and lifelong learner." However, when Longfellow is quoted in saying "the love of learning, the sequestered nooks, and all the sweet serenity of books," I want to imagine that education focuses upon the love of reading, of a lifelong search for truth, of the enjoyment of nature and of one's fellow human beings (*Learning Results*, 1997, 11). When Risinger in 1992 is quoted as saying "the study of human past with all its triumphs and tragedies is necessary to understanding of contemporary society and the issues facing humankind" (*Learning Results*, 1997, 81), I would like to think that we are working together to create a more sane, healthier, and harmonious world. The reality is that "a self-directed and lifelong learner" is simply the euphemism for saying that students must be prepared for complete retraining for nine different careers during their lifetime. They can expect to be laid off as their companies downsize or go entirely out of business. They must also be prepared to learn how to use the newest technologies as older forms become quickly outdated.

A colleague of mine in the Augusta, Maine, school system, Sebouh DerSimonian, was struck by an analogy expressed in the *Maine Learning Results* by the president of a community college. That president said, "education is a train and students must be able to get on and off as their needs change" (*Learning Results*, 1997, 5). My friend asked whether we really, according to this analogy, want to place our students on a predetermined track? After all, railroad tracks are placed on a particular bed, laid in a specific direction, leading to a fixed destination. The destiny of the train is placed in the hands of a single individual, the engineer. Similarly the paths of preparation and their destinations have already been decided by the performance standards of the *Maine Learning Results*. Is that what we really want?

Having someone else do the navigation for our students is appealing to many parents and students. It is easier to have others make decisions for us than to have to make them ourselves. However, doesn't the purpose of education include preparing students to prepare young people to become self-reliant individuals who are able to lead responsible and fulfilling lives? Doesn't this imply independent, critical thinkers, self-disciplined individuals, reliable people who are in charge of their own lives? Are not these reflective people, appreciative and caring individuals who are socially responsible and active citizens?

Furthermore, according to the train analogy, what will happen to students who get off the train before it reaches its destination? May they stay in the town in which they disembarked? May they take a train back to the town from which they came? They might board a train for a different destination. However, someone else has also determined the destination of that train. If students become conditioned to others telling them what to do and how to do it, how can they become truly educated individuals?

If neither parents nor their children are encouraged to take charge of their education while many teachers passively adhere to established curricula in which they have only had an imaginary voice, some irreplaceable values are being lost. Therefore, this model of education is very dangerous as it creates the atmosphere of being manipulated, governed, and it fosters irresponsibility.

I can only too easily picture Thomas Jefferson and Horace Mann rolling in their graves as they see their ideas about education, though quite different, being bastardized by corporate America. Jefferson hoped to educate youths so they could foster the principles of democracy. Today the educated power elite sometimes openly and probably more often subconsciously manipulates people worldwide to believe that corporations are democratic.

In fact, multinational corporations resist those national dictators, like Saadam Hussein who nationalized the oil industry in Iraq, because they interfere with the corporate ability to make profits.

Horace Mann must be horrified at the thought that his hopes for public education to eliminate poverty, which would abate social-class conflict and decrease crime and violence, turned out quite the opposite as capitalism reinforced the greed for material consumption and wealth. Mann would be terribly disappointed if he were to discover that local school boards, like Madison's, following the example of the state, are insincere when they claim to promote education. By placing greater demands on schooling while at the same time cutting the budget, they are in fact reducing educational opportunities for students.

In order to meet the objectives of the Goals 2000 Educate America Act to improve the ability of the U.S. economy to compete in international trade by producing better educated and skilled workers, students must be disciplined. Felicia Briscoe, Larry Cuban, Joel Spring, and other prominent, contemporary educators have observed that discipline implies being able to master the new basic skills required by business and industry and reflected in the national standards movement. Discipline also suggests that students have to learn compliance to this new system. Since schools are seen as the front line by which American corporations will remain competitive, according to Felicia Briscoe, "One of the fundamental ends of the new efficient, pervasive, and invasive school disciplinary regimes is to form students whose knowledge, ability, dreams, and moral vision are shaped toward economic ends. These programs are designed to create students whose desires, habits, and abilities will make them better workers" (Briscoe, 2000, 67–68). Briscoe explains that by gaining a communitywide commitment, a cooperative effort between parents, teachers, school administrators, law enforcement officials, and business leaders, a disciplinary approach can be developed that manipulates students to the goals expressed in national standards. According to Briscoe, "these disciplinary programs seek to penetrate more deeply into students — seeking to be kinder and gentler because that is more likely to shape the student within and seeking to instill a sense of self-esteem that is dependent upon school standards" (Briscoe, 2000, 66).

5

ANTI-ESTABLISHMENT, YET TRYING TO MAINTAIN DISCIPLINE

Although I felt trapped in a system I believe hampers youths from reaching their full human potential, I tried desperately to be a firm disciplinarian in a traditional school setting. At the same time I attempted to practice a philosophy that is contradictory to the system. As a result, I was able to identify with, understand, and feel empathy for marginalized students.

Discipline Defined and Its Application to a Working-Class Community

The word *discipline* according to *Webster's New Collegiate Dictionary* suggests "training which corrects, molds, strengthens or perfects." It also means "control gained by enforcing obedience or order, as in a school or army, hence orderly conduct," or to "train in self-control or obedience to given standards." It is even used to chastise; punish. It can also mean "control gained by enforcing obedience or order, as in *school* (emphasis added) to teach as obedience," as compliant students who do what their teacher tells them to do. Submissive students learn to become loyal, law-abiding citizens, who dutifully and without question, serve their country. This may include serving as soldiers who have been drafted into military service. Students are also conditioned that, should they violate any law, punishment will be the consequence. Compliant students, dedicated to the system, learn to become leaders. As such they may become public servants, elected by citizens, to create and uphold laws that are supposed to comply with the democratic principles of this country. They may also become supervisors, managers, and eventually CEOs of a company that devotedly carries out the policies of their firm.

Since Madison, a mill town, and the outlying communities that make up the school district are working-class communities, the school is going to reflect these values. Social class is determined by the way in which a person relates to the production process in society: as a worker, as a manager, as an owner, as a corporate executive. For example, working-class people have less autonomy in their work, less responsibility in decision making, even in the creative process related to work, and only hold low-level supervisory positions — if any. Therefore, a person's occupation and income level help to identify the social class to which an individual belongs.

The curriculum and teaching methods at Madison High School reflect a working- to lower-middle-class environment. Since working-class jobs demand that employees are told what to do by their supervisors, whose authority itself is limited, they are taught from the earliest age how to follow orders. Therefore, Jean Anyon, who demonstrates that curriculum and teaching methods reflect the social class that they represent, accurately observed that for a working-class community, "the procedure is usually mechanical involving rote behavior and very little decision making or choice . . . . Most of the rules regarding work are designations of what children are to do; the rules are steps to follow" (Anyon, 1980, 262–63). This is certainly true of Madison. Although some blue-collar jobs as carpenters, plumbers, and electricians do demand some planning and decision making, they do not require the same degree of conceptualization and creativity that many professional jobs demand. Consequently, in contrast with the upper middle class, Anyon observed that upper-class students "are continually asked to express and apply ideas and concepts. Work involves individual thought and expressiveness, expansion and illustration of ideas, and choice of appropriate material" (Anyon, 1980, 269).

Even though several teachers have been promoting Advanced Placement classes, only very few students take these. None, to my knowledge has received high scores on the national exams. Only because of pressure from corporate America for schools to meet its newest paradigm that demands team building, critical thinking skills, and interdisciplinary learning, Madison High School is making some changes.

At least in the public schools with which I am familiar and from my experience as a teacher in a working-class community, the emphasis traditionally has been on demanding obedience to established standards and punishment if students do not comply to the rules. That means the students must do as the teachers demand. They must do the busy work so that they will pass the tests. If they do not comply, they will be punished.

My Conflict with the Administration

My conflict with the administration arises in part because I believe the focus of discipline should be on that portion of the definition that develops strength and aims toward perfection. This aspect of discipline is similar to the manner in which ancient Chinese draftsmen mastered line drawings of plants, people, animals, and natural surroundings. As a result of years of articulate observation and devoted discipline they learned to create with incredible simplicity and speed the most graceful, accurate, and beautiful images of people and nature. In other words, I am concentrating on facilitating a form of concentration that nurtures the sensitivity and humanity of our students. The aspect of discipline that helps individuals to become self-actualized persons, who have learned to think independently, to question authority, and to courageously stand up for the ideas and principles in which they believe, caused consternation among my administrators.

I was obsessed by discipline. Even though I realized that discipline for the sake of control was poor and ineffective pedagogy, I felt I had to maintain proper classroom decorum or face being fired. I did not want to experience the humiliation and financial hardship of being expelled from my job. After all, I had a wife and small child to support.

Holding views that deviate from the mainstream made it very difficult to win the support of students and administrators who were neither familiar with the kind of thinking I expressed nor were they willing or even able to adjust to it. At least subconsciously students sensed my dilemma and, therefore, I did have a harder time with classroom management. As much as some students liked me, the temptation to let off steam breaking rules was a lot easier in my classroom.

I remember those early days in the fall of 1969 as if they had occurred today. It was mid-September, less than three weeks since the beginning of the school year when I left the auditorium feeling dejected following a study hall last-period-of-the-day with nearly 120 students. In the corridor I encountered the school's principal, a small, completely bald man, known by his students affectionately as "Chrome Dome." Fearing reprimand because of a noisy study hall, I feared this strict disciplinarian.

This hometown boy had made good. He had become a hero, even though he was of French-Canadian descent, who had witnessed the Ku Klux Klan during his youth. Not only was he a decorated officer during World War II, but upon his return to Madison, he became a successful football coach for his high school achieving victories against his school's arch rival, Skowhegan. Following a number of years as a physical education teacher, he was promoted to principal. I was, therefore, surprised when he reached out his arm to shake my hand. "I didn't think you had it in you," he said. "Congratulations!," he added, shaking it firmly. He referred to the fact that I had slapped a student in the face during the study hall. Had I done so today, in the last year of the twentieth century, I would not only have been promptly reprimanded, but suspended with pay until the investigation had been completed and then fired. If lucky, I would not face legal charges brought against me nor have to appear in court, but at the very least my teaching career would be over forever. The emotional trauma undoubtedly would be awful.

When students misbehaved in my class, I felt as if I were the target of their frustrations. Standing in front of the classroom, I imagined that they saw me as their controlling father or some other authoritarian male figure with whom they had problems and toward whom they felt anger. I sensed a combined feeling of anger, guilt, and empathy. Even so, somehow, I had to deal with classroom management since the authorities judged the best classes as being the most quiet. During my first year in Madison, I expressed in my journal anxieties about discipline. I wrote:

> I am alone in the teacher's room, except for Mrs. Stuart, and I am worrying constantly about study hall. The last few minutes were unruly. Why is it that when I tell a student to be quiet, when I am standing in front of him, he will make murmurs, and others near by will whisper. I thought that when they saw the teacher, they were supposed to be afraid. I simply do not know the answer as how to handle this. I've tried to be calm and quiet. Yesterday worked better than today; yesterday I was calmer than today. But I did sit at my desk, did change seats. This worked relatively well, but at the end, I lost more control. I tried to quiet the crowd from my seat, by calling names. But after the eight-minute bell rang, more and more found they could whisper. I was tempted to make a general announcement, but am glad I didn't. Unlike Mr. Baldwin, the kids would have laughed at me. To send kids to the office would be a sign of weakness. To keep kids after school plays little role because they do it over and over again. I must try to try to keep calm, because, it is when they can excite me, and they did succeed a little today, it gets noisier, and then things go badly.

While beleaguered with discipline, I felt caught between having to teach the textbook and relating the subject matter to the issues of the present to which, I hoped, students could relate. Although I tried my approach through discussion and reading, I was always disappointed and frustrated when the kids just didn't get "turned on." I wrote in January of that first year:

> This week I have tried to talk generally about the reasons people go to war, then look at the horrors of World War I by reading a terrifying description of trench warfare, and then look at the causes for the assassinations at Sarajevo. This I think was a good plan, but somehow it didn't work. War is horrible. I want the students to feel why Serb terrorists assassinated the Archduke at Sarajevo. I tried to discuss this by showing how we as people stick to our own groups, thus making it more understandable why national groups as the Germanic Austrians, the Magyar Hungarians, and the Greek Slavs each wanted so strongly to belong to their own groups: similar languages and customs. Then when the Archduke went to Sarajevo with the intention of saying that he will be willing to make some minor reforms that the Slavs, regarded as inferior by the German people, would be allowed some role in the empire's government, that the Serbs who wanted to make their country more powerful by luring their Slavic kinsmen to them from the Austro-Hungarian Empire, was a cause for jealousy, because the Serbs were afraid that the Slavs in the empire may become content. I wanted to discuss these problems in relation to the different groups to which they belonged. The sophomore girls are bored stiff by everything I say; the boys expressed no interest at all. I am hurt when Robert calls me Bushy, referring to my wild mop of hair, and makes nasty pictures of me which he shows to the class in my presence.

As I look back over those years, it is clear that I was not a status quo teacher, and therefore, was either very well liked by some students and parents, or was hated by others for the ideas I represented and the challenges I cultivated.

As a high school student I recall experiencing anger toward most of my teachers for the power they seemed to wield. It appeared that they were determining my future by judging me with tests and grades. I felt they were trying to mold me into something that I did not want to be, but wasn't able to define exactly what that might have been. As a teacher I didn't want my students to share a similar experience with me.

Even as an adult my anger toward authority figures in the classroom persisted. During one of my early years of teaching in Madison, I took a course for recertification on China, a topic that has always fascinated me. I sat in the front row of the small classroom. The teacher, a tall young fellow often wearing tight blue jeans, stood directly in front of me. As much as I liked him and as well as I did academically in his class, I still felt resentment when he told me what to read and tested me over the reading and on his lectures.

I Am Still Beset by Schooling for Humanity

Although I had taught at the European equivalent of A. S. Neill's Summerhill, the teaching methods at the Ecole d'Humanite had become quite traditional. However, the very year I started teaching at Madison, together with several others, my wife and I responded to an ad in the *Maine Times* seeking people interested in starting an alternative school. At the initial meeting the concept of the "New Day School" was born. Within a year it was off and running.

I was deeply impressed by A. S. Neill and Paulus Geheeb but also by Jean Jacques Rousseau's *Emile*. Rousseau wanted to mold a conscientious citizen for a free state. To do so, he encouraged children's spontaneity at a very young age, caused them to learn to suffer and helped them develop a responsibility to others.

I found it exceedingly difficult to implement these concepts at the high school level. I had not studied, for example, John Dewey in depth to realize how to motivate turned-off kids. Still, I persistently tried to get them to think and to question. I believed in the concept of democracy and democratic schooling. In trying to pursue these ideas in a generally hostile environment, I was truly, according to Helen Epstein, fulfilling the role of the martyr as victim.

For instance, in March 1974 I wrote the following little piece "To be a Non-conformist" for the *Madison Bulldog*, the school's newspaper, which happened to be a project of the business track students.

> "Whoso would be a man (woman) must be a nonconformist."
> Bosh. First of all a schoolteacher would never make an original statement like this. After all, the teacher's job is to make conformists out of students: people, who will nurture the economy of the land and actively partake in its government, i.e., vote responsibly. Secondly, if the teacher did quote a person, he (of course a male) must be from the last century since teachers have a tendency to live in the past and are incapable of comprehending the ways of today.
> "Whoso would be a man (woman) must be a nonconformist."
> Bosh. You are right. First, the statement is not original to this teacher. Secondly, this teacher did quote a person from the last century. He quoted New England's essayist, Ralph Waldo Emerson.
> "Whoso would be a man (woman) must be a nonconformist" is relevant especially today in a society whose unique characteristics are quickly being

lost to the effects of many technological inventions. This causes us in Maine to wear the same fashions, adopt a similar lifestyle, and hold similar jobs as those living in California. We are too easily led into the crowd, enjoy the sensational, dwell on the superficial, and neglect the hard and often lonely struggle to know ourselves, to become independent thinkers, to become those who will not give under pressure the principles we have developed and believe to be right. Rather we tend to go through life callously, pushing aside into our unconscious minds the wrongs we have done others by expediently following the demands of group pressure. We do this because the group gives us security that we are not readily able or willing to give up.

"Whoso would be a man (woman) must be a nonconformist" means that we have to learn to ask questions, to doubt rather than blindly believe. We cannot take for granted that the teacher knows everything, nor can we arrogantly imagine that we are all knowing. We cannot simply stand on the statement: this person is wrong; I am right. To be able to come to such a judgment demands years of thinking, reading, questioning, and experiencing. It means more than developing an understanding for one's peers and elders; it means developing the wisdom so that one has empathy for others.

If you partake in a group, it is adamant to know why. Many of you have been urging reforms at school. My first reaction is, Great! You will be challenging us as teachers to make courses interesting and relevant to your needs, demanding reading and writing assignments that stimulate your thinking and lead to meaningful class discussions. Sure, I realize as a teacher I get carried away with the idea of the perfect classroom situation. Nevertheless, I am basically pleased with your demands: "We want equal rights!" This is understandable and can be justified: i.e., you wish to be treated with respect as young adults, not as objects who occupy numbered seats, onto whom sarcasm is sometimes used and you cannot retaliate. Alas, when I find out that equal rights means being able to grow beards and mustaches for the boys since the teachers are allowed to do so, having a smoking area to poison your bodies just as the adults have, I become disappointed. Since you now can grow beards, wear Bermudas, and at the state level can now legally drink alcohol three years younger than before, you seem to feel you have not only gained equal rights but have gained greater potential to become individuals since you now can do your own thing.' I believe you are mistaken.

I see these developments as a reflection of the direction in which I believe our society is heading: superficiality and impatience. These demands of yours are ignoble since they are irrelevant to the true self of each person. They are largely an indication of wanting to be cool, belonging to the crowd, and demanding to be part of the fad that is "in" at the present moment. It is exciting to realize the power you have as a group to bring about change. However, the changes that you are making are basically self-destructive. This is not just you at Madison High School; this is all of us in affluent, contemporary American society. We adults must be included herein, as we too often are seeking the easier and superficial path to happiness. I say these demands are self-destructive because they are techniques in which we pass off taxing intellectual demands by becoming freer from any form of discipline that makes us think and work. Thus, we place our demands on the superficial level, in your case beards, naked belly buttons, and smoking privileges, rather than the person. Finally, the substances that some of you and us inhale or swallow means to help pass over that which may be disagreeable.

I am not asking that you abstain from cigarettes, alcohol or marijuana. I am suggesting that you stand above these, that you be as completely conscious of your motives and activities as possible. I am suggesting that to become independent of the group's security much knowledge and experience must be gained. This is not an overnight affair. It means developing an inner security. This inner security means that you must develop skills, knowledge and wisdom.

Recently, several of my students were disturbed because they did that which was easier for them, not that which was right. They visited an elderly gentleman, who very powerfully stated that he favors the impeachment of President Nixon. He asked each student to give his/her opinion. The students quickly agreed that they favor the impeachment of the President. Later they admitted having said this because they knew this is what he wanted to hear. "We were afraid to say anything different." I contend that had a person studied the impeachment issues in some depth, he/she would quietly be able to give some information as to why he/she believes at this stage of his/her thinking the way he/she does. They probably would have gained some respect from this elderly man if the statement were based upon thought and knowledge rather than upon emotional fervor.

To carry the above idea further, during World War II many German citizens partook in the atrocities of the Nazi concentration camps and death chambers. Many of them despised the cruelties they were carrying out and hated themselves for it, but for fear of becoming unpopular and of the possible consequences not only from their superiors but also from their own group members, they continued to commit their atrocities. They had not yet developed that inner strength necessary to be able to stand up for their principles.

"Whoso could be a man (woman) must be a nonconformist." That is a wise man or woman who achieved this state of being by means of a slow, arduous process: patience, intense learning, precise observation of people and nature, and self-discipline. When you become a nonconformist, you become yourself. You no longer are a number in the crowd in which you have been for a long time before. Nobody can take yourself away from you. You achieved it; it is yours forever. You not only have achieved real security, that all of us need, you are happy with yourself, and you are even a benefactor to humanity. Was Emerson not a wise man even though he lived in the last century?

At the same time, the ideas that I was expressing and the need to think and to write good, thought-through answers were an anomaly for my students, especially those in the lowest track. That certainly was understandable. After all, they had never been taught to question, to think critically, and to write as a means of self-expression. Furthermore, their parents and relatives, many of whom had never completed high school themselves, had had similar schooling. Like many of their parents before them, a large number of these students found school to be an unpleasant ritual they had to endure in order to receive a diploma. All too many had to bite the bullet in order to survive the humiliation they received from teachers and fellow students. Being submissive was the name of the game.

I Am Nearly Fired

My fear of being fired nearly came to reality by the late 1970s, nearly ten years after I had started teaching at this small, rural Maine mill town high school. At that time rowdiness among students became common throughout the school. On several occasions cherry bombs were ignited in the toilet bowls in the boys "basement." Students were smoking cigarettes in the bathrooms. Some kids came to school high on drugs. In those days, though, "the war on drugs" including the DARE program sponsored by the local police department had not yet come to town.

During the first week of September in 1978, the superintendent of schools continued a paper trail to try to fire me that he had begun the previous winter. The emotional strain of losing my first wife to a car crash in May 1977 and my younger son the following May of injuries stemming from that accident, certainly didn't make matters any easier. The superintendent resented a controversy that brewed because a student complained about foul language in Ron Kovick's *Born on the Fourth of July*, which I used with my lower academic-track students. Nor did he appreciate the fact that I was awarded a grant to purchase a potter's wheel and art supplies for my social studies classroom. Since he couldn't find grounds to get rid of me because of my academic methodology and my political leanings, he concentrated on my apparent lack of strict discipline. On September 8, he wrote complaining about my inability to manage a study hall effectively:

> I was most distressed to hear from Mr. Yerxa that problems which you and Miss Richardson experienced with the study hall situation on 9/7/78. As you are aware, we are very crowded this year and need the full support of all teachers to keep things under control. It is imperative that we can count

on you to carry your weight in the monitoring process.

If students see that they can get the best of you in a study hall, it is certain that they will try to take advantage of you during your classes as evidenced by the problem you have already had in your class this first week of school.

We talked about "student control" problems last year and you assured me that you would take courses during the spring to improve in this area. I also made it clear that your continued employment depended upon your ability to control the students.

In a letter he had written to me earlier that year, James Hennigar's true colors shone brightly:

Finally, I cannot help but feel your personal appearance, the appearance of the classroom and your philosophy of providing a democratic classroom all contribute to the management problems that you are having with division A. It is imperative that you address these three areas seriously if true progress is to be made in student management.

It is understandable that Superintendent Hennigar took this position. He believed that the teacher must reflect and uphold the normative values of the community, the state, and the nation. After all students are the next generation who are supposed to uphold and procure the longevity of a strong capitalist economy. During his superintendence in SAD #59 he quickly climbed toward the top of the AMWAY pyramid. Currently he is the CEO and fundraiser extraordinaire of the Goodwill-Hinkley School located 20 minutes east of Madison. The Hinkley School was founded in the early years of this century as a charity school for poor and orphaned children. It is now a thriving boarding school for troubled youths.

At a time when youth appeared to question the status quo and challenge authority more than ever before, while the American economy was experiencing recession, Hennigar couldn't tolerate a teacher who wasn't a team player. I have no doubt that he was responding to what Felicia Briscoe observed as the two themes on which school discipline is focused on, "increasing the domain of coherent intermeshing disciplinary regimes and increasing the international economic competitiveness of the U.S. business" (Briscoe, 2000, 64).

Hennigar also observed my classes. Alas, he was unable to verify the charges brought against me. In October 1979 he wrote:

I observed a class of freshmen students who were involved in a writing assignment. The students attended to the task and there was no evidence of behavioral problems. At the conclusion of the period, we discussed the fact that I had not observed paper-throwing, nor students hanging out of the windows, no back-talk from insolent students; there was no apparent abuse of bathroom privileges on the part of the students, and certainly no obscene comments about you in fact, there were no disruptions of any kind.

He did note that his presence in my classroom may have contributed to the students' good behavior.

Although according to proper procedure, it should have been up to my direct supervisor, namely the high school principal, to try to get rid of me, Hennigar continued his battle against me until the end of the 1982 school year. He then left Madison to take the helm of the Goodwill-Hinkley School. However, a few days before the school year ended in June, he called me to his office. He handed me my entire personnel file for me to keep while apologizing for not recognizing my ability as a teacher. He noted that his son, Robert, whom I had as a student that year, appreciated my approach to teaching social studies.

In spite of the pressure from the superintendent, the principal, "Chrome Dome" continued to write positive evaluations of me. By 1980 his time honored authoritarian methods were no longer working. During one of those remaining years that he was still head of the school, I recalled in my journal the following incident:

> At lunch break two of my period four classmates, Tim and Randy, left the school building in somber recession, not their usual noisy, frolicking selves. When students gathered in my classroom for the first period after lunch, the following conversation took place:
> "They got kicked out of school," said Fred. "Yeah, I seen 'em coming out of the office."
> "Why"?
> "'Cause they ripped off a toilet seat and broke it."
> "No kidding."
> "Can't even take a shit without Chrome Dome gawking at ya."
> Chuckling among fellow students, their buddy, Joe, looked solemnly out the window: "I broke one, too, but I ain't got caught."

As more students entered the classroom, the now familiar assertion was heard amongst them:

> "Hear what they done in the boys' basement"?

The student remarks continued, escalating with profanities for the school, its principal, and teachers.

On another day, as the principal left the school at noon to go to his home directly across the street, two boys simply picked him up, held him in the air momentarily before setting him gently back onto the ground. Under pressure from Superintendent Hennigar and because of poor health, he retired at the end of that year. In the fall he successfully campaigned to be his district's representative in the state's legislature. He held this position until his death a few years later.

The following principal was basically friendly toward me, but he carried out the wishes of the superintendent to observe my classes frequently. His evaluations of me continued to be positive. Within a year, this gentle man was fired for habitual drinking on the job.

When Superintendent Hennigar departed, I could breathe a little more easily. Other principals continued his threatening ways but with considerable less consistency. The very year I resigned from thirty years of teaching at Madison High School, my principal wrote in his annual evaluation that, "Mr. Solmitz needs to control the class so that a positive learning environment is maintained," and that he "does not implement school policies and procedures." Nevertheless, at the final school assembly of that year, June of 1999, I was honored with the "Teacher of the Year" by the senior class. It was a particularly great reward for this anti-establishment teacher, who had had these students only when they were sophomores, two years previously, and only a few of them as juniors the following year. After thirty years I finally felt validated by those who truly count: the students.

Trying to Control Students Remains the Name of the Game

When I started teaching, students who were placed on an academic warning list because they were failing one or more classes were forbidden to go to the school's library during study hall. This same policy still exists thirty years later. In the fall of 1998, for instance, a sophomore girl ran for the office of class president. Just before the election, after a couple of weeks for gaining signatures of support, the principal told her that she was ineligible for office. She was told that she had been on the restricted list during the last quarter of the previous school year.

Some teachers routinely give students after-school detention if they fail to get their homework done on time! If they do not report for the teacher detention and then fail to report for "office" detention, they are assigned Saturday detention. Failing to appear for Saturday detention, they are suspended from school for three days. At least these youths, who are encouraged to hate school, are rewarded with a three-day vacation from those who turn them away from the joys of learning.

Rarely was a student ever suspended during the early years that I taught at Madison High School. Students pretty much bit the bullet by submitting to authority. Although the age to drop out of school had just been extended by one year to age sixteen, due to legislative action that spring, still those students who didn't fit into the system dropped out as soon as they could. There were jobs available then that didn't require a high school diploma:

cutting wood to feed the pulp mills for making paper, employment at other factories related to the wood industry, i.e., making dowels, or finding employment at one of the shoe factories. Until about a dozen years ago a high school diploma was all that was needed for a boy to get a lucrative job at the local paper mill. It certainly helped, even if he was a poor student in the lowest academic track, if his dad worked at the mill.

Questioning the system always causes trouble. This is because the nature of a hierarchical structure demands obedience to all persons who have higher ranks. If one person's authority is questioned, that individual is considered a weak link in the structure. Weak links are considered dangerous as the system may collapse. Therefore, many who hold positions of authority believe they must do everything to maintain control or else their own job is jeopardized. When people in authority feel threatened, they try to tighten their hold upon those who are accountable to them.

Back in 1969, one boy, a senior by the name of Johnny, committed that cardinal sin. He managed to get hold of an article "The Student as a Nigger" written by Jerry Farber. At that time Farber was a Professor of English at California State University in Los Angeles. Johnny found the article at the Community Action Agency, the local office of President Johnson's War on Poverty, in nearby Skowhegan. A person at the agency duplicated the paper that Johnny circulated around the school.

In this article, Faber attacked educational institutions as being oppressive and openly discriminating where students were considered inferior humans, namely "niggers." Therefore, students were unequal to their professors and school administrators in every sense. For example, at Cal State faculty and students ate in separate dining halls. If a professor were to eat in the student cafeteria, his colleagues regarded him as a "nigger" lover. Students were also required to use separate toilets from the faculty. Although students could vote in national elections, they were disenfranchised at the university level. They had no say as to what courses were offered or which courses they were required to take. They had to address their teachers as *sir*, *doctor*, or *professor*. If they did not parrot back the information that the professor had dispensed, they would fail the course.

Since professors had been "niggers" throughout their schooling, they had become timid, gutless, and fearful people kowtowing to the whim of their administrators and legislators. Like their students before them, they had become conditioned, throughout their twelve years of public school, to follow orders, then again at the university, and at graduate school. In spite of their fear of students, the only place where they held power was in the classroom. Here, like gods, they wielded it mercilessly with their most powerful weapon—the grade. If students appeared to be bored and inattentive to their monotone lectures, they commonly had temper tantrums. Some even gave exams at 6:30 on Saturday mornings so they wouldn't have to give up their precious, scheduled, lecture class time.

Although students were angry by the time they entered college, they had learned early on to bite the bullet. Throughout twelve years of public schooling, they had been conditioned to submit passively to authority. Farber wanted his students to question, not to accept everything blindly. He lamented that students didn't ask that orders make sense. He was distressed that they had given up expecting things to make sense long before they left elementary school. He was frustrated because students accepted things to be true just because the teacher said they were true.

During these years, students had been programmed not educated. Therefore, by the time they entered college, they had forgotten the math and science they were supposed to have learned, hated literature, and writing. All they appeared to be able to do in Jerry Faber's class was to haltingly ask how to fold their themes and whether to place their names in the upper left or right hand corner (Faber, 1967).

Johnny discovered early in kindergarten that teachers had their favorites. Those who were most obedient and who learned easily what the teacher expected and did well on tests, were favored. In addition, coming from a family that had a reputation of being low class and rowdy didn't help him. As the years progressed he discovered, like Farber said, that school became ever more like a prison. As a high school student he intuitively predicted that it wouldn't be too long before Madison High School would lock kids in the building just like they had been doing in Los Angeles according to Faber's article. And how right he was.

In the spring of 1999, following the shootings at Littleton, Colorado's Columbine High School, the back door of the school was locked. Initially the janitor scribbled a note stating the door would be locked at 7:30 a.m. Shortly thereafter, the principal posted a formally printed sign notifying students that "for their protection" the door would be locked at 7:30 a.m. Of course, the intent was to keep students from skipping out of the building during the day as well as to prevent unauthorized people from secretly entering the school.

The significance of this story is that Johnny was never listened to. Besides feeling validated for having been given a copy of "Student as a Nigger" by a concerned employee of the regional Community Action Program (CAP) agency and distributing it throughout the school, there may be another message as well. Johnny identified with oppressed students since he had been marginalized throughout his schooling by teachers, classmates, and townspeople who represented a higher social class than he did. Instead of nurturing Johnny's interest in learning, the manner in which he was treated by the school system turned him off from school and aided and abetted his rowdy behavior.

Now Johnny is 49 years old. After leading a "hell-raising" lifestyle, according to his mother, he finally married a few years ago. He has one child who is two years old and another just seven months. He works in the construction business in Texas. Imagine how different his life could have been, had he been given the nurturing and encouragement to find a path early on that would have been emotionally fulfilling. Although Johnny was never suspended from school, had he challenged authority in the way he did then, today he most definitely would have been suspended. Should he have challenged the suspension, he more than likely would have been expelled.

Zero Tolerance Policy toward Violence Worsens the Situation

Since our schools react after the fact, i.e., a trend of school violence that finally has penetrated middle-class American schools, they are clamping down ever more harshly on students. Even before the banning of chains, which are now considered weapons, students at Madison High School and at other schools were forbidden from carrying backpacks between classes. These allegedly pose a safety threat to students and teachers. Furthermore, the color black and so-called Gothic clothing is frowned upon.

Unfortunately, school administrators and all too many teachers do not realize that some of the clothing and ornamental fads have a strong message. The black clothing worn by some is a clear indication that these youths feel oppressed and depressed, put down, unwanted, and not listened to. The message is often a cry for respect, for trust, and a yearning for others to care about and understand them. If it is considered by some as rebellion, that is accurate only in the sense that this is these youths' way of getting out their message that they are in pain.

Shortly after the Columbine tragedy a ninth-grade student at Madison High was suspended for wearing a bandanna to school because in her words she "had a bad hair day." The assistant principal had her removed from class by the police because she defied his authority and told him to, "shove it." In a write up of the incident in the local newspaper the assistant principal was quoted as saying:

> "The language was the main reason. She used inappropriate language."
> Maines (the assistant principal) added that the girl was asked several times
> to remove the cloth bandanna from her head. Once disciplinary action was
> taken, he said, he was worried the girl would become angry. "I didn't want
> her angry and walking around the school," he said.

Maines said, with the current atmosphere of disaffected students taking their rage out on other students, he took no chances. "You don't know what an angry student may do," Maines said. "It's a safety issue." (*Waterville Morning Sentinel*, 1 May 1999, 1)

The assistant principal suspended the same girl for the last ten days of school because she had thrown a book at him. Why? He wouldn't let her leave school early to attend the funeral of a rowdy kid from a neighboring school district, who had been killed in a car accident.

Eva, Columbine, and Ostracism

A prime example of a bright and interested student, who has been marginalized by school officials, was a sophomore student at Madison High School, Eva (not her real name). Eva was an honor roll student. She was well read, having completed recently several books by Aldous Huxley, as well as E. M. Forster's short story "The Machine Stops," and Orwell's *1984*. Besides being intelligent, she had great insight into the functioning of schooling that has as its prime purpose to prepare youths for the workforce. She was critical of a school system that was more concerned about supporting the status quo than encouraging students to ask questions and seek answers, and to find their own paths in life. She questioned what she considered to be the narrow-mindedness of most of her teachers and administrators, their desire to prepare students to fit into little neat boxes, and the jobs and careers demanded by business and industry.

Her mother continues to drive a school bus. Her father is disabled, having been severely injured some years ago on the job at the local paper mill. He is partly paralyzed and in constant, excruciating pain. He doesn't understand his daughter who has been an avid reader since she was a small child. He can't understand why she wears chains and black clothes. Besides yelling and screaming at her, he has on various occasions, since she was small, beaten her. After such an assault, within a month following the beginning of the 1998/99-school year, Eva ran away from home. Her mother, who previously had been verbally abusive, passively stood by whenever the father flipped out of control. She notified the police of her daughter's disappearance.

Several students talked with me about Eva, fearing that if she were returned home, her father would continue to be abusive. Together with a friend of hers, a fellow classmate who is artistic and appreciated Eva's search for answers, I searched a run-down neighborhood in the near-by City of Waterville in which I live. Unable to find her, we reported her plight to the Department of Human Services and notified several area police departments not to bring her home. The following day, two of her friends, who do not fit the status quo, came to Waterville to find her. By a stroke of good luck they found her at the first tenement apartment they approached. They brought her to my home together with a truly good friend with whom she was staying. Their relationship appeared platonic. After all she declared her sexual orientation to be lesbian.

This seventeen year-old young man, Chad (not his real name), with whom Eva stayed and still spends every weekend, and his younger brother dropped out of high school. Chad is a kind fellow, a prolific reader and writer of prose and poetry, a heavy drug user and a victim of bi-polar disorder, who has on various occasions been institutionalized. His father, a drug user, recently married a girl who had just turned 18. He had met her while she was a patient at one of the institutions to which his son had been interned. Initially his son and she had been dating. The father has been institutionalized for substance abuse. The mother also has her fair share of emotional issues. She is now attending Narcotics Anonymous.

Both Eva and Chad immediately agreed to notify the Department of Human Services of Eva's circumstances. The next day they came to my home to meet with a caseworker accompanied by a state trooper. It was agreed that Eva would stay with the girl who had found her and this girl's mother until a better solution could be reached. The following Monday she was back in school. Within a few weeks she returned home. A restraining order had been placed on her father by the court system.

Immediately upon her return to school, Eva was hassled by the administration. She had to remove the dog collar around her neck, the chain dangling from her waist, and the chain around her wrist. She tried to reason with the principal who simply told her that chains are dangerous and for the safety of other students she must remove these or face suspension. She reluctantly agreed. However, she still wore black clothing.

At mid-quarter, when warnings were issued to notify parents that their children are failing one or more classes, Eva, like all others who failed a course, was placed on a restricted list. In spite of faithfully making up the assignments missed during her absence and receiving high grades for these, she was still punished. Among the consequences of this restriction was that she had to remain in her homeroom during the daily-20 minute activity period. Since she didn't comply and failed to report for detention, the assistant principal suspended her. Knowing very well why she had run away from home, he still wrote a letter to her parents explaining the reason for the suspension. Her father beat her again. At this point she left home to live with her friend in Waterville. Only following the beginning of the second semester did she return home so she could attend Madison High School.

Since her second return to school she was not only harassed by the administration but also by other students. The administration continued to hassle her about her clothing. They demanded she take off a spiked collar she had been wearing, which she did. A senior boy, a popular football player, hung a bar of soap on her locker to mock her body odor. When she finally complained in writing to the principal about this incident, he reluctantly had the student apologize to her.

A few weeks later, following the Littleton, Colorado, shootings at Columbine High School in the late spring of 1999, the same boy approached the principal in his office. He told him that Eva had a hit list of 10 people whom she was going to kill. Because he believed he was on that list, he felt his life was in danger. Immediately Eva was called to the office. Her backpack and person were searched for weapons. Her locker was inspected. No drugs or weapons were found. As rumor spread quickly throughout the school and the community, students were afraid of her. Frightened parents called the school.

Eva articulately expressed her perception of the Columbine shootings when she participated on a panel discussion in my classroom to process the tragedy. This did not enhance her popularity among some students and staff. Since this subject was not discussed at the school as a whole, and only briefly in a smattering of classes, I asked the newspaper reporter for our area to cover any one of my class discussions. I felt the general public should know at least how one teacher tried to address this situation. The reporter happened to cover the class in which Eva was an active participant. During the discussion Eva drew out the anxieties of several students. At one point she said that she had no more sympathy for the kids who did the killing than those who were killed. One girl, president of the sophomore class, a stereotypical so called preppie jock, broke out in tears and left the classroom for the office. Within minutes the principal stormed into the room beckoning the reporter to come out into the corridor immediately if not sooner. Upon returning, the reporter meekly, like a reprimanded student, took her seat at a student desk. A brave young girl asked her what the principal had said. She replied: "He told me that I may not print this story nor take photographs because I do not have written permission from each student. The same girl, Susan (not her real name), then said, "Mr. Solmitz, write up a permission slip. I'll photo-copy it, and each kid bring it in first thing in the morning." This was done. Promptly the next morning the great majority of students brought in permission slips. The following morning a tame article, that failed to reveal the controversy that had taken place in the classroom, accompanied by a photograph of Eva and several other class members was published on the front page of the regional paper.

Before I could reach my classroom that morning, the principal stopped me in the hallway and gave me a formal letter. In it, he asked whether I had secured parental permission before taking up a controversial issue in class noting that he had already received parental complaints about one student's participation in the class discussion. He was also upset that I had not sought his permission to have a newspaper reporter cover the classroom discussion. He was particularly perturbed because the reporter had "lied" to him when she promised not to put recognizable photographs of Madison High School students in the paper.

Of course, when a reporter comes to take pictures of student athletes or those who will participate in the junior/senior fashion show, no questions are asked, comments made, or restrictions placed on the reporter.

Maybe it was good that no mention was ever made of Eva's controversial statement. It is unlikely that the reporter would have explained why she had made the comment she did and even more unlikely, I believe, that the majority of readers would understand why she said what she did. Eva was suffering from years of painful experiences. She never received sympathy from others. On the contrary, upon her return to school in January, she was excluded more and more by teachers and fellow students. It is understandable that she could not feel sympathy for those who were killed.

At the same time the principal handed me his letter of reprimand, he informed me that several parents had complained that their children didn't feel safe in my class with Eva present. One parent permanently removed her daughter from my class. Unfortunately, the administration, the parents, and their children couldn't understand Eva's pain. They simply saw Eva as a prime example of the student who fosters violence because she was not like their children who fit the status quo. She became the stereotypical kid who might bring a gun to school and who might endanger if not kill their children.

Later during the same discussion, Eva noted that in Serbia and Kosovo, a vicious war was currently raging. She was distressed that American airplanes were dropping bombs, and missiles were fired from ships killing large numbers of innocent people. "Our government is doing this. Isn't this worse than the Columbine shootings?" Another girl stormed out of the room in anger.

Eva, who questioned the use of violence, is both bewildered and amused by the fear she allegedly caused among students, parents, and educators. Even so, she noted that her older brother, whom she refers to affectionately as the "Red Neck," when he was a student at Madison High School in the early 1990s carried a gun in his pick-up truck that he parked daily in the school's parking lot. Academically at rock bottom of his class, an occasional discipline problem, he enlisted in the army upon completing high school. He was sent to Bosnia only to return home disappointed that he hadn't had the opportunity to kill anybody.

Eva explained that such a reaction was not unusual for him. After all, their father taught them that violence solves problems. He even demonstrated how to make bombs. These bombs were very effective in getting rid of ground hogs that raided their garden. However, as the stories about his daughter spread like wildfire throughout the community, he told her that he would gladly make bombs that could be used to send a strong message to those who were harassing her.

Eva completed her sophomore year as an honor roll student. She did not want to return to Madison High School. She did not like the new principal who had just been appointed. This man, raised in a hard-working woodcutter's family from which all five sons attended college, had been teaching math at the school for twenty-nine years. Nicknamed "Thrasher" because in the past, when it was possible to get away with hitting students, he was known to have thrown chalk, books, and blackboard erasers at those who didn't pay attention in his class. He reportedly even physically threw one boy against the slate chalkboard cracking the slate, though only bruising the unlucky lad. An authoritarian by nature, he especially had no patience for students like Eva who questioned authority.

Eva was granted a superintendent's agreement to attend a small, rural neighboring high school. With such an agreement she would not have to pay tuition of close to $5,000 to attend another school system. Eva's experience at the new school appeared little different from that at Madison High. The administration continued to harass her about wearing chains and objected to her clothing style. During the first quarter she earned straight "As." The principal, who reminisced with her about his free thinking years during the sixties, praised her as the brightest student in the school. By November, however, she had been expelled from Carrabec High School because a teacher had pushed her buttons too far.

During a lunch break she asked the teacher on duty whether she could go to her locker that was directly opposite the cafeteria door. The teacher said she needed a pass. Eva, unable to persuade the teacher that she should be allowed to go to her locker, said, "Damn you!" For this, the teacher gave her detention. As she returned to the cafeteria she muttered, "I want to kill you all." Even though her teachers spoke with the principal in her defense, for uttering these words in violation of the schools "zero tolerance policy," she was promptly expelled. SAD #59 and SAD #74 administrators and guidance personnel worked out an arrangement so that she would only have to attend an English class every other day at Madison High School. Her German teacher volunteered to tutor her in German. She would complete her remaining classes through the adult education program at night. A compromise had been reached. Eva would be able to graduate a year ahead of her class, and the school systems would be rid of a controversial student. Of course, she would not be permitted to participate in the formal graduation activities.

I do not believe that Eva would ever bring a bomb to school or shoot the place up with a high-powered gun. However, as schools alienate students further, try to control them with power tactics, and fail to listen to their messages, more Columbines are likely to occur.

Instead of trying to understand the message that these students are trying to tell us by wearing trench coats, the color black, and chains and using drugs, administrators' knee-jerk reaction is to alienate them even further. They feel threatened when students adorn themselves in unconventional clothing and hairstyles suggesting that they will not comply by fitting into the status quo mold. These same administrators and teachers do not seem to realize that when students call in bomb scares, a frequent occurrence in Maine public schools in the fall of 1999, they are sending a strong message, though inappropriately, that school is not meeting their needs. Administrators in particular want to assure anxious parents in their community that their school is safe and that they will do everything possible to assure the physical safety of all students. For instance, following the outburst that occurred at Columbine, the students who were friends of the two boys, who went on a shooting rampage at the school, were informed by the administration never to return to the school again. They allegedly were told that it was for their safety that they would not be allowed to return. However, by failing to listen seriously and take to heart the messages of already cynical students, they are unwittingly creating the chemistry that may trigger more Columbines.

At Madison High School the new principal successfully won the support of the great majority of students. Like Joe Clark, the principal depicted in the movie *Lean on Me*, who turned around a violence ridden and drug infested school in an inner New Jersey city, Colin Campbell tried a similar approach in his first weeks as principal at Madison High.

Campbell gave seniors privileges for the entire year that they previously earned only during the last few weeks of school. In addition, on the first day of school he issued each student a Madison High School T-shirt. He ordered Madison High School sweatshirts for the faculty to wear each Friday on dress-down days. His athletic director organized traditional rallies for athletic teams held prior to the end of classes on Friday afternoons. As principal, he appears to continue the pattern he had demonstrated when he was a teacher of patronizing the college prep students and pandering to their parents, who largely represented the upper socioeconomic group of the community, at the expense of the less motivated students. During the first week of school, he executed his mandate for stringently obeying school rules by suspending several students who failed to comply. In other words, by rallying students and teachers around school spirit, he was able to unite the school community. In this way he could more easily mandate compliance to the norm. By this time, most of the marginalized students had left the school. At least temporarily, the image of Madison High School once again emerged as a nice, little, cohesive school that offered students different paths that might lead them to lucrative occupations.

6

DISSIDENCE CONFRONTS
THE STATUS QUO

Since the general public, business, and industry, as well as state and national legislatures perceive schools are failing in their mission of keeping students in line, especially since school shootings that climaxed with the Columbine tragedy, school administrators panic. They want to give the public the impression that their schools are safe havens for all students. Therefore, they want to exert their image as strict disciplinarians.

However, the rebellious behavior, low academic scores, and the high dropout rate of lower track students is not the result of a lack of self-discipline, stupidity, or their inability to see a bright future at the end of the tunnel. These kids, often the very brightest and insightful of the school population, simply see no point in playing the system's game. They see their chances of trying to reach the aspirations of the college prep. student as far too slim and therefore not worth the effort. The social strata from which most teachers and administrators initially came and to which they currently adhere foster this.

Fear of Big Brother Outweighs Common Sense

All too many administrators feel they must take a tough stand by "expelling" some youths who dispel the image of the compliant student. Then, they find themselves in an awkward position. If they expel a student, they lose a considerable amount of state subsidy for that youth. Furthermore, they are by law required to provide an education for all youths until the age of eighteen. They certainly do not want to have to pay extra money to have these kids tutored. So in many instances they take this apparent tough approach to appease a frightened public and to demonstrate that they really mean business. Frequently, though, they let the students come back within a matter of weeks. When they return, the students are usually required to sign a contract that they will abide by school rules and will pass their classes. However, these contracts are not always enforced, especially if the students, who have been expelled, represent the status quo.

Drug use is a big "no-no" in school these days. After all marijuana is illegal. The principal, the assistant principal, and the guidance counselor searched the lockers of three boys who they thought might have marijuana and then brought these three lads to the office to search their backpacks and persons. They did discover a smattering of drug paraphernalia, i.e., some papers in which to wrap marijuana and a little bowl for smoking. On one boy they found less than an ounce of marijuana. The police were promptly brought in. These boys were immediately sent home and were required to appear with their parents at the next school board meeting. They were "expelled" for the remainder of the quarter, about six weeks.

The staff referred to this board action jokingly as "suspulsion," a combination of suspension and expulsion. Teachers of these boys, of whom I was one, were required to provide weekly assignments, correct, and grade these immediately on the date they were handed in. The boys were told if they so much as failed one course, they would not be readmitted to school. Each of the boys failed two courses. Each was readmitted. Upon return, each had to sign a contract that he would pass his courses and that there would be no discipline problem. Each boy failed at least one course and was allowed to continue at school. Two of the boys finally did drop out on their own accord.

Several weeks following this incident, the principal arranged to hold an all-school assembly with the local police and the state police's canine unit. The state police dog demonstrated how easily it could sniff out marijuana from a locker or on a person. The principal, cheered on by the applause of the majority of the faculty, threatened to bring in the dogs unannounced to eradicate drugs from the school.

There are two messages to be garnered from this assembly. The first is that if it is announced ahead of time that the drug dogs will be brought in, then the majority of students who use drugs will be more cautious about bringing these to school. So when the dogs actually are brought in, it can be reported in the press that Madison High School's zero tolerance for drugs works! Imagine, if no prior warning had been given to students about the possibility of a raid by canines, the newspaper heading might have read: "MADISON HIGH SCHOOL A HAVEN FOR DRUG USE." Congratulations! The principal has once again saved the "good image" of the school. The reality is, that even though the superficial image of the school may have been preserved for a little while longer, the social and economic problems that haunt us continue to flourish unabated outside the school walls.

This concept is not new at all. For instance, in 1978 the superintendent of schools announced that the school day would end at 1:40 p.m. instead of 3:10 p.m. How wonderful that sounded to both students and staff. However, the reason was not to please the students and teachers, but to respond to complaints from the local citizenry. One person, who had driven by the school during the noon hour, was offended to see a girl and a boy necking on the front lawn of the schoolhouse. At least one merchant complained that during the lunch hour students, who bought pizza, sandwiches, cold drinks, and cigarettes (at that time teenage smoking was still legal) had been stealing items from his store.

The superintendent's solution was simple. First, keep all the students in the school building at lunchtime and reduce the lunch period from one hour to thirty minutes. Second, eliminate the half-hour activity period at the end of the day. During this time, before the buses arrive, students could leave or get extra help from their teachers. Now students would have three minutes between the bell that dismissed school to board their busses and quickly be whisked out of the public's eyesight.

The new high school, following a statewide trend, was located in the countryside a mile and a half out of town. Although the argument given publicly was the need for more space to create a large out-of-doors-athletic complex, it seemed that an equally important reason was to preserve the image of the school as a safe haven for the students.

The school board, administration, and educators found it easier to ignore the growing alienation, loneliness, and frustration of youths than address it. For instance, curriculum development that would cause more students to become excited about learning was never considered. Ah, but there was a solution. More and more students were suspended from school for disciplinary reasons. Rather than cause trouble in the school, they were now free to roam the streets. Furthermore, the students and the community at large lost the school as a social, athletic, and academic centerpiece for the entire town. After all, the old high school had a beautiful wood paneled auditorium and a spacious stage, a large gymnasium, and adequate athletic fields.

The school assembly made it clear that teachers, who bitterly complained about the constant barrage of evaluations and documentation imposed by administrators to make sure they toed the line, were often the very ones who applauded bringing in the drug-sniffing dogs to hold students accountable for their behaviors. These teachers seemed to be unaware that the principle of trust, so important in a democratic society, were being eroded by the watchful eye of Big Brother. In addition, by holding students accountable in this way, these administrators and teachers instilled in their students mistrust of adults and alienation and crushed any sense of responsibility. These were, of course, the very reasons why many youths turn to drugs.

Alienation in a Consumer Oriented Society

Although I am focusing on alienation primarily among kids from working-class families, pain and suffering, including alienation, occur regardless of class difference. Some students from well-established families are alienated. That was particularly true of the two boys who went on the shooting rampage at Columbine High School. It is also true that some popular students suffer from severe emotional pain, some of which may have its roots in childhood trauma.

It is not a prerequisite to experience pain in order to be a caring and sensitive person. For example, the president of the sophomore class, who left the discussion on Columbine when Eva expressed what appeared to be less than sympathetic remarks about the Columbine students, is actually a genuinely caring individual. Her tactic to survive in the system is to be part of the elite group. At times she was silly to the point of being disruptive in my class, a behavior of hers unheard of in more conventional classes. However, the reader will discover in the next chapter that she was open to and even adopted some of the democratic approaches we explored and developed in her class in order for her to pursue a specific goal.

Alienation from parents, teachers, and administrators among all social classes of students is common. Although on the surface many students are friendly and cooperative, they do feel anger toward those in authority. The reasons are very simple. By demanding obedience of youths, these adults try to impose their traditional values not readily accepted by kids. They do not nurture their children emotionally and communicate with them at the feeling level. In other words, they are not in touch with their children's feelings, thoughts, and experiences.

Parents and their children spend little time together, even if they are in the same home. According to Ron Taffel, "Family members may be spending time *near* each other, in the same house, engaged in parallel but separate activities, and not remotely doing things together" (Taffel, 1999, 29). He gave the following illustration to support his point.

> Mother, for example, may be supervising her 5-year old in the bath while calling work to arrange a meeting for the next day; sister is e-mailing several buddies and talking with yet another friend on the phone; Dad (if he lives at home, or if it's his weekend with the kids) is busy finishing up a report, looking up every 10 minutes or so to announce it's nearly bedtime to whatever child might actually be listening. (Taffel, 1999, 29).

Not only do kids grow up today under very different circumstances from how their parents did, they have found new heroes and idols to replace them. The rapidly developing technology that introduced television to their parents' generation now exposes youths to the boundless world of cyberspace. Living in a consumer based and entertainment oriented society in which young people and adults, too, demand instantaneous gratification, it is not surprising that youths feel emotionally disconnected from grown-ups. It is much more difficult for both adults and youths to adjust to these technological changes emotionally than it is physically.

Mantak Chia, a teacher and practitioner of Taoist healing methods from Thailand expressed this dilemma succinctly:

> There are so many wizards of the computer, stock market, test tube, and spectator sport, but so few of the art of life. Our race spends its brief span fiddling with statistics, black boxes, noxious chemicals, and above all, with meaningless words. A majority of Americans daily pass more than six hours in a mesmerized trance induced by a colored shadow dancing in a box of glass. These machines have inadvertently become instruments of our own destruction: a TV programmed mind is not a free mind. Too few devote even one second to entering deeply the great current of life hidden within ourselves. Yet all the technological energy is eagerly sought in an apish imitation of the electrifying ecstasies found hidden within the body and mind. (Chia, 1984, 7–8).

Many parents support their kids' materialistic interests. Somehow these may subconsciously replace their feelings of guilt for not spending undivided time with their children. Some help their children to buy "Nike" shoes, "Gap" clothing, or whatever is in style. These are very expensive products earning enormous profits to the corporations that produce them. Parents often introduce their children at a very early age to computers and computer games. Kids become glued to these devices that bring them into galaxies unknown to many adults. At the same time, they are out of their parents' way for hours at a time. Therefore, parents have no idea as to what is going on in the minds and lives of their children. Communication began to break down in early childhood.

With the lack of communication and nurturance from understanding adults, kids are caught up in a conflict. Since they no longer receive undivided attention from their parents, they want instant gratification from entertainment provided by the newest computer gadgets and games to instantaneous friendship. The advertising media have caused them to seek new heroes and idols to replace their parents, i.e., in sports stars whom they see on TV wearing name brand sneakers and clothes. All too often their spiritual and physical needs are appeased through drugs, alcohol, and sex. For all of this they need money. This is not easy to come by especially since states like Maine have legislated that no student in school under the age of eighteen may work more than twenty hours per week at a job. Therefore, to gain the money necessary to supply their expensive desires some students become involved in the illicit drug trade.

Kids long for the emotional security that their parents and teachers want them to have. Since communication has broken down, all they get are attempts by adults to control their lives alienating them further. After all, attempting to control kids in an authoritarian manner while at the same time letting them have the material things they desire, is much easier than giving them the nurturing attention and understanding they so much need to become self-assured, curious, caring, and energetic individuals. Jasper (not his real name) is a case in point.

I got to know Jasper because his mother had told me that her son is a computer whiz. When I had computer problems, I called Jasper. He was always polite, prompt in coming to my home, and helpful in resolving the problem.

Jasper did not attend Madison High School but another consolidated school near Waterville, the city in which I live. I am writing about him, a middle-class student, who is not representative of Madison High School, because of his socioeconomic class, and because he experiences loneliness because of lack of communication with his parents. Like other teenagers, he is a product of American capitalist consumerism interested in making money to fulfill his materialistic desires.

Jasper is not a so-called marginalized student. He is now eighteen, tall, handsome, and exceedingly well mannered. He continues to be an honor roll student. He has a brown belt in karate, continues to take weekly classes, and teaches this martial art to small children. He is well liked by his classmates and teachers. He is interested in different cultures, having traveled with his Spanish class to Spain, and he has developed an interest in the Chinese occupation of Tibet. He appreciates my Chinese wife's Chinese cooking so much that he requested that she write out the recipe so he could make dumplings for his mother.

Jasper's parents are New Yorkers. So in Maine lingo the family is considered "flatlanders." His mother is a practicing Jew. Her grandparents came from Russia fleeing during the 1905 revolution there. In fact, Jasper is proud to be Jewish and relishes his limited knowledge of Hebrew. He attended Hebrew school for five years. His father is Catholic, the grandson of Polish immigrants. He is a well educated professional.

As much as Jasper loves his parents, relations are strained. Both parents continue to be strict with him and his thirteen-year-old brother. In fact, Jasper is angry at them. In his words, "they are trying to control my life and constantly interfere with it. They don't understand me and my ways." Therefore, he doesn't tell them what he does. It was only because his math teacher, a friend of his karate instructor, overheard a conversation that he and his friends were going to camp out overnight on his parents' fifteen acres of land and drink alcohol that she reported the incident to his karate teacher. The sensei telephoned Jasper's parents. Needless to say his parents were furious. They told him that if he does "bad things," he was old enough to go to jail and they wouldn't bail him out. His parents do know that he smokes cigarettes. They naturally frown on this habit not only because it is unhealthy but because Jasper is asthmatic. Apparently, they aren't aware that he chews the stuff, too.

At one point I asked Jasper what he wanted to do when he graduated from high school the following June. He replied that he wanted to enlist in the Marines. After all, since his parents seemed reluctant to pay his college expenses, the Marines would pay a large percentage if he enlisted for four years. Furthermore, he believed that by being a Marine, he would become a stronger man. He still might change his mind and go directly to college particularly one at which he could party heartily.

During our conversations it turned out that he knew Eva and Chad quite well. "How do you know them?" I asked. He explained that he gave names of high school students to Chad who then sold them drugs. Jasper received a percentage of the profit from Chad for each deal that he helped arrange. Since he was not actually trafficking in drugs, he believed he was safe from arrest. He did admit that on occasion he did smoke dope but had never tried anything stronger.

I asked Jasper why he had become involved with this trade. For money he said. He wanted to buy more computer parts and games. Name brand clothes were expensive, too. And after high school he wanted to take another school trip to Spain and spend an extra week there. Working one day a week at Wal-Mart didn't provide him the money he needed. He said he made much more money through the illicit drug trade and therefore was able to make a down payment for the forthcoming trip to Spain.

Will Jasper become a druggie and a loser? NO. He simply has found a way to survive in a consumer oriented materialistic society. Will he get in trouble with the law? Probably not, though he may have some close calls as the following incident illustrates.

Chad and he were standing together near city hall in the heart of downtown Waterville. Chad dressed in his usual Gothic style: dyed turquoise hair and wearing a quilt adorned with chains. As a police officer came up to them, Chad passed drugs to Jasper. The officer searched Chad for drugs. Obviously, the officer found none on him. Because Jasper didn't have the appearance of a druggie, the officer never bothered to search him.

The message from this illustration suggests that society judges people by their outward appearance not by the depth of their being. When a kid like Chad senses this, of course, he is going to feel unaccepted, discouraged, hopeless, and even angry. Nobody, he can effectively argue, understands him. Of course, he will feel more alienated and likely escape into the quasi-comfort of drugs. Jasper even observed that Chad does not like to sell drugs. He does it only to have food on the table since, without a high school diploma, he is unemployable.

Jasper is experiencing a conflict of values. On the one hand, he would like to go to a party-hearty college, to have a good time while he is getting the education he believes he must get. At the same time, he longs for the discipline that he experiences through Karate and which he believes he will get in the Marines. The conflict is caused by several forces that are tearing at him from all sides.

Success in America today is defined by a person being an affluent consuming member of the middle class who has vast material wealth at his or her disposal. It also implies a form of passive relaxation stemming from entertainment. Therefore, Jasper eventually has to earn a lot of money and have plenty of credit so that he can have what he wants instantaneously. After all, money not only purchases the materialistic lifestyle to which he has been conditioned through manipulative advertisements on TV and in popular magazines, but it also provides him with the status of being a successful member of middle-class America. At the same time, Jasper, the teenager, is rebelling against the control that comes from his family, teachers, and karate trainer. Sometimes the control is subtle, i.e., don't watch "R" rated movies; don't drink alcohol; get good grades; stay away from drugs and the "bad" people who use them; earn money to pay for college. It costs nearly $30,000 a year to attend a good private college such as Colby, Bates, or Bowdoin in Maine. This amount is very high for Jasper, considering that his parents are state employees, and their income does not make it easily possible for him to attend one of these colleges. To illustrate my point, the average wage in Maine is about $22,000 a year.

Since Jasper's parents, like so many other folks along with many school teachers and administrators, do not seem to understand and heed Montak Chia's message, they will continue to widen the lack of communication between themselves, their children, and youths, in general. Instead of tackling the causes of these problems that lie deep within the consumer oriented and materialistic based socioeconomic system that Americans appear to cherish, they attack the symptoms of a failing culture by trying to control young people. They, for example, insist that movies and lyrics by popular rock groups be censored by labeling them "R" and "X" without acknowledging that these are often produced by multinational corporations that realize huge profits from them. Many parents, school administrators, teachers, politicians, and others fervently uphold anti-drug laws and advocate severe punishment for use and trafficking not only of hard drugs but also of marijuana as well. Even so, they fail to make the correlation between students like Jasper who market illegal drugs as a way by which to satiate their materialistic desires and work to earn money for their college expenses and those who are habitual drug users.

Finally, Jasper feels that he needs to take control of his life. The only way he knows how is to continue to be controlled by his parents, teachers, and his karate instructor. He has never really been allowed to develop responsibility. Responsibility is the result of nurturing parents and teachers who encourage their children to make new experiences. It means that children are able to share their good as well as bad experiences with their parents, their teachers, and their peers. Accompanied by empathy and support children do develop responsibility.

Jasper will graduate from high school with honors. If he doesn't go to college immediately following graduation, he will get his college degree upon completing his stint in the service. Undoubtedly, he'll make a lucrative career in the high-tech industry. He will be a family man, well appreciated at his job, and a caring individual. He will soon give up tobacco. He will lead a healthy life. After all, it was Jasper who recently urged me to buy a protective screen for my computer so the radiation won't damage my brain!

The Relationship between Pain and Social Class

Much of the pain from which students suffer in school undoubtedly has to do with issues of social class. Our schools, public and private, are geared toward preparing youths to become gainfully employed. By becoming self-reliant, as opposed to being dependent upon welfare, they can be avid consumers who keep the economy on a roll. Those students who come from low-income backgrounds, whose parents do not value a college education for their children, like Johnny, are immediately designated as losers from the time they enter kindergarten. When they enter high school, they are assigned to the lowest track.

Because many of these kids have been told that they are failures throughout their schooling, some simply become lethargic and eventually drop out of school. Others have discipline problems and take it for granted that they will be suspended which implies given a short reprieve from the horrors of school.

Because of low-self esteem, some boys and girls bully other kids. As much as they feel looked down upon by more than a few teachers and by fellow classmates among the preppie-jocks, some feel a need to pick on kids weaker than themselves. A common target is the little nerd boy. He might be stuffed into a locker or his books may be thrown into the toilet. Other targets are students in the special education classes some of whom severely lack any kind of social skills

According to Fine, Weis, and Addelston (1998) white working-class males "are drenched in a kind of post-industrial, late twentieth-century individualism" (149). Because they are adversely affected by deteriorating economic and social conditions, they "scour their 'local worlds' for Who has robbed them of their presumed privilege — finding answers in historically likely suspects, blacks, women and sometimes gays" (Fine et al., 1998, 150). Therefore, it is not surprising that boys, particularly from the lower economic group, tend to be outwardly homophobic. They are apt to be authoritarian, controlling in their relationships with girls, often emulating the attitudes of their fathers. Because of insecurity, they tend to enforce the norms of male sex-role behavior and fear any change of the male sex-role. Gregory Lehne supported this concept in his article "Homophobia among Men" (1976). He noted that "homophobia is a threat used by heterosexist individuals to enforce social conformity to the male role, and maintain social control. The taunt WHAT ARE YOU, A FAG? is used in many ways to encourage certain types of male behavior and to define the limits acceptable to masculinity" (Lehne, 1976, 1).

It was only in the spring of 1998 that the first student at Madison High School came out of the closet admitting that she is lesbian. Apparently a great athlete, she was not severely harassed. However, in 1999 a sophomore boy admitted being gay. Although he was a student in the "elite" college prep group, he was not one of the preppie-jocks. He admitted that the ridicule he received came primarily from boys in the lowest academic track. I discussed with him various diplomatic forms of action we could explore ranging from an all-school assembly program with follow-up small group discussions on harassment to directly confronting these boys together with the guidance director. Although he constantly reminded me that their taunts didn't bother him, he chose to work together with several other students and myself in developing an all school program. (See chapter 8).

Many homophobic boys tend to be racist as well. Although they make the politically correct statement that they are not prejudiced against Blacks, they often admit to unwillingness to date a girl of color. However, some blatantly spurt out that they would have no problem having sexual intercourse with a girl of color while drunk or stoned at a party. Until just a few years ago, such boys said they would refuse a blood transfusion in a life or death situation from a Black person. Now most are willing to do so having learned in their science classes that blood from people of color won't change their appearance.

Race is another issue that is contentious. In the early months of 1999, three siblings from California came to our school. All three showed signs of having had a tough life. They appeared streetwise, sullen, and even angry. As the complexion of the two boys was darker than most of the lily-white students at the school, they were harassed as being "Spics," even though they were of Portuguese descent rather than Puerto Rican. However, of course, using epithets as the one mentioned is never acceptable.

One noontime in the lunchroom, three junior boys, in the lowest-track division, taunted them with racial slurs and obscenities. The two boys launched back with anger. At this point the assistant principal intervened. Instead of pursuing the taunters, he yelled at the newcomers. The two brothers, already humiliated and angered, were not about to be blamed for their behavior. Apparently, they yelled at the assistant principal telling him they would fight it out with him. He promptly told the office secretary to call the police. Because of the threatening behavior of the two brothers, he succeeded in suspending each for at least five days. That afternoon, after talking with the older brother, I called the hate-crimes unit of the attorney general's office for the State of Maine. Upon investigating the situation, they were able to get the assistant principal to reduce the number of days of suspension assigned to the brothers. However, still no school administrative action was taken against the perpetrators.

All too often girls from the lower social economic strata, who usually belong to the lowest academic track, are labeled as sluts, even by their own peers. Some are disposed to demean other girls verbally. On occasion, humiliating comments relating to these girls are inscribed on the walls of the girls' toilets.

Since the dominant social groups determine what is valued in the educational and social systems, the subordinate, or lower-class groups do not meet the criteria established by the dominant ones. Therefore, the self-esteem and academic performance of these lower-track students often suffers as a result of their social status. In reality these students are not inferior; they are simply judged as deficient by the standards established by the school made up of members of the small dominant class in the community, state, and nation.

Teacher Adherence to the Status Quo Alienates Some Students

Teachers and their administrators reflect the status quo of the middle class. Even if some have been raised in this social stratum, they have become middle class. Like the college prep students, who most favor teaching, they were members of the same elite when they were in high school. On the whole, school was easy for them. They did what the teachers asked, did well in feeding back the information that their teachers dispensed to them. They raised their hands in class, answered the teachers correctly, and mastered short answer, matching, and multiple choice tests. Many were elected members of the National Honors Society. Numerous played sports. Some were involved in drama, public speaking, and debate. More than a few teachers held class office while in high school and were active in a wide variety of organizations that ranged from the Key Club to Science Club to the Drama Society. Naturally, they feel an affinity to those students whose socioeconomic background, ability to comply with the system, and aspirations remained well within the range of the status quo.

Many administrators and teachers alike appear to champion the concept of the student who receives the "student of the month award." This type of student excels in academics, sports, class activities, and community service. They represent the all-around good citizen who will succeed in today's corporate world. If they do not go into business and strive to become corporate executives, at least they will become "productive citizens." They may become lawyers, doctors, or scientists who will further the stereotypical image of the United States as a prosperous nation with few if any social and economic problems.

Because many teachers feel that they are servants of the community in which they work, they believe they have an obligation to uphold its values. When Eva once handed in an assignment to her English teacher to analyze a poem or a song, her analysis of a song written by the rock band Dead Kennedys was handed back to her. The lyrics of the song were unacceptable to the teacher, even though she agreed that its message about our violent, sex driven society was relevant.

The teacher, with whom I spoke, explained that even though she may have allowed her teenage sons to listen to such songs, the obscene language in the lyrics did not represent the values of the community. When asked what the values of the community may be, she answered rather romantically, that they represented the conservative views traditionally held by majority of the people of this little, staid New England community.

Two years before, a girl published a poem that explored the beauty of making love as a spiritual experience in the school's second issue of "Paw Prints." An elderly woman, the chief cook at the school, found the poem offensive and promptly reported her concern to the administration. The entire paper was banned. Upon telling the story to Gerry Boyle, a columnist for the regional paper, he wrote the following piece for his column entitled "According to Boyle." In it he expressed sympathy for the lack of understanding that many teenagers experience in their relationships with adults, especially their teachers and administrators. He empathizes with their yearning to be heard and understood.

"School paper runs afoul of grandma"

The first edition of paw prints, a student publication at Madison Area High School, got mixed reviews.

Some students thought there were too many poems and stories and that too much of the poetry was about dark stuff, like teen suicide.

Coeditors Jennifer Trask and Katrina Stewart didn't really agree, but they said they would lighten up a bit.

"Our intent was not to depress you," the editors wrote in the preface to issue No. 2 published last month. "We just wanted you (not so much students as adults) to understand what it is like to be a teenager in 1997."

So the last issue led off with a haiku-shaped poem about being confused and lost, something any teenager can relate to. There was a poem narrated by someone in a mental hospital. And perhaps because the paper came out on Valentine's Day, there was another matter of great interest to teenagers.

Untitled, it started off like this:

Lately I've been dreaming
A perfect dream of you
I touch your face and feel the
  Moist warmth of your mouth
  Upon my finger tips
  I find it impossible to keep my lips
  From you
  Our bodies pressed together
  I can't get enough of you and
  Your hands travel down my hips
  Undressing is a slow torturous
    Battle that we soon conquer
  And become yet closer
  Burning flesh entwined so tightly

We pulsate as one.

And so on, for another 24 lines that include references to pain and ecstasy, naked bodies, and love.

You've got it. The S-word. Sex.

"But if you read into it, it's about more than sex," said Trask, a 17 year-old junior. "It was about two people becoming one. It was about love, but it was more than the physical aspect. It was emotional and spiritual."

The poem was written, though not based on firsthand knowledge, by a student named Tasha. Tasha, a junior who is 16, loves photography, writing, and The Grateful Dead, and dreams of someday shooting pictures for Rolling Stone magazine. But now Tasha is at Madison High School, where her artistic endeavors had barely hit the newsstand when they already were causing a stir.

According to Tasha, Trask, and others at the school, 300 of the freshly printed (copied and stapled) papers were put on a table that morning.

About 30 papers had been taken when the alarm went out.

"I was in class," Tasha said, " and they came in and they said they took our paper and they were going to burn it."

Which wasn't true. The papers weren't burned, just confiscated.

"Essentially, this is a publication that wasn't filtered through the normal channels and I had to pounce on it first and ask questions later," said Vice Principal William "Pete" St. John.

Well, questions were asked, at least by Trask and Tasha, who pronounced themselves appalled by the school's action. Trask, admittedly, lost her temper with St. John and was handed three hours detention for using inappropriate language.

St. John, at the school last week, stood by his action.

"We wouldn't have printed that in pictorial form or any other sort of artistic form," he said. "We would censor lyrics like that if they wanted to play them at a dance or before a baseball game or something like that."

St. John said he wasn't criticizing the poem's literary merit, and said it might be well suited to another publication. But he said the poem was too graphic for younger students, and for the rural Maine communities the school serves and reflects.

And the poem was about teenagers and sex.

Most parents, he said, don't want the school "to moderate that discussion for them."

"It's got to pass the grandmother test," St. John said.

Literally, according to Trask and Tasha.

They said they understood that the first alarm was sounded by an older woman who works in the cafeteria and picked up the paper that morning. St. John said that may have been a misunderstanding stemming from his use of the cafeteria worker as an example of the kind of sensibility students should consider.

Either way, the poet herself said she doesn't get it.

"I'm just kind of surprised because I didn't think it would be that big of a deal," Tasha said. "I don't understand why they would ban the paper because of a poem about sex, a poem about love."

I think I have an idea.

For one thing, I think the administration knew that some parents would have been less than pleased to have this poem read aloud at the supper table by their freshman girl or boy. Some parents would have been as hot as the poem is, by their standards, steamy.

In fact, yanking the kids' paper may even have reflected what the parental community would have wanted, but it raises other questions, such as:

Do we think 15-year olds really don't know what goes on around them? Whom are we kidding? Ourselves, not them.

One Madison High School teacher, David Solmitz, said the issue was about freedom of expression for students, about tolerance for others' view in a democracy. Solmitz passed along some proposed legislation on student expression, which Augusta lawyer, Jed Davis, has given to House Speaker Libby Mitchell.

The legislation would give students the right to publish and say what they want, unless it's obscene, libelous, invades privacy, or incites students to riot.

A "grandmother test" is not included.

But it was at Madison High School, and though I can understand why, I still wonder what message this sends kids. Teen suicide is a fitting topic, but an innocent and honest poem about sex and love gets yanked?

But really, folks, this little skirmish in Madison just reflects the rest of us. We don't talk to kids about sex in our culture, except, of course, in the din of videos and blue-jean ads. When sex appears it's usually in the context of some sort of violence or degradation. You won't see a breast on TV, but you will see a barrage of brutality.

Sex and love? On prime time, the two do not coexist. When was the last time you saw a made-for TV movie about a couple happily married and doing you know what.

For the last 50 years? Isn't it funny that we don't talk about sex with the next generation, when without it, there wouldn't be any next generation at all?

But it's happening all around us. As you read this, somebody is experiencing just what Tasha wrote about in her poem for a Madison High School creative writing course.

"I did pass it in, and the teacher didn't have any problem with it at all," she said.

"Did you get a grade?" she was asked.

"I got an A." Tasha said.

Two naked bodies wrapped up in
Each other's arms
It's so beautiful
Your breathing is so peaceful

The rhythmic way my head rises
   And falls on your chest soothes
Salvation surrounds us
   We have shut out the hatred
   of the outside world
   Our love is all that matters. (Morning Sentinel, 3/9/1997)

Because of their own middle-class background, their revered status as students of the college preparatory group, and their adherence to the values of the norm, all too many teachers do not like and have difficulty working with lower-track students. It is these students who are least appreciated by most of their teachers. Therefore, they perform to a "T" to meet the labels given to them even before they entered kindergarten.

These are often kids, like Johnny, who come from low-income, broken homes. They may be bright, but they are seen and treated as troublemakers. They are not motivated to learn within the conventional system. Often they are discipline problems. They are all too frequently criticized for their use of profanity and for their coarseness. They are the students who are most likely to be suspended frequently and even expelled. In Madison, by the time such boys reach high school, they are often referred to as "Skidder Boys," because of the work boots and flannel shirts they wear that identify the men who work in the logging industry.

Some of the girls in this group are stereotyped as low life. Although these girls may be less of a discipline problem, they are no more motivated than the boys. Often it is kids from this group who make the "Court News" section of the newspaper for losing their driver's license for OUI (Operating Under the Influence), for breaking and entering, and for burglary. Of course, we don't hear about the rare few of their classmates in the college prep group, who years later, as successful professionals and pillars of their community, are charged with embezzlement, tax evasion, or even pedophilia. Most of the lowest-track kids will get minimum wage jobs. A few might end up on the welfare rolls.

Low Self-Esteem Enhanced by Tracking
Fuels Emotional Problems

Even though some students' problems are socioeconomic, others are cultural, and a large number are home based, teachers and administrators must understand and respond sensitively to the reasons why so many students do not function effectively at school. To be able to do so, they should have a basic understanding of psychology. Take, for example, the case of Frank, a sophomore at Madison High School during the 1998 to 1999 academic year.

At age thirteen, this bright and sensitive boy was already in trouble with the law. On one occasion the police discovered a package of unopened bullets that had been stolen from Madison's police station. Frank recalled that he was lucky that the gun he and other boys stole from the police station was never recovered, and no evidence was found that he was involved in the actual burglary. Nor was he ever nailed for removing the steps to the police station on a Halloween night.

Frank liked to party. He, like his father, was a heavy beer drinker. Some kids described him as coming close to being an alcoholic. He also used drugs, relying primarily on marijuana but was also an admitted user of the hard stuff. His mother, whom I recall as a bright and involved student in my college preparatory class, did go on to college. However, she returned to Madison, had two children from two different men, and became addicted to crack cocaine. At the same time that she tried to raise her two sons, she worked hard to further her education. As a result, she was not home all that often, leaving Frank to his own devices.

When I had Frank in school, during the 1998–1999 academic year, he was in the lowest academic track. However, in my government/economics class he was a prize student. He got involved in projects, especially one on problems at the Maine Youth Center. He read articles on complaints about the Center brought forth by Amnesty International. He read up on the history of the state's reform school and brought to class a couple of his friends who had been incarcerated there for participation in a lively panel discussion. He spoke articulately about more humane means of reforming youths by showing appreciation for the good things they do rather than always emphasizing the bad.

Due to the fact that Frank skipped a lot of school, his mother, out of desperation mid-way through his sophomore year, sent him to live with his father. This huge man, especially, when drunk, was both physically and verbally abusive. He, too, had his share of unpleasant encounters with the law. He seems unable to hold a job since he is usually fired within a short period of time.

Frank, eager to get to know his dad more closely, asked him about his experiences during the Vietnam War. Since he would not share these with his son, Frank read books and rented numerous Vietnam era movies. He was particularly moved by Oliver Stone's films: *Platoon, Between Heaven and Earth*, and *Born on the Fourth of July*. At Frank's suggestion, we invited several Vietnam veterans to share their experiences and thoughts about the war with the class. Frank was deeply engrossed in these discussions, raising thoughtful and thought provoking questions.

Frank had a girlfriend of whom he was exceedingly possessive. He often

left session to drag her out of class or meet at an appointed time in the corridor. He never let her out of his sight. It was reported that he was both verbally and physically abusive to her. For roaming the halls without a "pass,"
for skipping school, for failing to report for after-school and also for
Saturday detention, and for talking back to the assistant principal, he was
frequently suspended. Because of a school policy that says if a student miss-
es more than ten days of school, he or she will automatically fail all courses, in mid-May he had to appear before an appeals board consisting of the
assistant principal, guidance counselor, and a teacher. Naturally, the days
for which he was suspended were counted as days missed. Since he wasn't
granted a waiver, he had to appeal to the principal. That appeal's process
never materialized.

In early June, within an hour before the end of the school day, the assistant principal, with whom Frank had numerous confrontations, approached
him in the hall. He did have a pass. However, since he had his backpack
with him, in violation of school policy, the assistant principal in his words
"made him take it to the office so it could be searched." Lo and behold, an
unloaded gun, two unopened beer cans, and a small amount of marijuana
were found in the bag. Within minutes three police cruisers descended upon
the school.

The assistant principal took great pride in announcing to the staff at an
emergency faculty meeting how he enhanced safety at the school. He noted
he had already submitted the paper work to the superintendent to have the
boy expelled from school. By having him sent to an adolescent treatment
program, he felt he did a good deed in helping the lad work through his problems. (Frank was released within three days). However, it was only through
questioning on the part of a teacher at this meeting that we learned the boy
had no ammunition with him, that he was of no danger to anybody other
than himself. He intended to use the gun on himself.

It was very evident that Frank was experiencing severe depression. He
looked for relief in drugs. Anything he could do straight, he could have more
fun doing buzzed. His abusive relationship with his girlfriend was a sign of
low-self esteem if not depression. Neglect and abuse by parents only added
to his despondent state of mind and low self-esteem.

According to Terrence Real in his book *I Don't Want to Talk about It*
(1998) a traumatized youth, in Frank's case by his father's rage, becomes a
tormentor himself. At the same time his parents' emotional neglect caused
him to hate himself and feel powerless as well as shame. Real, by reflecting
on his own life, suggests a similar pattern adopted by Frank. The difference
is that Frank never had even the cultural encouragement to pursue college
from his parents as Real had from his. Even so, the similarity between Frank
and Real is obvious: "Cold blackness has been my companion for decades.

Through my teens and twenties, my unwillingness to sit still inside that darkness drove me into drug abuse, wildly inappropriate relationships, risk taking, and petty crime" (Real, 1998, 251).

The last I heard about Frank was that he had a new girlfriend and was no longer attending school.

Had we as teachers and administrators understood Frank and responded appropriately to his background, we might very well have been able to work with him through his depression that caused him and others serious problems. Had we developed a trusting relationship with him, there is no doubt that he would have responded positively. For example, he told me that his English teacher had given him a book on the Vietnam War that she had found at a yard sale. He read it voraciously. Obviously he was touched by her thoughtfulness. In Frank's case, and undoubtedly in many others as well, the "tough" stance, that all too many "educators" take to uphold their image as strict disciplinarians, only antagonized him more and continued to deflate his self-esteem and enhance his despondency.

Real tells us that "one of the ironies about men's (boys) depression is that the very forces that help create it keep us from seeing it" (Real, 1998, 22). Since men are not supposed to show pain, if they do, they most likely feel shame. Even their family and friends may feel that shame. Therefore, by keeping their pain secret and hidden deep within themselves, the effects are often physical illness, alcohol and drug abuse, domestic violence, failures in intimacy, and self-sabotage in their careers. By externalizing their pain, men are more likely to feel victimized by others and release their distress through violence. All of these factors appear to have affected Frank.

Girls, on the other hand, internalize their pain. They tend to blame themselves and as adults "draw distress into themselves" (Real, 1998, 24). However, when girls experience pain, as is evident among high school girls, they will turn to their friends for comfort. Often I have excused a girl from my classroom because she was in distress. Without exception another girl would accompany her to the "Girls Room" where they could talk.

On the other hand, Real notes that when boys disclose depression, they are frequently met with outright hostility from their male peers. Such boys are alienated from other youths. They often have few or no friends. They seem to hide within themselves. Often as a teacher I sense a lot of anguish, while at the same time many of these boys appear to be numb. They suppress their emotions since they simply do not know how to handle them. Real explains, since boys are ostracized from showing their feelings, they can only manifest their pain externally. In this way, they avoid the outward signs of depression. However, this behavior drives them into covert depression. They turn against themselves and even lose their capacity to feel anything at all.

As teachers we are neither trained to be therapists nor do we have the time and energy to work extensively with young people in helping them overcome their often deeply rooted problems. Since many teachers have not had sufficient training in psychology, it might be worthwhile for schools to hold workshops on such psychological issues as teenage depression, its symptoms, and how to deal with them. Certainly, continuing education courses for teachers could be offered in this field. For instance, we may learn not to take youthful misbehaviors personally. Such training may also help us understand how to deal with a troubled boy or girl so that we may be able to help avoid or at least effectively defuse a difficult situation. Finally, we should have sufficient knowledge as to whom to refer a student with problems, be it the school guidance counselor or the school social worker, should the school be fortunate enough to have one employed. In some rare instances, students may have to be sent to the principal. Once a student realizes that the teacher genuinely cares about him or her and is skilled in dealing effectively with his or her conflict, then the student gradually develops greater respect for and trust in the teacher. These are important factors that help make a teacher a successful educator.

Simultaneously, though, teachers need to have fundamental self-knowledge. Teachers should know why certain students push their buttons, why they favor some students over others. They must also understand why they wanted to become teachers. With this knowledge it is important for the teacher to explore those forms of discipline they wish to pursue to fulfill their own professional purpose. Do they simply comply with the traditional norm of classroom management that says that if the teacher isn't in control of the class, the result will undoubtedly be chaos? Doesn't the same philosophy also warn that children need to be told exactly what is expected of them or face the consequences? Does a teacher often use this approach to maximize time on task and obedience to authority? What might happen if the teacher's primary objective were to motivate young people about the joys of learning and to foster a greater depth of understanding? Would the results be negative if teachers tried to develop mutually respectful and trusting relationships between themselves and the students? Would such a relationships also allow students to genuinely appreciate the uniqueness of each of their classmates? Will the students be able to grow, to become in Pindar's words who they are? (Kohn, 1996).

Discipline Upholds Mainstream Community Values

In order to adhere to and maintain the established standards of the school and community, the school focuses primarily on discipline. In this way the school appears to imagine that by trying to control youthful behavior, it will successfully mold students into compliant but competitive, marketable employees or lucrative employers. However, the rebellious behavior, low academic scores, and the high dropout rate of lowest-track students are not the result of a lack of self-discipline, stupidity, or their inability to see a bright future at the end of the tunnel. These kids, often the very brightest and insightful of the school population, simply see no point in playing the game of the system.

Alfie Kohn in his book *Beyond Discipline: From Compliance to Community* (1996) explores why the traditional pattern of discipline is ineffective. Trying to control student behavior with the carrot and stick approach, reward or punishment does not create healthy, independent thinking, or self-actualized individuals. He notes that this approach is negative. At best it can only accomplish temporary compliance. Teachers and administrators can only manipulate a student's actions. They cannot and do not help a student to become a kind and caring person. I have already offered evidence from my own experience that punishment "can't possibly have a positive effect on that person's motives and values, on the person underneath the behavior" (Kohn, 1996, 26). Kohn argues that punishing the same students over and over is deeply rooted in rigid values. Adults are in charge and students must be obedient, even if they perceive the adult to be in the wrong.

Kohn explains that punishment never solves a problem; it only makes it worse. The more one punishes a person, the angrier the person becomes. Since the need to punish intensifies, a vicious cycle is underway. That is why at Madison High School the assistant principal is so much hated by many students. It is the same ones whom he detains and suspends time and time again. No wonder students accuse this man of being on a power trip. What might have happened, not only to his relationship with students, but to their own development had he tried to reason and negotiate with them? Wouldn't the values he would be teaching here be more in tune with the principles of a democratic society? Kohn realizes that "punishment actually impedes the process of ethical development. A child threatened with an aversive consequence for failing to comply with someone's wishes or rules is led to ask, rather mechanically, 'What do they want me to do, and what happens to me if I don't do it?' a question altogether different from 'What kind of person do I want to be?' or 'What kind of community do we want to create?'" (Kohn, 1996, 28).

Last year a student of mine, disheartened by the antagonistic relationship between many students and some teachers, including the assistant principal, did a research project for my government class in which she visited two alternative schools; one public for "at risk" students and the other a small, private venture, comparing their approaches to discipline to Madison High School.

This student became a mother before she completed high school, she suffered from bi-polar disorder, and she had been a patient at an adolescent treatment program recovering from substance abuse. Furthermore, she displayed a slew of behavior problems for which she was frequently suspended, and she was labeled as a slow learner and placed in the lowest academic group. Now married to her child's father, she is attending college. Clearly, the reader will find Marianne to be an insightful, open-minded thinker, whose point of view is articulately expressed and should be taken seriously. In a March 1999 essay she wrote for my government/economics class, she compares the authoritarian approach to students at Madison High School with a more humane attitude at a small, private alternative school, Evergreen-Sudbury, in Hallowell about an hour's drive from Madison:

> I started this project in hopes of reaching a compromise between the students and teachers to make Madison High School run smoother....
>
> The reason behind this project is Madison Area Memorial High School has recently been struggling with many problems. The students feel that it is the result of the authoritarian approach of the vice-principal, teachers, and staff. We think such problems like truancy, tardiness, and passes have been handled incorrectly.
>
> I feel the way rules are enforced by the staff is the major problem in the school. Though I agree that the rules are reasonable, the handling of the infractions border on abuse. Throughout the year I have observed the authoritarians, the ones that are to be the mature adults in the situation, [are] often yelling at, degrading, and making fun of the students involved. This leads to many more problems, personality conflicts, and it just magnifies the situation. While the student maybe shouldn't have broken the rule at all, once the damage is done, it is up to the adult to de-escalate the situation and bring things back to normal.
>
> An example of the problems we've experienced within the school would be a situation that happened last year. A student and teacher were in the hallway, and they were arguing about something the student had done. When the teacher was done hollering at him, and turned around to walk away, the student then made an offensive, obscene gesture to her. Another teacher in the hall saw this and reacted immediately. The student was brought to the office and sat down in front of everyone. The teacher with whom the student had been fighting and the teacher who had witnessed the gesture, ganged up on him. One got in his personal space, finger in the face, and began to holler at him using words like "punk" and "hoodlum." Meanwhile, the principal and other teachers stood watching silently. The student received three days suspension and the teacher's actions were overlooked. I, myself, was sitting right next to this situation as it happened and feel it was very inappropriate. . . .

While I visited the alternative school, I made it a point to notice the way students were treated. They seemed to have a fine relationship with the staff. I asked about why they thought they got along. A response I got was that the teachers treat the kids as though they are adults. Each teacher is referred to by their first name and is the first one to stick up for the kid in a problem. . . .

Equality in the schools seems to be quite important. Maybe not a first name basis for a public school, but definitely listening skills are required to get anywhere in life. Maybe when a student is obscene, the teacher can pull them away from everyone, maturely talk about the situation. This way the student will feel respected and the relationship will improve.

At the alternative schools, when a problem occurs, it is approached in a mature and understanding manner. Both the student and staff member sit down to give points of view and let each other have their turn in talking. The staff talks without prying into the personal business of the student, which brings about trusting and understanding relations in the school. Maybe, the alternative school can be a good example to the public schools. In the alternative schools, a student is treated very fairly. But this isn't a one-way thing: the student treats the teacher with respect. Like I scratch your back, you scratch mine kind of thing, but all respectfully portrayed. If the students at Madison High School learned to become more respectful and mature, then there wouldn't be as many problems in the first place. Things would be just as peaceful with a less stressful atmosphere.

Still the thought of the alternative school's approach of teaching and policies on certain things, I feel would not be good to use for public schools. First, the extreme change would come as quite a surprise to the district, and the students would become very destructive. They might not even attend regularly because it would be like a field day (every day) to them. Even so, some of their structures and policies would be quite a relief on everyone if the public schools filtered in some new rules. High school, as the teachers say, is supposed to be a wonderful learning experience. Some of the adults in our lives believe it is supposed to be the best years of your life. So why make school so much like hell? Of course, the students, too, have a part in the way things are handled. They have a part in what rules are made, just by the way they act or present themselves.

So if everyone wants a better school, then everyone should try to take part in cleaning up attitudes, behaviors, and teachers, too. Maybe, Madison Area Memorial High School can view or research the alternative schools along with others to learn new ideas. Maybe, they could even adopt some rules and regulations to help make school for kids more enjoyable and less stressful for the staff. They should try to talk to the student and see their point of view and build a trusting relationship with them. They should try not to yell or fly off and bring themselves to a lower level than maturity. Maybe, they will see that honey attracts more flies than vinegar. Finally, the students become more mature themselves, follow the rules, and better quit complaining about how bad it is.

Marianne's essay effectively illustrates the debilitating effects of many years of authoritarian rule on students, causing many to take more blame for their actions than they deserve. Kohn acknowledges Marianne's insight by demonstrating that the more rules the school makes, the more students, like lawyers, try to find loopholes through which they can escape. Teachers, then, become police officers trying to enforce these rules. They are not facilitators for students in their search for knowledge and meaning. Because rules divert back to punishment, teachers do not solve problems together with them, nor encourage them as a group to resolve these. Rather teachers simply enforce the rules often resulting in unfortunate consequences for the students.

To try to make sure that students comply with the goals of the school, rewards are given if students achieve high grades. Not only are these students recognized at an assembly attended by the entire student body but also their names are also listed on an honor roll that is printed in the regional paper. Some parents even have bumper stickers on their cars noting that their child is an honor roll student. One such bumper sticker reads, "My child is on the honor roll at Benton Elementary School, 'just can't hide my pride.'"

Local businesses such as the Pizzarama will give honor roll students a discount on their next purchase of a pizza. Honor roll students pay less for automobile insurance. In the spring of the year when seniors are accepted at college, their acceptance is announced to the entire student body over the school's public address system.

For students who are not successful, such recognition of the compliant achiever weakens any desire they might have to succeed in school. If this is not enough, they are further punished. As already noted, they are restricted from use of the school's library, unless given a pass from a teacher indicating that they will actually be doing research for that class. The work must be shown to the librarian before leaving the library. Students on the restricted list, during study hall, must study the full 80 minutes. They may not even whisper to one another.

Kohn states that the

> only way to help students become ethical people, as opposed to people who merely do what they are told, is to help them construct moral meaning. It is to help them figure out for themselves and with each other how one ought to act. That's why dropping the tools of traditional discipline, like rewards and consequences, is only the beginning, It's even more crucial that we overcome a preoccupation with getting compliance instead of bringing students in on the process of devising and justifying ethical principles. (Kohn, 1996, 67).

The direction in which public education is currently moving makes it increasingly difficult to achieve Kohn's practical ideal. For example, school administrators and teachers control students even more heavy-handedly in light of increasing school shootings in middle-class community schools like Columbine. In addition, they are concerned with their schools' reputation resting heavily upon broadly published student achievement scores.

However, in order for our students to achieve the very skills that the *Maine Learning Results* want them to acquire, it is necessary to adhere to Kohn's pragmatic wisdom. In Maine the skills and goals "with which each student will leave school" according to the Guiding Principles of the *Maine Learning Results* are that the students have:

- the ability to communicate clear and effectively
- the ability to learn under self-direction and throughout their lives
- the ability to solve problems creatively and practically
- the desire to be responsible and involved citizens
- the ability to work collaboratively and to do quality work
- the ability to think independently and the desire to be informed

However, Kohn explicitly explains that the primary objective of a teacher should not be simply to get students to comply. Rather he states the teacher must "first maximize the opportunity for students to make choices, to discover and learn for themselves, and second, creating a caring community in the classroom so that students have the opportunity to do things *together*" (Kohn, 1996, 68). He warns that there are now programs available that allow the students to come up with the very rules that teachers have in mind. Such decision making, of course, is deceptive, as it does not empower the students to think for themselves, independently, and for the good of the class as a whole. Instead of fostering the principles of a democratic classroom, these programs are created to cause students still to try to please the teacher.

Kohn suggests, as the Guiding Principles of the *Maine Learning Results* imply, that the role of the teacher is to engage the class in discussion about the ways they would like their class to run, and ways in which all class members, including the teacher, feel comfortable. Through a process of discussion, which includes the ability to listen and respond to others, the end result cannot help but be positive.

Ideally, students should learn to reach decisions by consensus. After all, decision making through voting remains a contest among students. There are winners and losers. Naturally, the losers have less commitment to the class than the majority. Therefore, no real sense of community, which includes the ability to appreciate and trust one another, has been accomplished. By helping students to become active participants in their own social and ethical development, the teacher is really putting the Guiding Principles of *Maine's Learning Results* into practice. Students are learning to discipline themselves rather than be controlled by others.

Democratic schools should encourage and empower students to become independent thinkers who are able to listen to and respond with appreciation and understanding to the thoughts and opinions of others. Together, they develop the ability to create an environment that is harmonious. In the following chapter, using my own experience as a classroom teacher, I hope to demonstrate that it is possible to teach a classroom democratically and to enhance the very principles throughout the school upon which our democratic nation was founded.

7

AN ALMOST
DEMOCRATIC CLASSROOM

I believe that a major part of my work is to nurture a sense of community among my students. Therefore, I could not just teach about democracy. I had to put it into practice in my classroom. I tried to motivate my students academically and to empower them to become socially responsible and active citizens of their school and community. To accomplish these ends, recently I developed the curriculum around the ideals of Maine's newly adopted *Learning Results* by incorporating a wide range of activities. Students created their own classroom rules within the limitations established by school policy. They facilitated problem-solving processes as conflicts arose within the classroom. When broader, school related issues came up that disturbed many of them, they learned to confront the administration diplomatically. Academic projects brought students into the community to explore and seek solutions to local problems. Although it was particularly difficult to create a sense of community in a school that is conducted in an authoritarian manner, this chapter provides the trials and tribulations my students and I encountered as we swam against an autocratic current.

Experiential Learning in a Democratic Environment

Michael Apple and James Beane (1995) correctly observed in their book *Democratic Schools* that as high school students we learned that democracy is a form of government involving the consent of the people and equal opportunity. However, we never explored the conditions that are central to democratic schools. Among these are:

1.   The open flow of ideas, regardless of their popularity, that enables people to be as fully informed as possible.
2.   Faith in the individual and collective capacity of people to create possibilities for resolving problems.
3.   The use of critical reflection and analysis to evaluate ideas, problems, and policies.
4.   Concern for the welfare of others and the "common good."
5.   Concern for the dignity and rights of individuals and minorities.
6.   An understanding that democracy is not so much an "ideal" to be pursued as an "idealized" set of values that we must live and that must guide our life as a people. (Apple and Beane, 1995, 6–7).

I wanted my students to experience the difficult reality of living democratically. By immersing them into the world of direct experience, I could incorporate the concept of teaching for social responsibility. Sheldon Berman in his book *Children's Social Consciousness and Social Responsibility* (1997) explained the purpose for teaching social responsibility:

> Educationally, teaching social responsibility incorporates the development of social skills, ethics, and character. Although it also includes developing political knowledge and skills, it gives primary attention to the way we live with others and our responsibility for furthering the common good. Therefore, unlike citizenship education, social responsibility cuts across the curriculum and the culture and organization of the school. It adds to the commonly accepted notion of citizenship education the concepts that young people must be able to work with and care for others, that classrooms and schools need to embody and nurture a sense of responsibility through their organization and governance, and that these themes can be integrated into all areas of the curriculum. (Berman, 1997, 9)

My students needed the opportunity to meet face-to-face with all sorts of people whose cultures, ideas, and lifestyles are foreign to them in order to overcome the prejudicial conditioning with which they have grown up. For instance, many students have been socially conditioned that certain religions are evil, i.e., Moslems are terrorists, while specific lifestyles such as homosexuality are sinful. Through direct dialogue with different people, asking questions, listening, and exploring ideas with the class as a whole, students gain greater understanding and are better able to accept differences. Since I was initially hired to teach world history and geography, this was an approach that helped to bring my classes to life.

I also needed to conduct my classroom as democratically as possible and directly involve my students to bring about desired changes in overall school policy. Berman said that, "social consciousness and social responsibility are not behaviors that we need to instill in young people, but rather are behaviors that we need to recognize emerging in them" (Berman, 1997, 39). All too often adults turn students off by giving the impression that they know just about everything better than their students. Such adults demand respect by trying to control kids through the use of fear. Therefore, Berman is correct when he states that "our conception of the child as egocentric, morally immature, uninterested in the social and political world, and unable to understand it has effectively deprived young people of the kind of contact they need to make society and politics salient" (Berman, 1997, 39).

In the mid-nineties I was required to drop world history and teach a new course called Government and Economics. Although I continued to expose my students to all sorts of different people, I realized that I could only make a course in American government relevant to my students by putting democracy into practice.

One of my first tasks to create a greater sense of community was to address the grading system. I dislike grades because they are not only a tool to maintain discipline, but a competitive practice by which the top students are rewarded with praise from both the school community and the community at large. Students who fail have been erroneously conditioned to believe they are stupid and do not deserve the recognition that high academic achievers receive.

As a public school teacher I had no choice but to give my students grades. Therefore, I devised a grading procedure to try to establish an environment whereby students could develop respect and appreciation for one another and the teacher as well. I graded equally for class participation and for written work. It seemed only fair to take into consideration that some individuals express themselves orally much better than they do in writing and vice versa. At the same time, I wanted to be sensitive to those students who are very shy in class and have a hard time speaking up. A point system was established by which each student had to earn three out of six points in order to pass for the day. The remaining three points were cumulative in order to achieve a higher score. This method encouraged students to attend class regularly. These were:

- *1 point for attendance*: being in the classroom with all materials (books, pens, notebook. . . .) and ready to start class at the sound of the bell.

- *1 point for attitude:* respect for yourself and others (according the policies that we agreed upon as a class.)
- *1 point for being prepared for class, trying to complete all work, working the entire period (reading, writing, oral participation)*
- *1 point for average work*
- *1 point for good work*
- *1 point for excellent work*

The average of these grades counted 50% of the quarterly grade. The other 50% was based on essays and research projects. The research projects were often presented orally. For these I would have to see the students' written preparation, i.e., notes and the bibliography. On occasion I did give an unannounced quiz. Essay tests were developed to help both students and myself to see how well they understood the concepts we were exploring and how effectively they could support a point of view with plenty of facts.

I, the "teacher king" had established nice principles such as encouraging students to listen to others and respond respectfully to what each person had to say. Such an attitude might help those quiet students gradually feel secure enough to speak up. However, these policies didn't come from the students themselves.

The next step was for the students to create their own rules. Apparently, though, this could only work if each student in the class agreed to abide by them, was resolved to abide by them, and was willing to enforce them. Should the students rely on the teacher to be the enforcer, they would take on little or no responsibility, continue passively to bite the bullet, or misbehave.

Introducing the Democratic Classroom

By the fall of 1998 I was ready to jump headfirst into making my classroom as democratic as possible. After two and a half months of summer break, I returned to school full of enthusiasm ready to implement the new ideas I had been developing over the summer. When my first government and economic students arrived, a middle-track group, one boy asked, "we hear this class is different — all you do is watch R-rated movies. You don't learn real stuff." I responded: "I'm so glad you raised this issue. In fact, as you can see by looking at the black board, this is really one of the issues I want to explore with you. That is, how do you learn best? How do you become a knowledgeable, mature, and wise person? Is this through direct experience, through books, through personal contact, or through a combination of these?"

At this point I introduced myself as a facilitator, one who supports all students individually throughout their learning process. Therefore, I explained, it is necessary for us to address these questions so that we can work effectively together. "I need to understand from where you come, and you should know my purpose for conducting the class the way I do."

Students said they learn best through discussion, through practical activities, through experience. "What about books?" I asked. "No, they are boring. We don't learn from books," one student said. "We use them only to cheat on exams." I responded: "Oh, isn't cheating a skill that you learn? So you are learning something? Practical experience"? Three boys, affectionately referred to by the class as the "Three Stooges," who had become a little disruptive, continued to giggle and even laugh aloud. I asked, why they laughed. "This isn't the way we are supposed to learn in school." One of the three boys took off his shirt saying it was hot. I asked what message he was trying to convey. Embarrassed, he quickly put his shirt back on. The first boy said that when the class is boring he either falls asleep or becomes disruptive. "So our discussion is boring?" I asked. "No way. It's weird."

At this point I suggested we get right down to the business as to what this class is all about, namely government. "To understand our government, we have to practice democracy in the classroom. Only in this way will you be able, I believe, to become willing and active participants in your school policies and our government."

I then handed the class the first assignment that included the following questions:

1. Name new and old laws that DIRECTLY affect you.
   Describe how they affect you.
2. Name new and old school policies that DIRECTLY affect you.
   Describe how they affect you.
3. Define *freedom*.
4. How do these laws and policies DIRECTLY affect *your freedom*?
   Identify these freedoms.
5. What can *you* do to change these laws and policies? Begin with school policies. Describe the process step by step.

Walking around the classroom, I noticed that most students were working diligently. The first of the three spirited boys piped up: "I don't know how laws and policies affect me." I encouraged him to take out his student handbook that he said he never reads. He did. Together we looked at the new policies. He was surprised. He then began to write. Almost immediately, he called me back to his desk asking: "Who will get this paper? Will I get in trouble?" I told him that I would be the only one to read his paper and assured him that he would not get into trouble. I followed up by asking him what he felt he was learning. He responded: "You are teaching us that we have rights and that we can make our school and our life better." I was delighted. Finally, when I asked the class at the end of the period what they liked about it, several students replied: "Neat class, I like the way we are involved."

At the beginning of the following class, the lad who appeared to relish being silly together with his two buddies, became actively involved in the discussion. He and other students took an active part in small-group work sharing their answers to the five questions from the previous class. They spent much of their time exploring how they could change school policies.

Of course, I introduced the process by which small groups would be conducted. The facilitator would listen, summarize, maintain open and balanced conversational flow, protect individuals from personal attack, focus discussion on the topic, make sure each person in the group was actively involved, clarify, encourage, and guide the group. The recorder documented points made during the discussion and conclusions reached. The spokesperson presented the group's ideas to the whole class. I also noted that there are several basic rules that had to be followed in every single discussion:

1. Everyone who is here belongs here just because he or she is here and for no other reason
2. Only one person may speak at a time
3. Before one person speaks again, all others must have the opportunity to speak
4. Listen carefully to what each person says
5. Respond directly to what each person has said
6. Look at the person to whom you are talking
7. Be open-minded to different points of view
8. Back up your opinions with as much factual knowledge as possible
9. No put downs
10. No foul or abusive language.

However, during the following class, facilitated by a student, the leader of the "Three Stooges" reverted back to his leadership role as the class clown taking the lead, encouraging his two buddies to crack jokes, and mouth strange sounding noises. At this point I felt I had no other choice other than to intervene and let the class address this issue.

Several students urged me to "take control" of the class. Two students requested that I send these boys to the office for punishment. Others suggested that they sit in front of the room for ten to twenty minutes so that they would be embarrassed. My feeling was gosh, no. This reminded me of public humiliation in China during the Cultural Revolution of the late 1960s and early 1970s where people, targeted as anti-revolutionary, were

paraded through city streets wearing dunce caps. Some class members insisted upon some form of humiliation. I raised questions as to the effectiveness
of such a policy.

The class unanimously adopted this discipline procedure, though I
believe several students passively went along with the decision rather than
making an issue. Maybe they couldn't believe that as students they had the
right to make decisions regarding their class. Possibly they felt the policy
wouldn't work anyway, and the teacher would take charge just like in every
other class. This course of action would be used for disruptive behavior
which included chatting, talking out of turn, silliness, rudeness, and disre-
spect.

1st offense — 10 minutes sitting in front of classroom facing the blackboard.
2nd offense — 20 minutes sitting in front of the classroom facing the
blackboard plus one half hour of detention during which time student
and teacher try to resolve the issue
3rd offense — referral to the guidance counselor
4th offense — sent to principal's office with a behavior referral form
completed by the teacher

Since the school authorities only allowed students out of the classroom with a name specific pass from the teacher and since the bathroom
could only be used for formally designated purposes, students came up with
the following procedure:

- sign-out and sign-in with the time of departure and return on a
  sheet in front of the classroom
- take appropriate girl's or boy's pass
- if out for more than five minutes explain reason to the class
- if not excusable, student loses privilege for next class; second offense
  means loss of privilege for one class and one half hour of detention
  during which time the student and teacher try to resolve the problem
- in case of a true emergency a student may leave the classroom even
  if another student is out.

It was agreed that any student as well as the teacher had the right to
assign "punishment" according to the class established rules. Within minutes
following the acceptance of this policy, the girl who had been moderating the
discussion gave one of the "Three Stooges" ten minutes in front of the classroom for booing her. He reluctantly did what he was told. When he returned
to his seat he was more cooperative for the remainder of that period.

Throughout the year the "Three Stooges" continued to be an interesting distraction. Students who took responsibility to try to "punish" the

"Three Stooges" found that they received little or no support from their classmates. Even though each had signed the agreement to which I attached my own signature, they continued to violate it. Several students said they would not stop any of these kids because it was fun to see them distract the teacher when the class was boring.

My department chairperson, as a young woman had been a liberal Catholic, now pushed for high academic achievement among the college prep students and had little patience for the lower-track students. She and apparently at least one other colleague complained on several occasions to the principal that kids from this class were roaming the halls and disturbing their classes.

Having exhausted all strategies agreed upon and feeling paranoid because of staff complaints about my "lack of control," with great reluctance I finally sent two boys with behavior referral forms to the office. One was given three hours of detention by the principal. The following class period he was just as silly.

We discussed control issues. Students came up with the idea that respect comes from the heart. Control, as they understand it, is doing what they are supposed to do out of fear of punishment. We related this concept to the large number of youths in the class who have been on various occasions stopped by the police.

I asked them how they felt the moment they saw the cops. They said they were scared, intimidated, angry, misunderstood, and not trusted. Some tried to run away. I asked what they said when they were questioned. Several admitted to the "offense," some said they lied, others said they were "framed" by friends who wouldn't take the blame.

I tried to draw a parallel to dictatorships — Stalin, Hitler, Idi Amin, Mao Tse Tung — when frightened people tried to save their own skin by turning their closest friends and family members in to the government. Some students were quite amazed at this analogy. Two of the "Three Stooges" participated actively and with interest in this discussion. However, no resolution was reached.

We then discussed these issues in relationship to the class contract we had created and upon which we agreed unanimously. It was the agreement of all that the contract was not working because some individuals failed to cooperate while others left the discipline in the hands of the teacher. Even sending these boys to the principal's office was of no avail. Finally, we arrived at the conclusion that I would give each of these fellows one half hour of detention every day. The agreement was reached but without the cooperation of the "Three Stooges." When they participated, in class, detention would be discontinued. When lack of cooperation began again, so would detention.

I decided that I would try to make special contact with Bruce, the ring-leader of the "Three Stooges." I discovered that he had the same free period as I did. The following morning on my way to school, I stopped at a bakery to buy a donut for Bruce. I suggested we meet in the cafeteria, the only available space, during this period. He agreed.

I told him jestingly that the donut was both a bribe and an indication that I admire his creativity, intelligence, and leadership ability. Therefore, I would like to explore with him ways in which he can conduct the class. He came up with a great idea for class that day. It was at the height of the Clinton-Lewinsky scandal, and he would hand out pieces of paper on which the students would write their definition of sex. Then the class would discuss these to see how similar or different they were as a means to understand the controversy over President Clinton's definition of sex. In this way, he argued, students could understand how language can be manipulated and how difficult it is to come up with a solid definition. During the class he ignored the silly comments made by his buddies. Both he and I were happy with the outcome of the class.

However, Bruce would soon be "suspelled" from school for having been caught together with two other students for possessing drug paraphernalia and a small amount of marijuana. During the time that Bruce was absent, the remaining "Three Stooges" were considerably more cooperative, and the class seemed to be more harmonious. Students who had been reluctant to speak up now contributed greatly to the class. Upon Bruce's return, the silliness resumed. Sometimes it was intertwined with a powerful and meaningful discussion led by Bruce and now and then assisted by his buddies who provided additional insight.

At the time of the shootings at Columbine High School in Littleton, Colorado, the "Stooge," who had noted that this class primarily watched R-rated movies, suggested we watch, write about, and discuss the movie A Clockwork Orange. He felt it showed many similarities to the Columbine incident. He perceptively observed that the particularly violent main character, Alex, came from a well-to-do, middle-class family similar to the majority of the students at Littleton. He agreed to work together with his buddies on preparing questions about the film. His classmates would first write about them and then discuss them in class.

Bob (not his real name) felt we should explore the reasons as to why Alex and his fellow group members felt no guilt following the horrific crimes they committed. Naturally, I added the question: "How might 'material consumption' that is our desire to buy more luxury items, i.e., big screen TV's, RVs, snowmobiles, expensive Nikes, play a role in the behavior of these boys?"

The students observed that the boys in the movie seemed to have everything they wanted and like themselves were pretty bored. They longed for some excitement. My students generally felt it was easy to get into trouble because many didn't see their parents often. Some parents quarreled much of the time. Others were overworked and tired and didn't want to have much to do with their kids. Several parents were mentioned as being heavy drinkers and when drunk tended to be obnoxious at the least. Other parents were divorced and living with a partner with whom the kids did not get along.

The "Three Stooges" accurately portrayed themselves as being the children of middle- and working-class people. One of their parents is gainfully employed at Madison's paper mill. Another parent is a middle-school principal in a near-by town, while his mother is an elementary school teacher in Madison. Only the third boy's parents would be considered working class.

When we held a discussion trying to define what is normal and where students in the class fit in terms of normal on the bell curve, each of the three boys was placed by his fellow classmates near the peak of the curve. After all, they play sports, are popular, and are fun loving. They basically are jocks but just aren't academic. It is for these reasons I assume that Bruce was handled more gently by the administration when he was "suspelled" than the other two boys, both of whom during the remainder of the year dropped out of school.

Disillusionment with life and feeling let down by adults and some of their peers may have caused the "Three Stooges" to stick closely together and act up. Although they were within the bell curve of the status quo, they never reached the curve's pinnacle in terms of popularity. This may have added to their feeling of loneliness and even alienation.

When a highly competent clinical therapist did activities with this class on race, gender, and class issues, which she had been conducting as a leader with the National Coalition Building Training Institute, these boys cracked crude jokes and were unwilling to participate. The same therapist was able to gain the involvement of every other student in this class as well as of all the students in my other sections.

Democratic Classrooms Add Vitality to My Other Classes

A student in another middle-level track picked up a weakness in the classroom management procedures I had previously been using. In the past, if a student and I failed to come to an agreement, I would call his or her parents. Should this approach fail as well, I would send the student to the principal's office with a behavior referral form.

A sensitive girl pointed out that sometimes if a teacher calls home the parents don't care. At the other extreme they may be abusive. One girl she knew came to school with bruise marks because her parents had beaten her severely with a stick following such a phone call. As a class, we decided that I would not call a parent, but instead would send the student to the guidance counselor. Should the problem not be resolved between the two of them, then the three of us could meet. Only should this effort fail, would I send a student to the principal's office. I told the class that I appreciated and could easily accept this approach.

However, I explained that some parents are eager to know about their kids, are understanding, and even helpful when the teacher calls home. In such instances, especially if parents wished me to contact them, I felt obligated to do so. I further explained that if I sensed the parents were concerned and understanding, I did not see this as a violation of our policy. No student expressed opposition. The policy was accepted.

By mid-winter the girl who raised my awareness and spurred the class to create a thoughtful and positive policy, dropped out of school. She came from a troubled family situation. Her on-and-off relationship with her boyfriend appeared abusive. In other words, one more student, who didn't fit the status quo, fell through the cracks of the system.

In the lowest-track class it was most difficult to get students to create their own rules. It is understandable that these kids took on the attitude of "I don't care." Why should they? Like Johnny, described in chapter 5, many students in this group, from the time they entered kindergarten had been dumped on and labeled as stupid by some teachers and fellow classmates. Some had been held back for a year due to poor academic achievement. They did not fit the norm of the school. After all, most came from the lowest strata of society. Many came from single-parent homes. If the mother did not work, she was on welfare. Others came from working-class families where alcohol and abuse were common problems. These students with low self-esteem were resigned to being reluctant followers and suppressed feelings they may have had. Finally, after much prodding and encouragement on my part, one boy in this group reluctantly took on the role as discussion facilitator. When I gave this group the rules I had created and used in previous classes to literally tear apart in small groups, many didn't bother. Nor would they read any contract before signing it. Most had given up on school years ago.

Betty Staley, a practitioner of Waldorf education at the high school level, observes that some adolescents never recover from their initial disappointment in life. Certainly, many students in this lowest-track group fit her perception. Although she believes that as adults some feel justified in abusing other people to compensate for the pain they had experienced earlier, I think she is closer to the target when she states that disappointment causes loneliness. The intensity of emotions leads, on the one hand, to depression and to acting out their frustrations without thinking, on the other. Therefore, she argues they are "capable of violent action. . . . Out of curiosity, they may be outrageously rude, set a house on fire, or even pull a trigger" (Staley, 1988, 8).

Shooting a gun in a classroom may be the result of loneliness and mis-understanding. However, the easy accessibility of all sorts of guns, I believe, is symbolic of technological advancements that have made them easily accessible to anybody including teenagers.

The presence of guns does not necessarily imply a growing tendency toward violence on the part of teenagers. In most rural Maine households, for example, guns are common objects.

When I polled my students, class by class, track by track, ever so rarely did a student raise his or her hand to indicate that his or her family had no gun in their homes. Most students reported that their families possessed from three to five guns. It was not uncommon to have students say that their dads collected guns. Frequently, such collectors had at least twelve guns, while a few had as many as twenty to twenty-five. If the parents were not collectors, they used guns for hunting. Most parents had at least one gun in the house for self-protection.

The bottom-line is that many students are lonely. Those in the lowest-track feel tied down. They have had far less encouragement than those students in the college prep group to explore new interests. They are less exposed to new ideas and to a wide variety of people and lifestyles. They have fewer chances to travel and not as many opportunities to explore different kinds of jobs. Their partners will most likely be people they have met while in high school or within the surrounding area. Because they feel tied down, they have a harder time with self-discovery. They often go from one low-paying job to another, feeling discouraged, stifled, and confined.

Naturally, the top-level track, my "A" group, showed the greatest signs for growth. As these students leave their small hometown for college, they have new opportunities to meet all sorts of different people, make fresh experiences, and develop new interests that may change the direction of their career and life.

In spite of their prominent status in the school and in the community, my "A" group was my most difficult class. Because they represent the status quo of the community and maybe out of a feeling of insecurity, many seem rigidly to adhere to the values of the school system to which most of the teachers and administrators adhere. Why shouldn't they? They are the ones who tend to receive the most recognition at the school, i.e., from "Student of the Month," to academic awards, to being elected class officers, and student council representatives.

Although traditionally, white Anglo Saxon protestant boys usually dominate, in this class it was a group of three girls. They seemed to enjoy the class, but they didn't take it seriously. Although they were the most outspoken about such rules as "one person speaks at a time" and getting other students involved, they were the ones who chatted most while others talked. They appeared to be the most cliquish, and they lacked the desire to hear those who were also outspoken but alienated from their class, the "A" group. One girl, a talented artist, approached me complaining that she did not want to be with the preppie girls because they ignore her, even though they pretend not to. She even spoke up in class to reiterate that her point of view was not being heard and that these girls snubbed her.

I felt I had to try to be especially objective and understanding with this class and particularly accepting of the three "preppie" girls. This was not easy as I still recalled feeling patronized and uncomfortable when I encountered this kind of girl during my high school years.

Student Projects Foster Social Awareness

Student involvement and participation in projects are an important aspect of teaching for social responsibility. Research conducted by Sheldon Berman has substantiated this statement. All three grade tracks were given the opportunity to do "political fieldwork." Berman reported that students selected a community problem that was of interest to them and worked either alone or in small groups to understand the problem and to effect change. "Thus the student could apply the concepts and skills learned in the classroom by extending the learning environment into the actual political structure" (Berman, 1997, 172).

My students could select from two different types of problem solving projects. The first consisted of a variety of local problems. These included:

- Is there a need to provide more recreational activities for youths in your community? What kind of activities would you like to see? How can this be accomplished?
- What is the relationship between taxes, the local school district's annual budget, and the quality of education in your community? What practical solutions are there to improve the quality of education in your community?
- What is the percentage of people who vote in your community? What are the reasons that people vote, do not vote? Is there any relationship in their responses to their profession, lifestyle, set of values, economic status?
- How much money does your community raise for local welfare? Who receives this aid? Who in the town government makes the decision to provide this assistance? What are the guidelines for recipients to receive the aid? Do the recipients have any obligations to the town upon receiv-

ing the aid? What are they? Is the assistance usually sufficient for the
needy person?

- Is police protection sufficient in your community? What are the usual
types of crime committed? By whom: male, female, age? Is any type of
crime on the rise in your community? What suggestions are offered to
reduce the crime rate? What training is necessary to become a small
town police officer? Is the required training sufficient?

- How does your community handle the mentally ill who live in the
community now that many are being released from state mental institutions like AMHI? Are both the mentally ill and the general public safe?
What could be done to provide better care for the mentally ill?

- Is school violence a problem in SAD #59? What is being done to deal
with a violent emergency should one occur? What suggestions can you
make to prevent such occurrences from happening and should such an
emergency occur, what should be done? Identify community values and
how these affect local policies such as education, welfare, censorship,
skateboarding, loitering, alcohol, and drugs?

- What kind of land-use plan and zoning ordinances does your community have? Do you feel these are needed? Are stricter laws needed to separate residential from business, industrial, and agricultural areas?

- Is the job market strong or weak in this region at this time? What kind
of job opportunities exist in this area? What kind of training is necessary
for these jobs? What is the pay scale? Is employment on the rise or is
unemployment increasing? Explain what can be done to reduce unemployment and to draw new businesses to this area.

- What is being done locally to take care of our veterans of foreign wars,
i.e., World War II, Korea, Vietnam, the Gulf War? Is this enough?

- The big paper companies like SAPPI are selling huge parcels of land in
this area. How does this affect the job market, your taxes, the environment? Once you have identified a problem, seek solutions to it.

- What is being done to take care of the elderly in your community? Do
they receive the care they need? Can they afford it? Does the care provided exceed the most basic? What suggestions do you have should you
discover a problem in this area?

- How does the juvenile court system operate in this area? Is it satisfacto-
ry? Is there a joint effort between the juvenile justice system, the school
system, and the community at large to provide a support system for these
youths to try to avoid recidivism? What research can you find that offers
a reasonable program that you can support?

Since some students were reluctant to go out into the community to
interview people, I also proposed general topics in government that students

might explore. They could research these in the library, use the internet, find actual cases, and arrive at their own conclusions. At the time I issued these projects, both President Clinton and the mayor of the near-by city of Waterville were facing impeachment and recall. No student chose either of these issues. Following are some topics that I suggested students might want to explore:

- Recent changes in U.S. immigration policy now being discussed, i.e., stricter controls on the U.S. Canadian border, policies determining the kinds of immigrants the U.S. shall accept, deporting immigrants who are good citizens but had committed a minor crime many years before, no longer providing education and welfare benefits to children of illegal immigrants in California.
- Is there a need for a Constitutional Amendment to forbid burning and/or other forms of desecrating the American flag?
- Religion in school: What is permitted, what is not? Recent court rulings: are these too restrictive? Why or why not?
- School choice: Should you be allowed to attend the school of your choice at taxpayers' expense? Options: voucher system, charter schools, home schooling. Should children who are home schooled be allowed to play sports and participate in drama competitions in their hometown schools?
- Freedom of speech: First Amendment
  Defamatory speech
  Fighting words
  In loco parentis in our public schools
- Freedom of the Press: First Amendment
  Radio and television
  Movies
  Obscenity and pornography
  Impact of the media on the public: from the press to advertising
  Censorship
- Freedom of assembly
  Limits on parades and demonstrations, e.g., Skokie, Illinois
  Limits on demonstrations on private property
  Prior restraint
  Picketing
    at labor unions or at abortion clinics
- Privacy versus Freedom
  Freedom of Information Act (1966)
  Privacy: child rearing, abortion to credit history, medical information
- Political parties

a. Major political parties: Democrats and Republicans
   Organization: local, state, national
   Nominating candidates
   Caucuses
   Nominating conventions
   Party platforms
b. Third parties: Green Party, Libertarian Party, Ross Perot's Reform
   Party, Communist Party
c. Political campaigns
   Campaign financing
   Campaign advertising
   Televised debates

- How to write and introduce legislation: drafting a bill. How a bill becomes a law. Referendum—bringing the legislation directly to the voters, e.g., Gay Rights referenda and Clear Cutting referendum in Maine
- Welfare and welfare reform: new workfare programs, federal programs now allocated to the states. Pros and cons of welfare reform
- The federal budget — how your tax money is spent. How the federal budget is created. How priorities are determined. This project can be done in relation to your country, state, county, and/or town.
- The Court System:
  Federal Courts, Federal District Courts: How these work; how judges are appointed; types of cases heard; examples of recent cases.
  U.S. Supreme Court: how it works; how judges are appointed; types of cases heard; examples of recent cases and decisions; how the Supreme Court justices interpret the Constitution. Why does the Supreme Court sometimes reverse decisions? Examples.
  Military Courts
- Different kinds of protest: civil-disobedience, violence, nonviolence, strikes, walkouts, boycotts, terrorism, vigils, demonstrations, petitions.
- State agencies and commissions that deal with a variety of issues:
  Maine Arts Commission, Maine Historical Preservation Commission, Maine Human Rights Commission, Maine Bureau of Mental Health and Retardation and Substance Abuse, Maine State Division of Motor Vehicles, Environmental Protection, Marine Resources, Liquor Commission, Medicine Board of Licensure, Labor Department: job service, labor standards, unemployment
- Rights of the Accused: Fourth Amendment
  Search and seizure
  Exclusionary rule
  In schools: locker searches
  Wire tapping

- Double jeopardy: Fifth Amendment
- Cruel and Unusual Punishment: Eighth Amendment
  Death penalty
  Guaranteed Right of Counsel: Sixth Amendment
- Equal Protection under the Law
  Discrimination, i.e., against women (the glass ceiling), against minorities (blacks, Hispanics, gays/lesbians, handicapped, the obese)
  Affirmative Action
  Harassment

Lower-level track students were more willing to tackle local issues and relate these to their own experiences than the college prep students. This preference may be related to some students' limited reading ability and therefore lack of interest in reading. It may also be because they learn more easily using a hands-on approach. For example, several boys from the lowest academic track felt there was a need for a skateboard park in town. Not only did they interview town officials, but they also designed the park and made a small model of it. They gathered information from the internet, went to a local lumber and hardware company to price their project, and designed the park so that it would satisfy both their own needs and budget restraints from the community.

Three students in the same class were particularly interested in school violence. They explored means by which to deal with this problem in their own school. By telephoning the state's emergency preparedness agency, they secured a copy of the School Emergency Management Plan. They also interviewed the school district's director of supportive services as to how SAD #59 handles such situations as bomb scares and unauthorized people in the school. He told them that the school system follows the emergency plan they received from the state. The students felt most of the suggestions reflected common sense and wondered why each category, e.g., bomb threats had a checklist that specified the action to be taken in response to such an incident. They felt under such circumstances most students would instinctively seek safety. We discussed the need for such accountability in a day and age when the school could be sued if procedures weren't carried out according to policy.

The three presenters believed that students who are turned off from school are more likely to be violent. Therefore, they led a discussion by asking each student to explain what each of them felt was wrong with the high school. Following is a partial list from this group of fifteen students:

- We are not treated with respect by teachers and administrators.
- Therefore, we don't care about the school and that's why we trash it.
- Constant restrictions on students lead to anger. We ignore the restrictions and get punished.

- It's not fair to punish us if we get bad grades, i.e., placing us on the restriction list.
- It's unfair to restrict us during the activity period that really is a twenty-minute-break for us to socialize.
- If we miss more than ten days of school per semester, the highest grade we can get is a 65 (70 is passing).
- It's unfair that we are given detentions for being late.
- Teachers and administrators don't trust us. Of course, we are going to skip school early, and then they lock the back doors on us.
- Preppies gain the highest respect.
- Tracking: We're in the C group so we get all the blame, all the "shit."
- The office never listens to our side of the story.
- Teachers have favorites.
- Teachers and the office (administrators) are not consistent with their own rules.
- Some students get a lot of help from teachers. Other times the teacher says to a kid, "Look it up in the textbook." Or we get a sermon, but students can't do the work.

The project leaders picked up on tracking as one of the prime factors why students release their anger at school. Several noted that they expressed their frustrations by kicking in the bottom of lockers, producing graffiti on the bathroom walls, breaking the metal bars that hold their desk and seat together and telling teachers and administrators to "fuck off." Others noted that they have been labeled as troublemakers just because their older siblings had been in trouble, because a parent was in jail, or because they came from a poor, rowdy family. "If we are treated badly, we are going to be angry. Do you really think we are going to 'give a shit' about this place?" seemed to be the consensus of the class.

The students followed up this discussion with the film *Lean On Me* featuring an inner-city, New Jersey high school principal who turned around his violence ridden school like a "caring, military drill sergeant." The students liked the drill sergeant approach for several reasons. They felt he had no other alternative considering how serious the problems at the school appeared to be. They felt that the kids who used drugs had to be removed. Since many of their parents and family friends yelled and screamed at them, they saw this as normal behavior. Kids generally adopt the same set of values as their parents and family friends. Like their parents, they believed in the death penalty and other forms of cruel and unusual punishment, even though <u>all</u> members of this class currently had a family member or friend in the state prison system, and many of these kids had been in trouble with the law. Thus, I was not surprised that my students accepted the principal's, Mr.

Clark's, technique of intimidating his teaching staff, frightening his students, and using coercive techniques to get them to become patriotic and follow his lead. In fact, most felt he did the right thing considering that his job was to salvage a school that had become tumultuous.

Since these students seemed unable to see the similarity between following Mr. Clark and those who followed authoritarian leaders in other nations, I suggested that we watch a short documentary on Hitler and the first part of the movie *Full Metal Jacket*. The latter deals with an abusive, army drill sergeant during the Vietnam War era. The students liked the idea. The group leaders would still be responsible for continuing the round table discussion. In preparation for the discussion, students would prepare some questions.

In answer to the question "What did Hitler do to achieve unity?" one boy responded. "He got rid of the Jews to establish his own Aryan race." I then asked whether there was any similarity between Hitler's actions and Principal Clark kicking out 300 "rotten apples" from the school. One boy replied: "But those rotten apples had been there for five years. They needed to go." Another student, who was monitored by the special education department because of learning disabilities said: "Hitler killed the Jews. Clark just got rid of the troublemakers from his school. He was not prejudiced against them. He just saw them as destructive to the school." A girl perceptively observed, as our school was in the midst of the eleventh-grade statewide assessment that week, "Mr. Clark kicked out 300 plus bad students because, if they were gone, then the test scores would go up. He was hired to bring up those scores." The special education department also monitored this girl. Another student asked whether by removing the "rotten apples" to the street, Mr. Clark was sending them and the community the message that they couldn't be saved. "Won't their behaviors become worse," he asked?

I raised the question as to whether Mr. Clark expelled these students illegally? If so, then did he transgress the law for the good of the school? One student felt that he had broken the law. If he really wanted to help these students, he would abide by the law and make sure each had a tutor since schools are responsible for all kids' education. Another said that the law should have punished each of those drug users and thugs. Just kicking them out was useless.

Students asked me to express my thoughts, which, naturally, I was happy to do. I told them that I could see their point of view that the drill-sergeant approach may be what these kids from the asphalt and brick jungle of the inner city might initially respond to. However, I didn't believe that schools were trying to train soldiers for war. The drill sergeant used humiliation to destroy his recruits' self-esteem in order to make them into "killers." Principal Clark used intimidation to obtain obedience. He also encouraged students in the school chorus to adopt a revised version of the school song created by students to rejuvenate the school spirit. Students, like soldiers, were shorn of their individuality to become a united front to achieve a certain purpose. In the case of the school, they proved that they could all pass the state's skill test. In war they were trained to defend themselves and eliminate the enemy. I questioned whether this really was the purpose of public schooling. Of course, students disagreed with my analysis. They expressed their ideas politely and with support especially from their own experiences.

I was particularly impressed by the analytical skills demonstrated especially by those students labeled as "special ed." Hoping to bolster their self-confidence, I sent notes to their parents acknowledging their analytical skills, insight, and ability to articulate their thoughts clearly.

Most of the students in this group did not particularly care for the assistant principal whose frequent confrontations with classmates often escalated into ugly scenes. Several said that he was trying to be tough and was only interested in himself, not the kids. They felt Mr. Clark, the principal in the film, really cared about kids. Our little school, they noted, does not need his style.

The college prep students were more willing to do bookish projects using library resources as opposed to the more hands-on approach directed toward local and statewide affairs. They chose such topics as the death penalty, censorship, and flag burning. By mid-year some students expressed concerns about projects. Several students said that since they did not have regular, daily homework assignments, worksheets, textbook assignments, and regular scheduled tests, they find it hard to take this class seriously. Deadlines provide the structure they need to gain more out of the course. A few wanted us to follow sequentially the textbook from which regular assignments were given.

We frequently got behind because the follow-up discussion to some projects took longer than expected. Two deeply involved students argued articulately against deadlines. They said they did the work because they were interested. They liked an approach whereby they took responsibility for themselves and were not repeatedly told, as in other classes, that they were irresponsible young adults. They felt that they could get everything done on time without being reminded. In their case, this was true. As we were a group of diverse personalities, I supported the need for deadlines. Some people worked better under the pressure of deadlines, while others could do without. If a time frame were not established, I feared we would be experiencing more confusion than we presently were.

One girl commented that when she decided to do a project on veterans, she had no idea as how to go about it. Although she chose to study the potential closing of the Maine Veterans Institution, she knew nothing about veterans, and just couldn't figure out how to do the project. Although she did come for help, she felt this project had little to do with her ambitions for going to college. She was afraid that since the curriculum in this class was different from that in neighboring high schools, where they only used the textbook and memorized the three branches of government, she wouldn't get into college. She felt she needed this background to do projects.

Several students immediately jumped onto her case. They said that they had learned all of this stuff in junior high and by now had forgotten it because it had no relevance to their lives. They never had a chance to put into practice what they had learned. Some argued that they wanted a combination of my approach with that of the traditional teacher. One boy got into a heated argument with this girl. He said that he is in school not to get grades, not to be trained for a job, or how to meet deadlines, but to find out who he was and what he wanted to do with his life. This brought great laughter. He was offended.

Several students joined the fray. Some wanted projects based upon the textbook. Others liked the approach we had been using. We finally agreed that the best use of the textbook is to gain basic text information before reaching out to the library for other resources. Then one popular girl suggested we debate.

The student facilitator asked how the class felt about this idea. Gradually, hand after hand was raised until all except one individual supported this idea. I expressed surprise that so many would choose debate expecting that others would select different approaches. I overheard one boy saying: "I might as well join in."

Then the facilitator asked the class what topics they wished to debate. Several were listed. The group agreed that by a show of hands the topics that gained the most votes would be the ones to be debated. The topics selected were drug testing and assisted suicide. It was agreed that I would prepare students on the process of formal debate. The next class would be devoted to research in the school library. Those who had signed up for each topic would find the Constitutional Amendment to which their topic was related and search for actual court cases. Then the students for each of the two topics would decide among themselves which side of the debate they would take.

Two students decided they wanted to do separate projects. The girl, who was concerned that neighboring schools utilize the textbook, decided to work out of the book, by answering the questions at the end of each section and at the end of each chapter. I agreed on the condition that she would do some exploratory work that demanded some comparison and critical thinking. Another student decided to do a project on political art by examining the work of Ben Shahn. I suggested she talk with his daughter, Abby, a powerful artist in her own right, who lived in the vicinity and worked with high school students as an artist-in-residence.

The first debate with the topic title, "Resolved: Drug Testing Is Legal," went well. The students were well prepared and accepted the challenge. A student moderated the debate. At the request of the class, ballots were issued to the remaining students in the class to determine the "winner." As much as I disliked this kind of competition to which students had been conditioned since their preschool years, I could accept it. After all, the way this class was conducted and the curriculum covered was a far cry from the traditional methods to which these students had been accustomed. Following the formal debate, there was plenty of time for each side to respond to questions and comments from the audience. In this way, the entire class had the opportunity to become actively involved in the discussion.

Students were less well prepared for the second debate. The subject was, "Resolved: Assisted Suicide Is Legal." One boy accurately observed: "There are three distinct groups in our class. No matter how good the points of any one of these is, how much they might agree with them, they will tear them down just to get back at the other kids."

The dilemma reminded me of the vicious conflicts in the former Yugoslavia. Under Tito's control it was possible to keep ancient, deeply rooted animosities under control. Once Yugoslavia broke up, as the "benevolent" dictatorship of Tito fell apart with the collapse of the Communist Block, the lid came off the pot. Old animosities boiled over with vengeance: Serbia, Bosnia, Croatia, and Kosovo. Genocide was among the atrocities that took place.

This appeared analogous to the classroom teacher as a benevolent dictator. It was possible to keep the lid on the pot. It was even possible, especially with a traditionally, well motivated college prep group to encourage a certain amount of learning: reading and writing essays that support a thesis. However, when I, the authoritarian in charge, allow the class to take responsibility for itself, ugliness rises to the surface. Even with active student participation, I had a hard time maintaining the ideals for which I had been striving.

When I became discouraged, I recalled former students telling me that they learned about respect and how to take responsibility for their actions. They, also, learned how to think, to question, and to methodically seek solutions to problems — personal, school, and community related. Ironically, the children of second-generation troubled youths whom I had as students, who tended to be difficult in other classes, were generally well behaved and involved in my classes. Above all their honesty and willingness to struggle with difficult situations in which they were directly involved, certainly was a redeeming characteristic that could only lead to better understanding and relationships. The subsequent example took place in the "A" group that demonstrates social concern and constructive action to seek resolution to a schoolwide problem.

Active Student Involvement
Enhances Social Responsibility

Remember the girl who had the bad hair day? Many students in the class were angry following the incident in which the assistant principal called the police to remove a girl who refused to take off her bandanna. Even though this was a 10th-grade college prep class, and the girl was in a 9th-grade, low-track class, students unanimously felt that the incident had escalated to unnecessary heights.

I felt that the students needed not only to air their frustrations but that they also should take on the role, for which my class was preparing them, as socially responsible and active citizens. In this case they would try to resolve a schoolwide problem. This project took the better part of four, 80-minute class periods.

Hans, who truly liked to moderate problem solving discussions, immediately volunteered for this position. During the first part of the debate students related what they had observed and heard about this incident. Some expressed anger wanting the assistant principal to be fired immediately. Two students suggested that the student body hold a walkout in protest. Another student suggested that whatever the class did, it should not be a vendetta against the assistant principal, Mr. Maines. Hans observed that trying to fire Mr. Maines or organize a walkout would be futile. Rather, he said that the class should try to come up with a strong proposal, maybe a policy, which the school board would adopt, to be followed by all teachers and administrators.

By the end of the second day, some students were beginning to lose interest. Others argued that the class was taking on more than it could handle since they believed it would be difficult to get a great deal of support. Hans and a few others felt that the class should draw up a petition to the administration with copies sent to school board members expressing their concerns about harassment and that students had no say in regards to school policy. The class unanimously agreed to do this.

However, the question arose, who should present the petition to the administrators? This turned out to be a very heated argument. Several students felt that those who were most active on this project should make the presentation. Others felt that the class president along with the project leaders, even though she didn't wholeheartedly support the proposal, should approach the principal with their proposal.

It was also suggested that the representative of the student government be among the presenters. She refused. This was the girl who felt at a loss because her class was not textbook oriented like those in neighboring schools. Her former friend, Eva, the outspoken girl in Gothic attire, asked why she was on the student government if she refused to take the class's petition to the administration. The outcome was that the two girls began calling each other names. Nina called Eva a "bitch and a psycho." When another girl told Nina that it was her duty to present the petition, she left the room in a huff.

Three students took it upon themselves to write the petition with specific proposals. The class reviewed these several times before agreeing upon a final draft that follows:

TO: Administrators of Madison High School: Mr. Testa, Mr. Maines, Mr. Collins and the Board of directors of S.A.D. #59
FROM: Those who have signed this letter which originated in a sophomore government class

May 21, 1999

We are bringing to your attention the fact that many students have expressed concerns about current issues in our school. Specifically, we have no say in regards to school policy and atmosphere. In addition, the harassment, threats, and lack of trust and respect especially shown by the administration disturbs us. We are doing something about these problems, but how are we to change anything, if it is only the students that want change? We realize that we can make these changes with the support of the student body and our parents, but we would appreciate your support as well.

The students have discussed the problems in our school, and have arrived at some conclusions and solutions. We hope that these ideas will be used and that further and more confrontational actions need not be taken. We feel that if these measures are taken, we will be able to change our school for the better.

We thank you for your attention and time and know that you will give these proposals your utmost consideration and action according to our wishes.

Proposals
We believe that we have come up with an effective way of dealing with harassment.

At the present time detentions or suspensions only cause the harassed person to become subject to further, if less odious, harassment and ostracism.

We feel the harasser needs to apologize immediately to the person that they have harassed. Then they are to see the guidance counselor on a regular basis for a minimum period of two weeks or if necessary for the remainder of the school year. The parents must be involved in the counseling of their son or daughter. For more severe and hateful kinds of harassment, we think the harasser would have the above as well as set a time of appropriate community service. If the harassment continues, we feel that legal action must be taken without delay by the school.

If students want to share their views on a subject or situation in a respectful way, they must be allowed to speak to the administration. In the past, we have been silenced and punished for sharing our feelings. Administrators need to realize that not all criticism is directed to them specifically and that criticisms are not always of a malicious or confrontational nature.

The class agreed that all members who so desired would sign the petition. Since I had all sophomores in my four remaining government/economic classes, students who had a free period during these times would present the petition to the other classes and secure signatures. Eighty-three out of eighty-seven students signed. Some, who initially refused to sign, did so after their friends had. Two students, a girl and a boy, who were in constant trouble with Mr. Maines, felt it was too risky to take part. Finally, with all the signatures in hand, Hans proceeded to the office where he met Mr. Maines. He asked whether several students could meet with him, the principal, and the guidance counselor to present a petition. He said that he didn't have the time. He also mentioned to Hans that he had been told that the students in Mr. Solmitz's class were trying to get him fired. Hans said that was the furthest from the truth. Mr. Solmitz's class, he explained, is a problem solving government class. Hans then spoke with the principal, who agreed to meet with the students. The principal apparently was polite, but handed the petition back to them, saying that he would no longer be principal next year and they should address those matters with his successor. I recommended that the students who had presented the petition to the principal, present it in person at the next school board meeting. However, they decided to send it by mail to each school board member. According to the minutes of the following school board meeting, no mention was made of the petition.

Following this experience in democratic problem solving, I asked the students to write a process paper in which they responded to several questions:

1. What provoked last Thursday's discussion on harassment, Mr. Maines, and a student involved in a school related issue?
2. Describe the process of this discussion from "venting" to "problem solving."
   a. Describe how the process evolved?
   b. What actually was accomplished?
3. Did you notice any resistance developing? When? Why? From where? Do you feel resistance building up in yourself? When? Why?
4. Describe in detail what you learned about a) human behavior, b) the democratic process?
5. What are the advantages to an authoritarian type of government?

6. What are the advantages to the democratic process?
7. Which system do you prefer? Explain why, carefully.

Some students said that the school only worked if the students felt good about it. Therefore, both students and administrators had to feel good about the school. Although the class came up with a reasonable proposal to bring about necessary changes, the democratic process was slow. However, most agreed that they didn't believe that the class would ever get to the point of total agreement. One person wrote that it was human nature to constantly change one's mind. When finally it appeared that a decision had been reached, two people changed their minds and "screwed things up again." Another student observed that one or more people become power hungry and take over. Several students noted that they liked the freedom of democracy but felt comfortable with the decisiveness of dictatorship.

Many students felt resistance built up because comments made were not always listened to, taken seriously, and even ridiculed. One student said the rudeness and lack of respect among some class members reminded her of politicians bickering with each other on C-Span television.

Inability to accept one another's opinions continued to be a problem for this group. Most acknowledged the fact that taking what others have said personally is a sign of human behavior. Many disagreed with Eva because she often expressed ideas that were disconcerting to others. She observed that the advantages of a dictatorship applied only to dictators and their followers. Anybody who disagreed was wrong and would be punished. "Yet the herder (dictator) and the sheep (followers) have the advantage of things going their way." Along with the herder and follower mentality Phil indicated that most people were "cowards, spineless machines, content to live under control, never taking responsibility to think. The resistance was coming from people just saying 'Oh, it's not that bad, we don't really care about Mr. Maines, and continue to forget about the violations that have already taken place.'" James continued to explain that people do not want to confront the powerful organization and have it get mad at them. In addition, he noted people would rather maintain the status quo because they fear change.

Another student noted that even the democratic process appeared to be like a dictatorship since the people who were supposed to be in charge, were actually subservient to the rules and structure of their political system. Therefore, he argued it was the lack of control by the people that would bring down the system if not even the nation.

Finally, Kevin (not his real name) expressed concern that the process was useless because even the teacher, I, had a vendetta against the assistant principal. He wrote with particular clarity and sociological insight as to how situations like the "bad hair day girl" came about:

April 20th, 1999 — Two young adults execute a dozen classmates at their school in Colorado, setting the stage for a wave of hysteria that is sweeping across our nation. From coast to coast, school after school, has been consumed by the flood. Ours is one of them. Built-up hostility between certain cliques is being unleashed at last. Even our administration seems willing to take part in feeding the prejudice — fueled fire which rages through the hallways of Madison High School.

So what can be done, when even our leaders are opposed to justice and equality. Many of the students seek to blame the administration for allowing these activities to continue, but to seek action would be futile. As a whole the student body is a frightened animal, basically snapping at whatever it can. We need to find fault somewhere for what's happening. Anywhere in fact. That. . . . anyone but ourselves. Mr. Maines is not the problem here in Madison, though our mob mentality allows us to blame him. Our anger is really being driven by the anti-authority views of a few students and the personal vendetta of our teacher. It should be obvious that many students have no personal interest to put this plan into action; we can't come to a solid decision regarding process, and very few of us are willing to take the burden of carrying the plan out upon themselves, regardless of how adamantly they seem to agree with it. What we're afraid to realize is that changing an outside influence is not going to solve the problem. The change needs to take place within ourselves. The hostility is ours. The hatred is ours. We are the predator as well as the prey. We are the criminals as well as the victims. When we can come together in unity, when we can overlook each other's flaws and differences, and achieve social equality, then our problems will be solved. As long as we avoid that truth, this war will never be won.

The beauty of Kevin's statement is that he felt free to express his point of view including his interpretation of my mindset and values and that he was struggling with his own personal conflicts. Just as he said that change needs to take place within ourselves, he was battling with his own resentment of authority. Although he did have a few friends and an occasional steady girlfriend, he seemed to be somewhat of a loner.

It must be difficult being the younger brother of the popular senior-class president. He, therefore, must have felt some conflict about the need to belong to a group and his own need for independence and self-reflection. Doing poorly in all of his classes, he said recently to me that he was bored and lacked motivation. He added: "I need structure. But the more structure I get, the more I rebel against it and don't do what I am supposed to do." The following year he attended a private preparatory school about an hour's drive from his home.

Shortly after our petition had been filed, the president of the sophomore class and another student drafted their own petition to the administration for which they sought student signatures. They hoped to arrange for a special student bus to take those interested in watching one of their classmates be Madison High School's first ever participant in a statewide tennis championship meet. After all, the school department provided a bus when the girls' soccer team advanced to the regional championship. The girls concluded their petition:

> We understand that the main problem is the fact that we would be getting out of most of our classes that day. But that wouldn't be a problem because we will immediately make up the classes and catch up on the work. Before leaving, we will get all the work from the classes that would be missed. [This is school policy for any field trip during the school day — my note]. We are always pushing for our school to get more involvement, "School Spirit," what a better opportunity? If we think about this logically and want to make an unbiased decision, why are we not providing a chance for this Madison High School girls' tennis team to be recognized? Why shouldn't we support the girls' tennis team as much as we would other teams?
>
> Thank you for your time, and we hope that the point made in this letter is clear. We also hope that the right decision is made — one that could make all the difference.

The administration promptly turned their petition down. I believe the principal and his assistant didn't want to set a precedent whereby students could get what they wanted by petitioning the administrators. They didn't relish students challenging their authority. Had the tennis team the same popular status as the football and basketball teams and had the coaches of these teams along with parents from the sports' boosters club requested such a trip, it most likely would have been granted.

A "Hands-On" Government Class Is a Firsthand Experience in Democracy

Trying to teach a hands-on course in American government is far from an easy task when the teacher has to swim against the tide of authoritarian control. In spite of criticism from the administration and some colleagues for not completing the entire mandated curriculum, I chose to place more emphasis on the personal development of each individual student following in the footsteps of progressive educators beginning with Pestallozzi and Rousseau and adhering to the ideals of Jefferson and Mann.

I believe that the democratic process, for example, that resulted in the student petition on harassment and respect, far outweighs the mandate to rigidly master all knowledge and skills mandated by the curriculum. The diverse viewpoints and insights expressed by Kevin and his fellow classmates demonstrated the importance of individual growth and development that arise through the exploration of ideas, namely the democratic process. The kind of clear thinking that evolves, including that of the teacher, leads to resolution. Should any action be taken? If so what should it be?

The teacher, who is the facilitator of this process, must have faith that change for the better will occur. The history of the civil rights movement in this country provides evidence for this faith. Had there been no federal mandate to integrate Central High School in Little Rock Arkansas, had not Martin Luther King and others taken nonviolent action to the streets of Birmingham, Alabama, the crusade for civil rights would have taken even longer than it has. It is the students' freedom to express their thoughts, their spontaneity, their endurance to try to solve problems, and above all their serious search for answers that truly fosters thinking and questioning individuals so necessary for the democratic process to survive.

Even though the formal debate process is helpful in developing listening skills and the ability to respond directly to what has been said by the opposing team, the need to develop greater understanding and acceptance of one another must continue to evolve. Of particular importance is that teachers are able to listen and to take seriously the concerns and criticism of his/her students. Realizing that students are different, that opposing points of view may be expressed through the concerns and criticisms expressed, the teacher can present different viewpoints to the class. Together they can come to meaningful resolutions. By responding positively to criticism, the teacher will model the kind of exchange that is necessary for such a class to run effectively.

The democratic classroom that encourages students to develop a broader understanding and acceptance of a wide variety of views, some of which are controversial, will be explored from a different perspective in the following chapter. Here students are introduced to actual people as guest speakers in their classroom. They are encouraged to dialogue with the guests about their ideas and beliefs many of which are new and foreign to many students. After all, for democracy to survive, students must learn to compromise but still maintain their beliefs so long as these do not infringe upon the freedoms of others.

8

ENCOUNTERS WITH CONTROVERSY

Early Encounters with Controversy

During my first weeks of teaching in the fall of 1969 at Madison High School, I naively and unexpectedly met controversy head-on. I was giving a course in geography at the time. It seemed to me rather futile for students to memorize the agricultural products, raw materials, and industries of each country they studied. I particularly wanted to expose them to the cultures of the country, its art, music, literature, beliefs, and values.

In those days it was taboo for a teacher to bring his entire class into the school library to gather materials. So I put together books that included literature, art, the landscape, as well as information about the government, business and industry, and education. Students either signed these out from the school in the library or from me if they came from my personal library.

As one group of students was studying England, I brought in my copy of A. S. Neill's *Summerhill* for a girl who wanted to become an elementary school teacher. I thought, what better way of introducing her to new ideas than this book? After all this was a famous English school. Her father seemed to take offense at Neill's insight that kids become difficult because of wrong treatment at home. He believed in firm discipline not in the exploration of life and ideas as practiced by Neill at Summerhill.

He called my principal to make sure that students never be exposed to such "filth" and that his daughter be given a different assignment. When the principal, Chrome Dome, politely mentioned this to me, I naturally concurred that the student be given other material to study. If the girl became interested in Neill's ideas as a result of this exposure, I believed, she might get the book on her own from some other source. If not, I hoped, that I had introduced her to some different approaches to education than the traditional schooling she had been experiencing. Maybe in the future she would be more open to less traditional methods of schooling than she had experienced.

Within four years of teaching at Madison High the laid-back superintendent who had hired me, retired. His successor, a rather abrasive fellow, decided to reform the curriculum. He notified teachers that we would all be teaching nine-week mini-courses starting in the fall of 1976. Students would rotate from teacher to teacher.

Although most of my colleagues resented this change, I jumped with glee at the possibility of teaching a course that I longed to try. I would be able to teach a mini-course comparing the utopian societies during the Jackson era with the communal movement that had come to its peak in the early seventies in the rural areas surrounding Madison. I titled it "American Social History: 1840 to 1860."

In contrast to solely reading about such mid-nineteenth century utopian societies as Brook Farm, Oneida, the Amana Society, and the Shakers, each week a different guest speaker addressed the class. Each of them talked about his or her own unique lifestyle. Guests ranged from a Mennonite preacher to hippies who had settled in the surrounding countryside as part of the back-to-the-land movement of the 1960s and 1970s.

One of our visitors was Jessie. She and her husband had grown up in Brooklyn. At age 22 and 23 they came to Maine to buy cheap land. Together with nine other families in 1970 they bought 120 acres of land in Canaan for $35000. They were poor; they didn't ask their families for help. The land they found in Canaan was ideal as it was not only affordable but had a lovely brook running through. It was large enough so should each family decide to have their own area, this would be possible.

They settled on the land in June, living in tents. They quickly realized that by winter they had to have a home. The only solution for so many people was to build one group structure. With youthful energy, they used bucksaws, bowsaws, and scythes. Most had had no experience with this kind of labor coming from middle-class families and being just out of college. They had studied how-to books on everything from organic farming to hand tools before coming to Maine. By November they finished their three-story barn and lived in it throughout the winter. The ground floor was for animals; the upper two floors were living quarters for the families. The families lived simply with very little money. They did odd jobs from mowing cemeteries to light housecleaning. They drove old trucks, VW Beetles, or dilapidated vans. However, without electricity and no bills to pay, they had enough money to buy the basic necessities of life, i.e., gas for the vehicles, some food, and clothing from nearby thrift stores.

As enjoyable as it was living together with nine families, tensions arose. Although they had a lot of fun together, including playing music and ping-pong tournaments, it was hard work to sift through and seek resolutions to the emotional problems that evolved. By spring Jessie and Paul moved out of the barn into a teepee they built next to the site of their present home. Like the barn they built the year before, they constructed their home out of salvaged materials for about $15,000.

However, Jessie's visit to my class stirred up a hornet's nest. Jessie, God forbid, nursed her infant son in my classroom. Word of her sin reached a local Christian fundamentalist pastor. Word spread like wildfire among regional fundamentalist preachers and the local Catholic priest. The superintendent of schools held a meeting with three of them. Although he noted that there was no criticism of the teacher, concern about the content of the course was raised. The superintendent in his letter to me wrote that three questions came up for which he did not have answers:

1. Do we have a course "The History of Christianity-Judaism?"
2. Do you have a recommended bibliography for American Social History? (I pointed out that I thought that it was the students' responsibility to develop their own bibliography but conceded that it might very well be that we had a general bibliography for them to use for topics.)
3. Is there a possibility that all the topics should be presented rather than allowing freedom of choice from the students? (Again I could not answer this one but conceded that it might be beneficial to see that at least all the topics in a course are covered in fairly equal measure.)

The superintendent then noted that the main concern of those present, other than the beliefs of the religious groups, was the topic—transcendental meditation and yoga. They felt these were aspects of satanic worship. The superintendent wrote: "I am afraid they are concerned because I did not agree to censoring any part of the [social history] course. (Personally, I don't feel I know enough about TM and yoga to either condemn them or defend them)."

He felt that the ministers at the meeting wanted "equal time" for their point of view. To this, naturally, I had no objection though, I wondered what the connection was between a hippie breastfeeding her baby in my social history class, transcendental meditation, and yoga. I immediately contacted one of the more vocal preachers, who attended the meeting at the superintendent's office, to speak to my class. This former New Jersey cop, with a huge scar on his forehead, accepted my invitation without hesitation. With no understanding of and no apparent desire to know more about Jessie's back-to-the land lifestyle, he tried to show how demonic "cults" were.

Although the students sat quietly through his presentation, during the following class several stated they felt Jessie was a warm and sincere person. They admired her courage to try this alternative lifestyle. They wondered why the reverend talked about demonic cults when Jessie had nothing to do with cults. In fact, some of these students asked whether we could visit them at their commune. This we did. The students were most impressed by the simple, peaceful lifestyle that Jessie, Paul, and their son were leading. They appreciated the wholesome meal Jessie had prepared to which they had made contributions. By this time, several families had abandoned the commune, while others built homes on the property. Years later I received a letter from one of the students who had participated on this trip, now a home decorator in San Francisco, saying that this trip was the most memorable experience of her high school years. It helped her become more comfortable and appreciative of other people and gradually come to terms with her then latent feelings of homosexuality.

In his letter regarding the social history course the superintendent foreshadowed the impending control over teachers holding them accountable if they dared stray from the details of the established curriculum as it was written and finally approved by the powers that be. He questioned me:

> How careful are you in making sure that guest speakers do not stray from generally accepted procedures in presenting material? Is there a possibility that the students select the more unusual controversial topics more than others? Is it possible that we should make sure that all topics are covered in equal manner?
>
> Since there are so many topics, is it possible that we might split this course into two distinct courses? One might handle the rather objective scientific topics mentioned in your outline: The other might be a straight, objective history of religions.

Although no further incident occurred during this superintendent's tenure, shortly thereafter, I ordered thirty-five copies of Ron Kovick's *Born on the Fourth of July* for a rambunctious, low-track class, in which we were doing a unit on the Vietnam War. I believed that the students would find this book easy to read. Some would be able to understand Ron's dilemmas because of experiences of their own relatives and acquaintances, who had served in Vietnam. Although many students became involved in the book, one girl complained to the principal that the book had "swear words." It didn't occur to me that in this class, in which students used "four letter words" more easily than Standard English, a student would be so offended that she would complain to the principal. The principal took grief from the superintendent for approving this book without first checking it out carefully. The superintendent wrote me a letter of official reprimand adding to the paper trail he had already started.

Tolerance Day

It all began in a ninth-grade social studies class in the fall of 1984 spurred by that summer's drowning of a Bangor, Maine, homosexual by three teenage boys. Aware that my classroom was always open to guest speakers of divergent viewpoints, students requested that a homosexual be asked to address the class. In order for the homosexual to be seen as just one of many minorities who are victims of injustice instead of being viewed as an object of sensational intrigue, it seemed relevant that the class develop an all-day program for the whole school on the subject of tolerance.

The students articulated the purpose of this project. They wrote that its intent was:

"To lessen prejudice toward people about whom we are unaware. By becoming exposed to these people of whom we have opinions, we will get to understand their problems and feelings and have an opportunity to talk to them."

"Tolerance Day" was supposed to have taken place in January of 1985, but the very idea triggered a controversy that stirred-up the community and even momentarily captured national attention. Even *Playboy Magazine* succinctly captured the essence of "Tolerance Day" which was supposed to recognize victims of intolerance. Although the school board permitted Blacks, Native Americans, and Jews to participate, it objected to the presence of a lesbian. The Maine Supreme Court ruled that the school board could cancel this one-day event because it had a wide latitude over the curriculum. Furthermore, the court feared that the local grange and a fundamentalist group, which objected to the presence of the lesbian, would disrupt the event.

Having successfully explored the region for willing participants for this program, I submitted a written proposal to my principal and shared it with fellow colleagues. The principal, who later became superintendent of the school system, circled the word "homosexual" among the many participants. He said that this proposal had to be presented to the entire faculty for its approval at the next regularly scheduled meeting. One teacher urged that the program proceed as planned; the faculty voted in its favor. Nobody cast a dissenting vote, fully aware that a homosexual was among the participants.

The go-ahead being given, I proceeded to formally invite participants for the event. The following week the principal interrupted my class, in his words "to confirm that the homosexual had been cancelled." Bewildered, I replied, "No!" He left only to return shortly with the message that he had scheduled a meeting for the following morning with the superintendent of schools, himself, and me. At that meeting the superintendent said that the program could proceed as planned only on the condition that the homosexual be uninvited. Unwilling to consent, I suggested that this exclusion signified intolerance and thus defeated the intent of a program on tolerance.

Had Tolerance Day materialized, the school day would have started with a panel discussion consisting of the fourteen participants for all 400 students. Each of the panelists would have had a maximum of three minutes to address the student body followed by a short question and answer period. The panel was to have been moderated by the commissioner of rehabilitation for the State of Maine. Following the assembly program, students would have adjourned to their regular classrooms. Willing teachers would each have had one of the guests as a speaker for each of their *remaining* classes of the day.

Frustrated by the superintendent's reaction, I contacted Jed Davis, an attorney with affiliations to the Maine Civil Liberties Union. Since the program was to have happened within two weeks, he set a hearing date in superior court. The superintendent, who then found it necessary to consult with the school system's lawyer, was told that he could shorten the program but could not cancel the lesbian. A compromise for a half-day program, attendance at which was to be entirely voluntary, was reached. In other words, the administration was willing to abandon a highly structured program for chaos in order to appease what it sensed to be a hostile mood in the community.

The press, having discovered the court hearing date, perceived controversy. The following day, Saturday, the regional newspaper ran the headline in the local news section "Lesbian Concerns S.A.D. #59." Although the compromise was reported, phones began ringing throughout the community within minutes of the paper's delivery at local households. So-called concerned citizens called a meeting to be held that very night at the local grange hall to seek the program's cancellation.

The superintendent of the Maine Christian Civic League presided over the meeting. Instead of allaying the fears of those who turned out, he aided and abetted their anxieties. Furthermore, he wrote to League members appealing for funds for "The Defense of Morality in Maine." He said:

> Homosexuals will turn to our courts and to our public schools in a vile and ungodly attempt to brainwash our children into accepting this disgusting lifestyle. . . . Make no mistake about it, militant homosexual advocates will not give up. . . . they try to tell us that they're nice normal people, just like everybody else. They are trying to convince naïve and innocent children that this is so. These homosexuals must be stopped before they completely destroy our American family and corrupt our children.

Even though less than 6,000 people lived in the area, the superintendent of schools in Madison and some school board members received each some thirty phone calls urging them to cancel the program.

At that Monday's regularly scheduled school board meeting, about 150 townspeople showed up in zero-degree (Fahrenheit) weather to protest the program. At the advice of its lawyer, the school board cancelled Tolerance Day on grounds of "order, safety, and security."

Stating that the "purpose of Tolerance Day was simple . . . to encourage the abilities of people with differences to live among each other" most teachers at the high school signed a petition drawn up by two of my colleagues. It was sent to the administration and school board members criticizing their position in this matter. A copy was mailed to and published in the regional newspaper.

Toward the end of the week a superior court judge in Maine's capitol city heard the case, brought by the lesbian and myself, for a temporary restraining order against the school board. The judge, who at one point during the proceedings said semi-seriously that the event should be called "Intolerance Day" because of the controversy, pressed the school board's lawyer to explain the reasons for canceling the event. "What is one good reason for not having Tolerance Day? What is the Board afraid of? Are they fearful of the speakers, the school, or what?" The attorney responded that he had had little time to discuss the case with the administration to determine why they took the action they did and urged the judge to deny a temporary restraining order so that the issue could be explored more completely.

Forty-eight hours later the judge ruled to uphold the school board cancellation because homosexuals are protected neither by the Maine nor the United States Constitution. Although he stated that he could not block the authority of the school board to cancel a program, even when it was "bowing to threats from those who wanted to keep their students from gaining a greater perspective of different lifestyles in the outside world," he did offer a warning. He said that the decision by the school board to cancel the Tolerance Day program "could only encourage further attempts to restrict the educational choices available to Madison students."

Having lost the first round, the Maine Civil Liberties Union attorney scheduled a full trial for early the following month, February. One of my ninth graders became a plaintiff in this case arguing that her right to hear the speakers was wrongfully denied to her. The school board based its testimony on order, safety, and security, noting that threatening messages of sabotage to the school furnace in the cold of January and other threats of violence were the reasons for the program's cancellation.

The same judge, whom I slightly knew during our college years at Bowdoin as we were both active members of the International Club, upheld the school board's right to cancel the program. He said "as the school board is the ultimate policy maker for the school, it is free to schedule programs and cancel programs where it desires to do so." He, of course, repeated his argument that gays did not enjoy any specifically protected status under federal law and under the Maine Human Rights Act.

Were threats of violence at the heart of the case? I doubt it. When the superintendent reportedly received threats of violence, did he immediately notify the police? No. Did he ever notify any other proper authorities? Apparently not. One of the organizers of the local protest, who fled to Maine from California to escape the freeways and homosexuals, wrote in a guest column to the regional paper, "I've had a fair amount of involvement concerning this matter since it became known to the public, and never heard, even in the most 'off the record' idle discussion any mention of addressing the issue, or any aspect of it, with violence."

It became apparent that an adept attorney redirected the issue of fear — fear of homosexuality to fear of children being the target of violence. Furthermore, it was obvious that the courts submitted to that notion, thus allowing a fear of terrorism to prevail over justice.

The Maine Civil Liberties Union immediately appealed the case to the Maine Supreme Court. The Court in Bangor unanimously upheld the S.A.D. #59 school board's authority just as it had 131 years before. At that time, it had championed the local school's authority to mandate the teaching of the King James version of the Bible.

Had Tolerance Day occurred without controversy, it would most likely be remembered by many students simply as an interesting program. However, at least at the time of the strife, students discussed the case within their families. Even though disagreement was expressed, avenues of communication might have opened up. If not, at least these youths had to ask difficult questions; they were forced to think. A large number of students signed a petition drawn up by a fellow student supporting Tolerance Day. The student who led a petition drive calling for the program's cancellation gave up her effort after a short time as she had gathered only a few signatures.

Even some parents were positively affected. For example, the mother of one student, a faithful Pentecostal since childhood, realized the hypocrisy of her church when she was asked to attend the celebrated meeting at the

Grange Hall to attempt to cancel Tolerance Day. She said she neither attended that meeting nor had she since returned to her church.

Although the students were denied the program, they learned firsthand that things they read about in textbooks still happened. Some also realized that the hysteria they sometimes witnessed on the news, for instance, when many in a community banded together to prevent a boy infected with the HIV virus from attending school, could take place in their own community. As a result of the Tolerance Day outcry, more students became accepting of homosexuality as a lifestyle expressed through the cliché "each to his own." However, homophobia is still, today, very much in existence among Madison high school students

The negative decision of the Maine Supreme Court had broad and chilling consequences as well. Support for the concept of a "Tolerance Day" program dwindled. The president of the local teachers association, a high school teacher, who did sign the faculty petition to the school administrators and the board of directors critical of their action, wrote a letter — upon learning of the Supreme Court decision — that was published in newspapers throughout the state. She wrote that Madison is a wonderful place in which to live and to teach and that teachers there do have a great deal of academic freedom. Another teacher, who had supported me during the crisis, said that it was a shame that sexuality was brought into the program on tolerance. She further expressed that ninth graders are too young to deal with the issue of sexuality as they are just coming to grips with their own sexuality. Students, she argued, should be inculcated with traditional values of our society.

Several parents demanded of the superintendent that I no longer teach their children for "moral and religious" reasons arising from the Tolerance Day dispute. Shortly thereafter, I was informed that I no longer would be teaching all divisions of world history so that their kids would have the option of another teacher. I was required by the superintendent to order a new world history textbook that he had to approve. I was also required to develop an outline of my course complete with goals and objectives that he had to approve. Finally, I was informed that a successful evaluation of my teaching depended upon how well I kept to the outline.

I also learned that the dollar is sometimes mightier than the moral campaign being fought. Such seemed to be the case for the couple who launched the moral crusade against my approach to teaching. They owned a local grocery store in which they sold such magazines as *Playboy*, *Playgirl*, *Penthouse*, and *Hustler*. By the mid-nineties big chain supermarkets put this small family run store out of business.

All of these examples support my contention that most teachers are reluctant to deal with any kind of controversial issue in the classroom. Now they realized that the state's highest court backed a local school board that

bowed to the interests of a vocal group whose viewpoint was narrow and blatantly discriminatory.

In order to avoid another Tolerance Day fiasco, my school board developed a policy specifically to deal with controversial issues; it had teeth. The
school board felt that the current policy was too vague. It simply stated that
"special lecturers, when qualified in their subjects, may be requested to speak
before classes and assemblies of students. Those requiring payment must be
approved by the superintendent in advance and shall be paid from the district funds." The new policy was drafted based on samples provided by the
Maine School Management Association.

Policy # 6144 stipulated that "a question shall be considered controversial when one or more of the proposed answers are objectionable enough to
a section of the citizenry to arouse strong reaction." To avoid any criticism
from the public that the policy might be biased against outside speakers,
especially those who could be considered controversial, the policy did say
that, "consideration of controversial issues has a legitimate place in the public school curriculum." Immediately thereafter, the policy mandated that
"outside resources that would be effective in reinforcing controversial issues
must have formal approval from the building principal and he/she from the
superintendent before any arrangement can be made." The request for such
an outside resource must be made at least one week before the guest's appearance. Parents had to be notified in a letter sent home through the mail
informing them of the controversial issue to be discussed and the speaker
who would be coming into the classroom. If parents didn't want their children to be part of the discussion, they had the right to remove them. The
policy stated that parents had the opportunity to review any material that is
used as part of the curriculum. They can either contact the teacher directly
or get in touch with the principal. Teachers were warned to

> be constantly mindful of their position of considerable influence in the
> classroom setting. In light of this, restraint and careful judgment must be
> exercised in stating personal opinions to which students might ascribe
> more weight than is intended, that might distort or destroy the objectivity
> of their viewpoint, or that might be interpreted as prejudiced, slanderous or
> self-serving. (6144a)

Even though I had to jump through more hoops in order to have guest
speakers, I accepted the challenge. They were a very special and valuable
resource. They represented aspects of the "real" world with which students
were either not familiar or toward which they had been conditioned by the
status quo to hold seriously biased viewpoints. At the same time I felt I had
to do more work with my students in dealing constructively with controversial issues. This meant that they had to recognize their own biases as well as
those in others and in their reading.

Learning to Deal with Controversial Issues

Although many teachers pretend to be objective by stating the facts of history, the way how facts are selected and others are omitted by human nature alone is biased. As a teacher I feel it is my obligation to state clearly to my students what my bias actually is. I also want my students to challenge my thinking. Therefore, I reward them by giving them a higher grade if they thoughtfully challenge what I say by providing evidence to support their point of view. I consider this a necessary component of "training" students to become responsible citizens of our democratic country.

Whenever any of my classes has a guest speaker, I ask them to complete a speaker/analysis sheet. Not only do I read these and comment upon them, but we use these as a basis for our discussion following the appearance of the guest:

1. Describe the main points the speaker made:
   a.
   b.
   c.
2. What did the speaker say that you agreed with? Why?
3. What did the speaker say you disagreed with? Why?
4. Tell something that you really like about the speaker?
5. Tell something you didn't like about the speaker? Why?
6. Did the speaker fit the "stereotype" of the profession and/or lifestyle he/she leads? Why? Why not?

I used a similar approach when I had students read articles from newspapers, magazines, and the internet. The students were asked to

1. write a summary of the article in which they
   described what the article was about;
   identified the article's main points;
   identified the author's point of view;
   identified the author's conclusions;
2. identify the author's biases; what factors might have caused him or her to hold these biases, for example, gender, age, ethnicity, nationality, beliefs, sexuality, profession, culture/ environment in which he or she lived and his or her experiences; explain how these may have influenced his or her point of view;
3. describe what you learned from the article that has a) *changed* or *challenged* your thinking, b) caused you to take action for or against something about which you read in or learned from this article;
4. describe what you liked or disliked about the article.

One of the issues that continues to be controversial is homosexuality. On various occasions I have had homosexuals speak with my classes. They have ranged from college students who belong to a gay and lesbian campus organization to a gay college professor. In each instance students were polite and respectful to the guests. Some realized that gays and lesbians were just like themselves except for their sexual orientation. Even though boys tended to be more homophobic than the girls, in our follow-up discussions not one expressed fear of being accosted by any of these individuals.

According to school board policy, I always had opponents to homosexuality express their point of view. These have always been men of the cloth. Not one ever strayed from quoting the Bible as to why homosexuality was wrong. Since students had been exposed to the painful struggles of gays and lesbians fighting discrimination and feeling ostracized by the majority, they often asked the minister to explore his own feelings about homosexuality in contrast to the biblical word. No pastor seemed to be able to express his own feelings. Experience has taught that students, who are able to reach deep within themselves to the feeling level, are able to understand the difference between beliefs to which they have been conditioned and their own genuine feelings. Their process of growth begins to emerge.

The legalization of marijuana always seemed to crop up when we explored the Constitution and its amendments. Some students admitted that they initially used pot simply because they knew it is a violation of the law. They enjoyed challenging authority, yet they wondered why marijuana, which was considered less dangerous than alcohol, was illegal?

This circumstance led to find out discussions as to how activities were determined to be legal or illegal. The process to bring about change ranging from how a bill was drafted to its acceptance or defeat to the referendum was analyzed. Students have examined actual drafts of bills and referenda, among them bills to legalize marijuana. With an attorney they explored the complicated legalese language.

Because Madison is the home base of the "Maine Vocals," a statewide organization that promotes the legalization of marijuana, students were eager to have a dialogue with its members in a classroom setting. Since some frequented the little office front of "Maine Vocals" right downtown on Main Street, I felt it was important that they participated in a well facilitated discussion with representatives of the organization.

The same principal who got cold feet because of Tolerance Day, approved a classroom debate in which the outspoken founder of the Maine Vocals sparred with the school's substance abuse counselor. This debate, which was videotaped, became rather hostile as the two opponents continuously attacked each other's person. The counselor demanded that the principal confiscate the videotape; the pro-marijuana advocate wanted a copy.

The students, however, were both amused and frustrated by the commotion over the tape. "What's the big deal about releasing the tape," one student observed. "After all, both participants made fools of themselves."

Since then I have found articulate, well-mannered spokespeople for the pro-marijuana side. The most eloquent pro-marijuana spokesperson was a well groomed supervisor at the paper mill whose daughter was the valedictorian of her senior class. He discussed reasons for legalizing marijuana especially for industrial and environmental reasons. He also showed the similarities between the prohibition of marijuana in the 1990s and the prohibition of alcohol in the 1920s. He also explored the purpose and organizational structure of the "Maine Vocals" with the step-by-step method this organization used to try to legalize marijuana within the democratic framework.

Usually within a week either before or directly following this presentation, a spokesperson from the state's drug enforcement agency presented the state's position opposing the legalization of marijuana. Inevitably, most of the students, including those opposed to the legalization of marijuana preferred the pro-marijuana spokespersons. In part this was because they symbolized a "forbidden fruit." They particularly liked the student's father who represented the status quo since he held a reasonably prominent position at the mill. He was conventional in appearance, spoke articulately, and was well prepared. He was open to questions and discussion and spoke fairly of the opposition.

One discussion with the director of the state's drug enforcement agency drew a lot of fire from all corners of the class. A student asked why the agency had raided homes at night, at gunpoint, and with dogs. He described an instance in his hometown of Starks in which a three-year-old child was traumatized by a 3:00 a.m. raid. Officers armed with rifles and accompanied by specially trained dogs stormed the house. No drugs or paraphernalia were found. The incident led to an intense study of the Fourth Amendment to the Constitution that dealt with search and seizure. The class then invited a lawyer to address the legalities of the issue.

As a result of these discussions a greater appreciation for the U.S. Constitution and the democratic process evolved. It also demonstrated the need to allow and accept opposing points of view and taught the methodical yet often slow process by which change can be brought about legally and without violence.

9

PASSION AND EXPOSURE
TO DIVERSITY

By personally experiencing other people's ideas, lifestyles, forms of expression, traumatic experiences, search for life's meaning, professional occupations, and their activities for relaxation, students were better able to understand themselves and others. In some instances these experiences motivated them to become social activists. As students actually immersed themselves into different forms of self-expression from Native-American culture to music and movement, some became aware of and enthusiastically embraced their own hidden potentials.

War Sparks Student Initiated Programs

After defining the concept of sociology, students chose the topics they wanted to explore as a class. Not surprisingly, the topic of war often arose. Among the selected projects were two Veterans Day Programs: One dealt with the survivors of war, whereas another focused on the effects of war on Vietnam veterans and their families. The Vietnam War remained of significant interest to students. Some of the students' fathers were veterans having a hard time dealing with their experiences. Others had relatives and family friends who had fought in Vietnam.

In 1988 the students decided that they wanted to interview survivors of wars. They had been using as a text a recently published book by Sam Keen entitled *Faces of the Enemy: Reflections of the Hostile Imagination*. Keen effectively demonstrated how nations and their peoples masked violence to legitimize war. From a psychological perspective he argued that "the wars we engage in are compulsive rituals, shadow dramas in which we continually try to kill those parts of ourselves we deny and despise" (Keen, 1988, 11). They also learned that in order to go to war, the enemy had to be dehumanized. It is possible, Keen argued, to kill a dangerous animal but much more difficult to murder another human being. He added that "In the image of the enemy, we will find the mirror in which we may see our own face most clearly" (11).

Having had several survivors address the class, including those of the Nazi Holocaust, Pol Pot's Cambodia, Vietnamese and American veterans of that war, a person from El Salvador, and others, class members decided that they wanted to host a Veterans Day program for the entire school. They also wanted to demonstrate that all people are human; it was governments, they believed, that created enemies.

For this event these survivors would share their memories with the hope that students would think about why a country goes to war and its effects on everybody. Among the presenters were two survivors of the Nazi Holocaust: a Christian and a Jew who were both born in Poland.

Although Ragnhild Baade was born in German-occupied Poland, her father was born in Latvia and her mother in Russia. Both parents grew up in Estonia from where they were forced to flee in 1939. She lived with her mother and grandmother, because her father, a teacher, had been consigned to the German army. Her trials began at age five:

> When we got orders to evacuate, we already could hear the Russian guns getting closer and closer. The military got us a horse and wagon from a farmer. My grandmother paid the farmer whatever she had. We had very little time to pack anything. We could only take so much on the wagon; we had to make selections that were very hard. I chose the ugliest of my dolls because no one else would love that one. . . . We left in this cold, cold January. It was the coldest winter ever seen in all of Germany, ice cold. My grandmother stuck my younger sister in a foot warmer to keep her warm. (*Morning Sentinel*, 11 November 88)

Ragnhild Baade's grandmother was a woman of fortitude. She was a lumberjack in Estonia and also ran a wood mill. She was divorced, unheard of at that time. As Ragnhild, her mother, and grandmother fled Poland, her grandmother helped an overturned sled. Ragnhild and her mother never saw her again. The line of evacuees had to continue.

> It was a never ending column. As far as you could see, the ditches were lit-tered with abandoned carts, and dead horses. Everyone was in such a fren-zy, they never would have let her back in line. So grandmother said to go ahead and she'd catch up. She never caught up with us.
>
> A truck with soldiers stopped us and told us one train was going out, but we couldn't take anything. We left the cart with a farmer and made it to the train station. There were people hanging off the train roof, anywhere you could hold on. They passed us through the window.
>
> I remember the SS on board and the women trying to hide their kids (fourteen and fifteen years old) who were being sought out as deserters. The soldiers were merciless. The children were pulled off the train and hanged. (*Morning Sentinel*, 11 November 1988)

In Halle, Germany, Ragnhild's family was assigned to live with another family. Since Halle was a large industrial city, it was constantly being bombed. The family had to continually flee to bunkers. Once the bunker that sheltered her took a hit. It took hours to dig out of the buried ruins. Ragnhild described the coming of the Russians as frightening. They were angry and took out their frustrations on civilians. They raped and murdered on the streets.

When her father returned from captivity by the British, the family moved from place to place until her father acquired a teaching post at the state university in Thuringia, East Germany. Ragnhild was ten by this time. Her father enjoyed his teaching duties until trouble started all over again. The military government asked him to spy on students. Her father was inter-rogated around the clock. The Russian commander threatened to send him to Siberia, her mother to Russia, and to separate the children.

Finally, the family, who had been making plans to flee, escaped on 31 December, 1951. "I was sworn to secrecy. It was the hardest time of all. I couldn't tell any of my friends. I left without ever saying goodbye." The fam-ily nearly got caught at the border. As the border patrol was changing guard, a guard dog began to bark. Ragnhild recalled: "We heard the guard say 'I really should investigate, but it's New Year's Eve and I want to get home, and they left."

Rachelle Slivka grew up in Vilna, Poland, experiencing anti-Semitism from her earliest memories. As a Jewess she had to attend private schools since Jews were not allowed to attend public schools. Jewish stores were boy-cotted as anti-Semites stood in front forbidding non Jews to enter.

On 1 October 1939, the German Army invaded Poland dividing the country in half between themselves and the Russians. Rachelle was fortu-nate to live in the Russian sector. Life became normal for two months. She could attend school again, but she had to learn Russian. Two months later

Russia gave this portion of Poland to Lithuania. A pogrom took place in which Lithuanians beat up and killed Jews. Then a period of normalcy set in. Again Rachelle could go to school, but she had to learn Lithuanian. Eventually the Russians reoccupied the area.

In June 1941, the Germans attacked Russia and took over Poland. Since the Germans couldn't identify the Jews, they managed to get the Poles to sell a Jew for a pound of salt or a pack of cigarettes. The Germans set up a Jewish ghetto. From here, if they didn't have yellow permit cards, they were taken outside of the city to a field where they were shot.

Three to four families shared a two-room apartment. There were no bathrooms, only outhouses. At one point Lithuanian, Russian, and Ukrainian police emptied a school and took the children away to be shot. Two months later the yellow cards were changed to pink. Those without the pink cards were killed. Rachelle recalled living in fear for two years. Then the ghetto was liquidated. Over loudspeakers she learned where to report without any belongings.

First she and others were taken to a field outside of the city where they saw three people hanging. They were told, that if they tried to break from the ranks, the same fate would happen to them. They stayed in the same field for a whole night. It was raining and cold. The men and women were separated. The men were taken to a concentration camp in Estonia where they were burned alive. Her father died there. Russian guards took crying children from their mothers and returned the dismembered bodies to the mothers. Some mothers killed their own children to save them from this fate.

The following day the women were taken in cattle cars to a concentration camp near Riga, 100 to a car, where they stood like sardines. There were no toilets. They were told that the camp was built over Jewish graves. The little they had with them was taken away. Their heads were shaven to make sure they wouldn't escape. They showered and were taken to barracks. In the cold of winter they slept on wooden boards without straw or blankets. Each morning at 6:00 a.m. Rachelle and the other women had to report for roll call. If they so much as moved a little, the whole group would be punished, having to stand at attention for a longer period of time. Then they went to work, digging ditches, building railroads, working in factories. They returned at 5:00 p.m. and were beaten by a German woman in charge. They had to seek permission to go to the toilet.

A year later they were taken to a worse camp in Germany. Here they were not even permitted to use the toilet. Nor were they allowed to wash themselves. Many died of typhoid and other diseases. Some women, who couldn't take the torture any longer, tried to escape and were electrocuted as they tried to break through the fence. In order to keep warm the women took the clothes of those who had died.

Ten months later, just before Christmas, the camp was liquidated. With trains and trucks unavailable, the remaining women were taken on foot through a bitter cold, snowy winter. For six weeks they walked from 6:00 a.m. to 6:00 or 7:00 p.m. They spent nights in barns or churches. If a woman tried to wet her lips with snow or attempted to help another person, she would be shot instantly. Rachelle said that women were dying like flies. Finally, they ended up staying in one barn for ten weeks until they were liberated by the Russians. This was in 1945. It took her four years to get to the United States where she had relatives.

Rachelle's husband, Jerry, told how he had survived the Holocaust. He had grown up in Poland, lived through the civil war of 1918, was a refugee many times over, and worked as a slave laborer in a coalmine in the Soviet Union.

Other refugees took part in the program. One fled his native Afghanistan; another escaped Pol Pot's Cambodia. Hung Hoang fled South Vietnam in 1975 with his family. Lila Balch talked of a return trip to war-torn El Salvador to visit her family. She recalled, "No matter where you go in El Salvador, you are met with a soldier carrying a big machine gun, guns pointed at people's guts. I was there two weeks and you'd be amazed at how quickly you get used to this kind of act." Nick Arkas, who was raised in the former Czechoslovakia and France, lived under Hitler and under communist rule before coming to the United States. His parents had fled Russia during the 1917 revolution.

Steve Bentley, a Vietnam War veteran, active with Veterans for Peace, who moderated the panel, spoke out against the atrocities of war. He challenged what he said were incorrect beliefs about "good guys and bad guys. . . . There are no good guys, no bad guys, just us guys." He explained how he grew up in a time, glorified by John Wayne movies, when the Japanese, Communists, and Indians were the bad guys, while the Americans were always the good guys, better than all other people in the world. "There's a line of good and evil that cuts through us all. We're living in a world where we spend billions of dollars annually on weapons while several million children starve to death each day."

Following the panel discussion, students returned to their regularly scheduled classes, where willing teachers allowed the guests to talk with their classes for several periods. The program concluded with a roundtable discussion of several students who reflected upon the day's experience.

Students explained that by listening to other voices and hearing the experiences of different people helped each of them develop closer human connections to others and taught them about their own feelings of fear, rage, and compassion. Even if only momentarily, the social consciousness of some students was definitely awakened.

From my perspective as a teacher, there is no substitute for encountering living people and learning about their experiences. Students were able to acquire greater empathy for those to whom they listened, be it the non-Jewish Pole, who had to flee her homeland at the onset of German occupation, or the Jewish Pole, who was persecuted by the Russians, Lithuanian, and Nazis. They heard from a Vietnam veteran how war not only destroyed other peoples, their cultures, and their biosphere, but also the soldiers themselves.

The Vietnam War

At various times over the years, students chose to study the era of the Vietnam War. We met regularly with veterans. In preparing for guest speakers, students drew up a series of questions. These were used as a guideline or if no questions arose spontaneously from the students:

Veterans
How did you feel about the war at the time of your entry into the service?
Were you drafted or did you enlist? Why did you enlist? How did you feel about being drafted?
Why did you go to war?
How did you feel about leaving your homeland?
What type of training did you receive? Was the training appropriate for what you experienced in Vietnam?
What outfit were you with and how long did you serve with them overseas?
What kind of people made up your outfit?
Describe a typical day in your outfit?
How did you feel about the civilians in the combat zone?
How did you feel about our allies? Are there any events in particular that occurred that you could share with us?
What kind of moral support did you receive from the U.S.?
After you were in the combat zone, did your feelings about the enemy change? Why? How about your feelings now?
What was Vietnam like? How was the weather?
Do people resent you for being in the war? How does that make you feel? How do you deal with it?
Do you have a lot of nightmares and/or flashbacks? What triggers them?
How did you get through the war? What mind games did you play with yourself, if any?
Did you experience military action?

Did you suffer from any wounds?

Do you feel ashamed about fighting? How do you feel about what you
    saw?

Do you feel the costs of the war (human and otherwise) were worth it?
    Why or why not?

Do you hate the "enemy" now, even though the war is over?

What part did the media play?

What kind of treatment did you receive when you returned home?

How do you feel your war-time service has affected your life? How have
    you dealt with it?

Wives of Veterans

Did your husband change from the way you knew him before the war?
    How?

Did his changing hurt your relationship? How?

Do people treat you badly because your husband went to Vietnam? How
    did they treat you?

Children of Veterans

Does your parent ignore (want to forget, not talk about) the fact that he
    was in the war?

Does your parent scare you when he/she has flashbacks, etc.? How do
    you deal with it?

Were you brought up to hate the so-called enemy? Do you now feel
    nobody is the enemy?

Was your father handicapped as a result of the war? How does he deal
    with it?

Since most of the veterans, who spoke with us, were experiencing Post-
Traumatic Stress Disorder (PTSD), students did considerable research on
this illness. A therapist, who treated veterans, spoke to the class and shared
her clients' poetry about their experiences. His poetry was particularly moving to those who heard it. Maybe, this is because, according to poet and ecol-
ogist, Gary Snyder, poetry is a way to express feelings more deeply and
poignantly than narrative prose or speech.

This therapist, who was the spouse of a Vietnam veteran, is now
divorced. She even said at the time of her presentation to the class that her
life was built around the symptoms of PTSD. Students met with other wives
of Vietnam veterans. Marietta was one.

She was married to a veteran for sixteen years before she realized it was
destroying her life. She was diagnosed as suffering from a secondary form of
PTSD passed on by her emotionally scarred husband. She told the class,
"Neither of you can help each other. You may want to say you're lonesome
and hurting, but you can't because you don't trust." She explained how her

former husband often had a faraway look on his face and in his eyes as if he were always in a dream world. She later realized that during these episodes he was experiencing flashbacks. Most of his nightmares were due to his fears of becoming insane because of the horrors to which he had been exposed in Vietnam. He would wake up at night drenched in sweat with clenched fists ready to fight.

Marietta described his frequent outbursts of rage when he couldn't get his way. When she no longer would accept his domination, he tried to control their daughter. Finally, she couldn't handle the roller-coaster life of one extreme to another. "Just when you think life seems normal again, he blows up, runs away or refuses to face reality. I am left alone again, to cope until he decides to try again and then find that we're back in the same rut — him running and me trying to cope."

Tom, in the very early sixties, was a student in the lowest-academic track in his class in a small Massachusetts community. He enlisted in the army even before the draft had been enacted. He wanted to follow in his dad's footsteps, a man he had never known. His dad, who had died shortly after he was born, had served as an officer in World War II.

The emotional pain of having a wounded soldier covered with blood, stumbling off a helicopter into his arms and die, was traumatic. Often when recalling that incident, this huge man, so gentle and peaceful, would break out in tears. Constantly hearing gunfire and having to sleep with a gun at the foot of his bed, caused this one time football player to wonder what war was all about. He now practices a form of Native American meditation.

Tom would sit through movies about the Vietnam War and share his thoughts and feelings about these. For example, the class watched the first part of Full Metal Jacket. While students initially laughed at the bullying manner of the drill sergeant, Tom told us that this part of the film showed little exaggeration. The exception was that Lenny, a humiliated and klutzy soldier, assassinated the drill sergeant and then took his own life. Tom explained that the purpose of boot camp was to break down all moral principles and values with which he and his fellow soldiers had grown up so that they would become killers. He was never debriefed.

Another veteran, Paul, shared his feelings about the film Hamburger Hill as it brought back chilling memories of his experience. Like Tom, Paul was in the lowest-track in his high school class in the neighboring town of Skowhegan. He was captain of the wrestling team and, in his senior year, was second in the state in his wrestling class. He weighed 167 pounds. After graduating from high school, he worked at his brother's gas station until he was drafted.

On 1 November 1968, in deeply forested hills, Paul's sixteen-man reconnaissance platoon came under heavy enemy fire. The man directly in front of him was shot in the face and killed. That man had been in Vietnam less than a week. The squad lieutenant's hand was blown off at the wrist and the sergeant, who had only a short time left in the country, dove for cover and froze up. Paul retrieved the radio from the wounded operator and when the sergeant refused to do anything with it, Paul decided that the time had come for him to take command. He called in air strikes and napalm and then went out into enemy fire to retrieve the wounded. For his action he was awarded the Silver Star.

Shortly before leaving Vietnam, Paul read in an edition of *Stars and Stripes* that his two closest high school friends had been killed that week. Upon returning home he met the father of one of his dead buddies at the local mom and pop store. The father, offended by Paul's long hair and flack jacket, wanted to know why Paul had survived and his son hadn't. This helped to trigger survivor's guilt. Paul has been diagnosed with PTSD and receives an allowance from the government for complete disability. He certainly showed all the symptoms of one suffering extensively from PTSD. He had trouble concentrating. He was depressed. He couldn't hold down a job. He was mistrustful, cynical, and restless. He no longer could control his temper.

Paul married, bought some land on an isolated hilltop several miles from Skowhegan where he raised his children, pigs, and ponies. He experienced fits of rage and was on occasion violent toward his wife and children. He became convinced that the local and state police were out to get him. He frequently had run-ins with the sheriff's department.

Paul still goes to the veterans hospital, more than an hour's drive from his home, for medical check-ups. He recently had an experience in which his file was exchanged with that of another veteran causing him to miss his treatment. He was angry. He explained that security officers escorted him out of the hospital as he "apparently had lost his cool." He remains bitter and angry about his wartime experiences, the lack of respect he is still shown especially by administrators at the veterans hospital and the limited amount of disability money he receives from the government. He is frustrated by recent cut-backs in service and the expressed intention of the federal government to eventually close Togus, Maine's only veterans hospital. In fact, Togus was one of the first federally funded veterans hospitals ever established. It was built immediately following the Civil War.

A class that studied the Vietnam War together with veterans in the fall of 1990 decided they wanted to host a Veterans Day program for the whole school by having a panel of veterans address the student body. They called it "The Never-Ending Saga of War: Vietnam After Twenty Years." The panel consisted of four veterans and three wives of veterans all affected by the war. Students put Paul's slides, which he had taken in Vietnam, to the music and lyrics of Billy Joel's *Goodnight Saigon*. Following the slide show, a student introduced the panel and moderated the discussion. She said:

> The purpose of this Veterans Day program is to give Vietnam veterans a chance to let us know of their experiences and feelings about the Vietnam War. We need to learn that there is more to war than shooting people in the jungles, and more than the Rambo image. Also we need to realize there is a lot of pain and suffering within the generation that grew up during the war, among people who are the age of our parents.
>
> It is important for us, the younger generation, to look at the Vietnam veteran as he was, a kid in war, and not like a baby killer as he was portrayed. We want to know that war is not the soldiers' fault and to realize soldiers didn't kill because they wanted to, only because they had to. At the same time, we need to be aware that war does kill and that soldiers, their families and friends become emotionally scarred by war.
>
> In order for us to get a sense of understanding of the Vietnam experience, we need to see all aspects of the war, not just the popular ones, as fighting. As we learn what the vets really went through, we will all gain respect for the Vietnam veteran who had a hard time in Vietnam. We want to understand these men so that we can really show them that we care.
>
> We also need to know how our government may have been misleading. We need to learn from the experiences of the previous generation so that these events won't happen again. Since we may be facing war in the near future (reference to the Gulf War), we need to hear the problems war causes because our class may be the first-choice pick.

One by one the veterans painfully and eloquently shared their experiences that held the entire student body's attention for two hours that morning. Bob, a Madison veteran and a former army engineer, was hit by friendly fire. He suffered from pain, pneumonia, cardiac arrest, and the loss of a leg. After fantasizing for years about taking revenge on the man who shot him, Bob finally called the man's home in 1988, only to discover he had died. He continued to wonder whether forgiveness could have helped him.

One veteran, a local police officer in Madison, proudly spent two tours as a helicopter gunner in Vietnam. He remained in the Army Reserves. He was eighteen at the time doing the two things he liked best—flying and shooting. Only after he was wounded for the first time, did he realize war wasn't just a game. Although he felt he had probably seen too much in his lifetime, he was at peace with his past. He said he killed only because he had to. It was either the other man or he who would die.

Steve, who had moderated our Veterans Day program several years previously, spoke eloquently. He had spent two years in Vietnam with the U.S. Army's 588th Combat engineers. Most of the soldiers, he explained, regardless of their political persuasion, felt that they had been lied to, used, and betrayed by the American people and their government. Some were angry at the Liberals for opposing the war and at such celebrities as Jane Fonda for going to North Vietnam to meet with the "enemy." Steve and others were angry at the Conservatives, the hawks who got us into the war. He resented the large corporations that made money off the war and politicians, who knew nothing about war, but who saw this as an opportunity to make political gains.

Steve shared two important lessons he had learned. The first was that in order to kill people, soldiers must be dehumanized. Therefore, boot camp was a form of psychological rape, to debrief soldiers of the biblical values with which they had been raised, to train them to follow orders, and never to think for themselves. Because he and his fellow combatants had been emotionally disconnected from any form of feelings, he explained that it did not take courage to pull the trigger of a gun or to drop bombs. They had been psychologically numbed.

The other lesson that Steve learned was what he termed "the biggest lie of all," namely, that the other people are less human than ourselves. He realized quickly that the enemy did not consist of slimy Gooks with one eye in the middle of their forehead and long teeth falling out of their head, but that they were people just like himself who laughed, who cried, and who had feelings. He asked why the United States government spent $900 billion a year on defense if our nation cared so much about justice in the world.

Steve expressed concern that our government had sold weapons to Saddam Hussein in the past. He observed that when we dropped bombs in Iraq, we weren't killing Saddam Hussein but innocent people. One veteran urged the students to be sure that what they would do was right before they did it. He encouraged them to ask questions that needed to be asked.

During the question and answer period some students' queries seemed rather insensitive. Several boys were more interested in knowing about tunnels and trip wires, movies and helicopters, and if it might work to send a sniper to get rid of Saddam Hussein. One boy asked if a war in Kuwait would be like the Vietnam War. Another wanted to know what he could do to urge his government not to go to war against Sadam Hussein.

The student who brought the program to a conclusion said that he felt that it helped all present to better understand the experiences of their fathers, uncles, and other relatives who served in Vietnam. He added that he and his fellow students had been affected by the war that happened 20 years before. After all, every veteran who suffered from PTSD directly affected at least four people around him. He explained that kids suffered when they saw the trauma their closest relatives experienced.

A girl told of her veteran father and of her mother who said that he had changed in Vietnam. He used to really be nice, but now blew up at anything. He hit her mother; he hit the kids; he cried a lot.

Other Guest Speakers

Having heard via the national news media how violent the militia movement was in some states, students were surprised to find that the Maine Militia represented ideas that were consistent with democratic principles. The organizer of the group, Mack Page of Belfast, handed out a leaflet that described the militia as:

> [a] well-regulated, unorganized group of private, unpaid local citizens, both armed and unarmed, to serve in time of natural disaster, civil defense, and in defense of self and state.
>
> In today's world, civil defense is more important than ever before. Hurricanes, Hugo and Andrew, Midwest floods, California earthquakes, and western forest fires are all devastating to individuals and personal property. A fast moving, well-trained civilian militia can respond and do so immediately. The citizens militia is an unpaid servant serving your local area in time of need or emergency.
>
> Constitutionally, a Civilian Militia is the final line of defense against all enemies both foreign and domestic. (Brochure of the Maine Militia, 1998)

The Maine Militia contended that it held both the United States and the State of Maine constitutions. "It does not tolerate racist, revolutionary or unlawful views or actions. . . . and likewise, espouses no religious views other than to uphold said constitutions which were intended to conform to Biblical as well as common law by our founding fathers" (Maine Militia Policy Statement). I wondered, though I never asked, whether Islamic law or that of any other major faith would be acceptable to the group members.

The three representatives of the militia, who spoke to my classes during our study of the U.S. Constitution, believed that the U.S. government was so corrupt that it bombed the federal building in Oklahoma City and used tear gas to ignite the religious compound in Waco, Texas. To support their point of view, they showed a documentary film, *Waco, the Rules of Engagement*, that displayed military tanks with ramming rods smashing into the buildings of the Branch Davidian compound. Government hearings were shown in which the Bureau of Alcohol, Tobacco, and Firearms (BATF) defended its raid on the Branch Davidian compound. At the same hearings, plenty of evidence, backed up by the documentary's videotaped footage, showed the well-armed BATF in a war-like scene attacking the compound. Evidence was shown that BATF agents' shots were fired through the metal door into the main building because the bullets penetrated the metal doors from the outside. BATF agents argued the opposite.

To counter the government's attitude that the Branch Davidians were dangerous, the filmmakers interviewed the county sheriff. He had kind words to say about the members of the sect. They were basically good people who simply had different beliefs from others and his own. They were always well mannered, minded their own business, and were never overbearing. They were clean and courteous. He admitted that they had many guns, but so did the local citizenry in Texas. He argued bearing arms was a constitutionally protected right. Although there was hearsay about inappropriate sexual activity on the part of the group's leader, the sheriff said that no arrests could be made unless there was proof.

Much of the following class was used to talk about the Maine Militia. Sure, some students felt that militia members were paranoid because they believed the United Nations was in the process of taking over the world and thereby creating a new world order. Since all too many students did not know about the United Nations, we later talked about its structure and the role it was supposed to play as the world's peacekeeper.

Some felt the Militia's belief that the bombing of the federal building in Oklahoma City in 1995 was a government plot was unfounded. However, the students had many questions about the government's siege at Waco in 1993. The question of search warrants was addressed. They wondered whether it was within the jurisdiction of the BATF or some other agency to invade the compound based upon sexual charges.

The discussion certainly generated a healthy understanding of the organization. It resulted in balanced views students held toward the Maine Militia. It demonstrated once again the need to listen to and to try to understand different points of view. Only with such comprehension was it possible to break from stereotypical images of the organization, diminish fear of it, and be able to enter into meaningful dialogue with these people.

One group of students exploring the manner in which the state government handles mental illness by gradually closing down state institutions and placing the mentally ill back into the community, examined the case of a young, schizophrenic man. In 1997 he had bludgeoned two nuns to death at their convent in nearby Waterville.

One of the students' mother, a mental health worker, knew the parents of this man. She arranged for the couple to address the class. Although the principal reluctantly approved the talk, he wrote on my application, "I believe that this is a real stretch to fit into content. I don't believe that these students have the background to deal with a subject like this."

One of the first things that Mark's parents did with the class was a role-playing exercise by which students could better understand the mind of a schizophrenic person. Each member of half the class was given a different phrase to read. The rest remained as the audience. All the actors read their separate phrases at the same time, louder and louder, as the mother tried to read a paragraph to them. The students became confused as to which voice they should listen. How could they distinguish that voice?

Mrs. Bechard was critical yet sympathetic toward the mental-health agency where her son was a patient. She explained how medication was supposed to calm the many voices he heard, but it made him feel lethargic, and he behaved rather like a zombie. Therefore, he apparently didn't always take the medications he was supposed to. Nor was he properly supervised by mental-health workers from the state-funded agency that was to look after him and many others with mental illness. Still, the mother had praise for the agency because she felt its clinicians and doctors did try hard to help her son. After all, the agency was underfunded and the employees, very caring people, were overworked.

The same group of students invited the director of the mental-health agency to speak with their class about this case as well as the role his agency played in dealing with the mentally ill. The director, too, lamented the lack of funding his agency received and the fact that his staff is overworked. He also raised the question to the students whether they or their parents would be willing to pay higher taxes, considering that many people felt their taxes were already too high, to care for the mentally ill. "Isn't it true," he added, "that every agency can demonstrate convincingly to you that they need more state funds? What will then happen if they all get the money they request? Won't there be a taxpayers' revolt? What will be the consequences of that?" Although students said they would like to support this program, many were concerned that if taxes became too high, they wouldn't be able to lead as comfortable a life as they now did.

A rather shy girl who became deeply involved in this project said that instead of going to school to become a computer technician, she now was interested in becoming a social worker. I introduced her to a social worker with whom she set up an appointment. According to both, the session went well, and the girl seemed interested in pursuing such a career. When I met her a year later at a shopping mall, she still expressed her desire to become a social worker. A further outcome of this project presentation was that it gave students a real-life understanding as to how a state agency worked, where its money came from, and the problems it encountered.

For the most famous speaker to come to Madison High School, I must thank my wife, whom I met while on sabbatical leave in China in 1993. She befriended the Chinese dissident Harry Wu when he spoke in the fall of 1997 at Colby College in Waterville. Having arranged several speaking engagements for him in Maine for later that year, he agreed to drop his $3000 plus fee to be able to address the students at Madison High School that December.

Some English and social studies teachers prepared students for his visit by having them read sections from his books and watch a videotape from an ABC news program. It documented, using actual footage taken secretly by

Harry Wu, how the Chinese government shot prisoners whose organs they sold worldwide.

Still some teachers and the administrators feared the students would be disruptive. My department chairperson wanted the lowest-track students to be kept in class anticipating they would interrupt the talk, thereby blemishing the good name of our little high school. I argued that it was important for the whole student body to hear Harry Wu. If we adequately prepared our students for his visit and show our faith in the students, they would at least be respectful and most likely appreciative. Hearing in person from one of the world's most renowned human rights activists could be a memorable and important experience for our students and staff as well. If we refused to let students attend the program, I reasoned, we would only be alienating them further and fostering the kind of behavior we were trying to discourage.

During Harry Wu's entire presentation, attended by the entire school population, a pin drop could be heard. Even the most rowdy students were attentive, realizing the courage that this man, incarcerated in Chinese prisons for nearly 20 years, continued to demonstrate by secretly returning to China to uncover the evils of the Laogai — the Chinese term for "labor" and "reform" prisons.

Students were amazed by his story. He lost his freedom at age 20 because he made comments that were construed as antigovernment. Of course, since his parents were members of the bourgeoisie and he was raised as a Catholic, the Chinese communist of the late 1950s held his personal history against him.

Wu's mother committed suicide following his arrest. His relatives were tortured, intimidated, and ordered to denounce him. During his nineteen years in twelve different labor reeducation camps, he was subject to physical and psychological torture and crushing labor quotas that determined whether he would be given food or not. He was even confined to a six-foot cement coffin for more than a week.

Field Trips

In addition to having guest speakers come to the classroom, students gained firsthand experience, understanding, and acceptance of other cultures, beliefs, and lifestyles through field trips. Over the years students and I have visited counterculture communes. For several years in the early 1970s I took the sophomore class to Boston's Museum of Fine Arts. My students and I visited two cultural communities: a Russian community in Richmond, Maine, and a Buddhist Temple in Portland.

Recently, I met a former student, whom I had during my first year of teaching in Madison. Before the end of the year, this student, in the lowest academic track, dropped out because she was pregnant. She never did complete high school. She said that her most memorable experience from less than two years at high school was a Sunday trip that she and several of her classmates had taken with me to Richmond.

This town, downstream of Madison and the state's capital, Augusta, on the Kennebec River, was home to a colony of Russians who had settled there in the early 1950s. They were refugees of the 1917 Russian Revolution. We attended a Russian Orthodox Church service. Not only was the entire ceremony conducted in Russian, but according to custom, parishioners stood throughout the service. The students stood quietly for two hours fascinated by the various rituals.

Relatives of famous Russians lived in the community at that time. The choir director was the grandnephew of Leo Tolstoy. Living with a community member, to whose home we adjourned following worship at the church, was an aged niece of Czar Nicholas. We completed the morning with a lunch of borscht at a little Russian restaurant.

We took this trip because we were studying Russian history. Upon returning to class on Monday I read the class a short story by Leo Tolstoy. Those students, who came on the trip, listened with attention and participated in a lively discussion. Gaining a glimpse of prerevolutionary Russia brought the curriculum alive to them.

For the past two years, I have taken my sociology class to a tiny Cambodian Temple located in the burned out shell of a house on the outskirts of Portland. At the temple we met with four refugees of Pol Pot's genocide. Ironically, when we visited there in April of 1998, we learned on the evening news that while we were there Pol Pot had died in Cambodia. As in any Buddhist Temple, students had to take off their shoes and hats and sit on the floor. They did this without question and with genuine respect.

One survivor related his story:

> My family and I left the city and took the road to Prek Phneuv. Along the way I saw the Khmer Rouge, soldiers waiting in groups of three and four; they searched people and took their watches, radios, glasses, gold stones. Some even took 500 riel-bills and threw them in the air. The revolutionary Angkar had put an end to money.
>
> We had great difficulty making any headway because of the enormous crowd leaving town and also because some Khmer Rouge kept firing shots to scare us. Many people died on the march: the hospital patients who had been driven out, the women who gave birth on the road, the war casualties. Along the way we saw many dead bodies scattered about everywhere — even in the pagodas — and the stench that came from them was almost unbearable.

Following the moving conversation with these survivors, we ate lunch together at a small Cambodian restaurant in the city. For several of the students this was their first visit to Portland, Maine's largest city, a 90-minute drive from Madison. I was particularly impressed that all the students, who were used to Burger King and McDonald's hamburgers and often threw away leftovers, ate all the food that was given to them. Most said that they liked it.

Police Sponsored Activities

Sometimes student concerns brought out their best characteristics. This was the case during the fall of 1980. Many Madison High School students were particularly unruly. Drug use was rapidly becoming more prevalent. Students tended to be more disruptive in the classroom and hallways. Cherry bombs were ignited in the toilets of the boys' bathroom adjacent to my own classroom. Students were frequently suspended, but little seemed to change for the better.

In my classes students said that they were bored. There was nothing for them to do in the town. They said when they hung around street corners, the police told them to move on; loitering was forbidden.

A student in a college prep group suggested that we invite the new chief-of-police to address their concerns. He listened attentively as students spoke out about the lack of activities for them in the community and the feeling they had that townspeople only complained about them. He spontaneously suggested that students from this class create together with him an organization he called "Police Sponsored Activities" (PSA). He would contribute some of his own money and help the students raise enough money to purchase a good sound system so that they could host school dances. The police department would provide an officer to be on hand at each dance.

Students were enthusiastic. Funds were raised; the equipment was purchased which was then housed at the school. Initially dances occurred twice monthly. They were well attended. The police chief, who liked to disco, brought his wife and together they danced with the students.

When the chief, a few years later, moved on to a different community, the organization continued. By this time most of the students involved were those who were in the lower academic tracks. Students elected their own officers, maintained the equipment, raised necessary funds to buy records and tapes. When the police officers became unionized, the PSA had to pay to have a police officer to chaperone the Friday or Saturday evening dances. This they willingly did. They continued to draw nearly one-third of the school population.

By the early nineties attendance at the dances dwindled; students lost interest, and the group faded into oblivion. However, the PSA was a prime example in which students and the police department worked together for the common good in a friendly and enthusiastic manner.

Seeds for the Diversity Leadership Institute Are Sown at Madison High School

Sometimes events occur in the community that affect students to an extent that they want to take action. Since high school students are generally inexperienced with social and political action, a supportive teacher can be helpful to them.

My role has been that of a facilitator. Upon identifying a problem, I asked the students what they felt needed to be done. Then we brainstormed to find ways how they could address these needs. Once an action plan had been developed, we approached it step by step. If, for instance, the students decided upon a school assembly program, I would accompany the delegation as a support person when they met with the principal. If letters had to be written, students drafted them. As an editor, I did offer suggestions. If phone calls were necessary, we talked about what needed to be said and how it should be said. Students then made the calls. As students and I worked out the details of the program, they introduced and facilitated the actual event. By using this skill-based teaching method to help students address a particular problem, I helped them to become self-confident, socially responsible, and active citizens. The seeds for the Diversity Leadership Institute (DLI) were sown as a result of an incident that occurred during the early evening hours of 4 November, 1991.

Three Madison teenagers covered their heads with white hoods made from pillowcases. They soaked crosses they had made out of wood in gasoline and headed toward the home of Rudi Harris, a Black youth. Together with his younger brother and his mother, he had returned to Madison, his mother's hometown. When the boys reached Rudi's home, they were chased away by neighbors, not before throwing eggs at their homes. As they fled, they abandoned their crosses.

Rudi, one of my sociology students, and other members of the class explored what they could do to harness this kind of deviant behavior. Although they concurred that Rudi, like many newcomers on the block, may have been tested, the racial tones of the incident couldn't be ignored. The aspect of racism only intensified as publicity about the incident spread throughout the state. An unknown person placed Ku Klux Klan leaflets entitled "An Introduction to the Invisible Knights of the Ku Klux Klan" on car windows. Beneath the symbol of the Klan was the caption "Grand Dragon of Maine and New Hampshire."

The students decided that an all-school assembly dealing with racism as well as an evening forum for the general public was needed. To the high school assembly they invited the regional vice-president of the New England Area of the NAACP along with several Blacks from Maine who experienced racial prejudice firsthand. The student, who introduced the panel, said:

> Racism exists everywhere, our state included. The recent incident in Madison awakened us to its existence in our town. Very misguided, we thought it was a leftover from the past.
>
> The majority of us have never truly been subject to racism. The issue summons us all, yet most choose to ignore it. In hopes of learning more about racism, we need to explore its causes and learn why it still exists today. Consequently, we will meet with people who have experienced it. They will share their feelings of the difficulties they experienced growing up simply because they are different.
>
> We hope this assembly will help us all realize victims of racism are permanently affected. It is wrong to judge people by the color of their skin.
>
> We need to create a "racial free" atmosphere in our school and community.

To the evening panel, entitled "Racism: No One Is Safe," a retired professor of Maine History from the University of Maine at Farmington offered an historical overview of KKK activities that were once prevalent in Maine. He noted that at its peak in the mid-1920s one out of three males was a member of the KKK. Roman Catholics and French-Canadian immigrants were the primary target.

An article in the local newspaper summed up the event with these words: "Comments from the gathering of area residents — some white, some Black or Hispanic, some young, old, male and female — showed that the message of the SAD 59 forum was clear and regrettably true — no one is safe from the pain of prejudice. But at the same time, residents agreed, no one is alone and with strength, there will be numbers to prove it" (*Morning Sentinel*, 20 November 1991).

Although these programs were a beginning step to try to lessen prejudice, students realized that their efforts had to continue. Being a founding board member of the Holocaust Human Rights Center of Maine, I suggested that students from my sociology class meet with the director and other members of its board of directors. By working together with a statewide organization focusing upon human rights, we might gain some new ideas as to how to progress. Furthermore, they might lend us support. I expressed my own bias to explore means by which to empower students and teachers through education to effectively reduce the factors that abet racism among youths. The students accepted my proposal.

We met late afternoons and on Saturdays at the Maine State Library in

Augusta. Patricia Stanton, a fellow social studies teacher at Maranacook Community School, brought several of her students to these meetings as well. Lieutenant Mark Dion of Portland, Maine's police department became an active participant. He was in charge of that city's innovative hate crime unit for which he gained national recognition. Together this group planned and successfully sought funding for the state's first Diversity Leadership Institute.

Held during the first weekend in August 1992 at the University of Maine at Farmington, 30 students from Madison, Portland, Lewiston, Gardiner, and other Maine communities joined together to celebrate diversity. The group developed appreciation and understanding for one another and cultivated peacekeeping skills. The success of the conference was particularly significant as the participants represented a variety of ethnic, national, cultural, religious, sexual orientation, and economic backgrounds that included among others African Americans, Cambodians, Vietnamese, Protestants, Catholics, Jews, and homosexuals. Among the chaperones was Madison's new, though short-lived superintendent of schools, Lillian Ingraham.

Workshop leaders included Dr. Elizabeth Kalau, who had never overcome the guilt that her father had been an officer in Hitler's army. A well-known Augusta, Maine, neurosurgeon talked about his own hate and anger. As a Jewish child growing up in Poland during German occupation, he spent several years living in a convent. A gay professor and author explored prejudice toward homosexuals. Mark Dion, the police lieutenant, led a workshop on hate crimes committed by kids that involved role-playing.

The participants bonded so well that they decided to meet regularly. During their monthly gatherings they developed plans for their second annual Diversity Leadership Institute.

This event, again held at the beginning of August, was expanded to four days and doubled the participants to sixty. The University of Southern Maine hosted the conference at its Portland campus. The students enthusiastically partook in many different activities, ranging from trust building exercises that included a ropes course, conflict resolution workshops, and cultural sharing. By 1999 the annual DLI conference, now regularly held on the Bates College campus in Lewiston, Maine, had more applicants than it could accommodate. The maximum couldn't exceed eighty participants.

Although students continue to develop the program as in the past, they now devise and lead most of the workshops and conduct all the activities during the four-day program. Former students, who had participated in the summer institute, come back to share the work they continue to do to combat prejudice and celebrate diversity.

As the 1993 to 1994 school year opened, two senior boys, who participated at that summer's institute, were so excited about the work they were doing there that they formed a DLI chapter for Madison High School. That year nearly sixty students participated. The two juniors who took the lead were energetic, well-organized young men who possessed natural leadership skills. With the volunteer assistance of one of the boys' mothers, an actress who founded the In Spite of Life Players, students developed interactive theater skits dealing with various forms of prejudice.

They gained recognition as they procured invitations to middle and high schools within the central Maine area. In addition to interactive theater, they developed other awareness heightening activities. For instance, with middle school students, they asked the kids to identify different cliques in their school, such as jocks, preppies, granolas, skidder boys. Then each of the DLI students would show how they represented each faction. Students seemed surprised that one person could belong to so many different groups. Then when they were asked to stand up to identify the many groups to which they had some connection, they began to realize the foolishness of identifying people through such classifications. DLI students also actively involved and challenged participants at professional conferences to which they were invited. These included conventions for guidance counselors and school principals.

Interpersonal tensions that came to light in 1991 with the attempted cross-burning incident did not slacken. They were similar to fears that had arisen in the 1920s toward East European and Franco-American immigrants who had come to work in Madison's textile mills and paper factory. This time, because tensions in inner cities multiplied while violence spread into the suburbs, people began migrating to Maine in search of a more serene lifestyle and safer haven in which to raise their children. Among these were Madison area natives who had fled the state in the 1950s when the economy took a nose dive.

At that time, textile mills were closing as labor and energy to run the mills were cheaper in the southern states. During the same period, new laws were imposed on dairy farmers requiring them to build special milk rooms constructed with cinder blocks and temperature controlled stainless steel containers to hold their milk. As a result many farmers in the 1950s and 1960s were forced out of business.

Maine natives returned to their hometowns to spend their golden years. Their children, grandchildren, and other relatives, all born and raised out of state, were drawn here by their Maine connection. In recent years, a few African Americans and Chicanos began settling in rural, central Maine. In the fall of 1993 the police were called into the high school to defuse a conflict between two groups of culturally diverse boys. The local young men clad in flannel shirts and work boots appeared to resist baggy clothed youths from such urban areas as Brockton, Haverhill, Lawrence, Lynn, and Quincy, Massachusetts. Their mutual lack of understanding led from name calling to property damage and threats of violence. A potentially explosive situation was brewing.

The *Maine Sunday Telegram* of 17 July 1994 reported the incident and described how DLI students developed a means by which to ease tensions.

> Mike Jacob wanted to grab Scott Fortin and beat him senseless each time the two students passed each other in the halls of Madison High School. Jacob considered Fortin a racist and a redneck because he suspected him of participating in a cross-burning in front of a black student's home. Fortin called Jacob a "fruit loop" because of his fondness for wild-colored clothes, rap music and street jive that he had brought with him when he moved up from Boston.
>
> Each of them had his own following. Jacob is Lebanese and, like several of his friends, embraces the styles and behaviors of the urban culture he was once part of. Fortin and his friends are white natives of rural Maine.
>
> When the bitterness between the two groups turned to shoving and defacing cars, students and faculty of the Diversity Leadership Institute stepped in to halt hostilities. The statewide student group, which promotes social harmony, helped the two factions to respect each other's differences, enjoy their similarities and build friendships.
>
> But it did not happen quickly. It was a grudging acceptance. Forced to sit face-to-face in a classroom and confront their hatred, the two sides glared at each other and yelled obscenities across the room during the first few meetings. Then, "We just started talking like normal people, and I'm actually friends with Mike now," Fortin said.
>
> Justin Kitchen, one of Fortin's allies, said the sentiment expressed by many was simply, "We didn't know you so we didn't like you."

During the summer of 1994 several Madison DLI students and I were invited to address the Governor of Maine's Commission to Promote the Understanding of Diversity in Maine. One of the students was quoted in the report, "We need to concentrate on learning about people.... with more personal knowledge things would work better."

I told the committee that teachers need to have courage to go beyond the accepted beliefs of their community. They should be willing and able to cause kids to explore issues to become more open-minded. Furthermore, they ought to expose their students to many points of view and many peoples and should whenever possible relate contemporary issues to history.

After the two leaders graduated and as tensions between students appeared to ease, the Madison chapter dwindled in numbers. For the next several years, there remained a core group of about fifteen students. Although a smattering of college prep students continued to participate, the majority represented lower-academic track and even several special ed students.

Lower-track students had never been encouraged or empowered to take leadership roles. They tended to be more reliant upon teachers, unsure as to what to do. Therefore, my role and that of a new drama coach, who worked with us, was to establish a structure by which the students felt comfortable. They came up with ideas and worked through these in order to create simple, interactive theater. These students also continued to adapt and develop their own games that addressed issues surrounding diversity.

As advisors to the group, we had to focus intensely upon listening skills. To be effective presenters, whether they were doing interactive theater or role playing and other activities with students, they first had to learn to listen to and respond to each other. Although their presentations weren't always as flowing and sophisticated as the ones by those students who had developed the self-confidence to relate more easily to different audiences throughout their schooling, these students felt justifiably validated by the success of their work. The group continued to do presentations at schools throughout central Maine as well as several programs for the entire high school.

In the spring of 1999 students were upset because of increasing harassment. Girls were bothered by both explicit and implicit sexual remarks made by boys. The three students, who had entered the school in the winter, tormented by others for their Hispanic appearance, drew sympathy and concern from DLI students. Determined that something had to be done, DLI students came up with the concept for "People Appreciation Day."

In their handout introducing the program to the staff, they wrote, "'People Appreciation Day' is a response to sexual harassment, especially inappropriate subtleties, and cultural and ethnic torment that are taking place at our school. This program is created, developed, and produced by Madison High School students." The students did invite several people to address the student body and faculty. These included the director of the Maine Human Rights Commission and an attorney who dealt with civil-rights cases. A counselor and students from nearby Colby College brought four students who articulately addressed issues of prejudice and discrimination on their campus.

Madison DLI students facilitated the program. They introduced the program's purpose; the speakers made moving speeches themselves and moderated the question-and-answer period. Although it was more difficult for the Madison presenters to admit to their schoolmates and faculty that they were victims of harassment than it was for the Colby students, they did get their point across clearly. Caitlin Malloy, a senior, gave one of the speeches. She had on occasion been teased because she was a celebrated classical pianist and lived in a very creative house built around a tree. She finally gained recognition from more students for breaking the school record of the girls' cross country team by landing first and second place in state championships. She told the assembled students, staff, and guests:

Diversity. It's everywhere. Whether you like it or not, it's a part of you and a part of me. Every single one of us is diverse, even if we don't think of it that way. The definition of diversity is "a point or respect in which things differ — variety or multiformity." It is for the same reason that diversity is so wonderful that it causes so many problems. Because every one is different, there are various things we believe in, do, come from, think, and look like. And through these multiformities conflict can occur. But it doesn't have to.

When you look down on someone for something that you think is weird about them — some differences that they have — just think about how they may be feeling opposite as you. If you make fun of someone because they like peanut butter and banana sandwiches, just think how strange the idea of eating peanut butter and grape jelly on whole wheat might seem to them. This is how conflict starts. A banana-lover might give a simple glare on the corner behind the fire station — the local hangout. Then at school a "I can't believe you like those" in an insulting tone of voice occurs. Later during a hard fought game of tetherball a playground fight may break loose!

"Banana-eating jerks!" shrieks a jelly lover and somebody ties some-one else's shoelaces together. . . . a nasty trick. The next thing you know, picketers are marching around the mayor's house. Signs read "Jellies make for fat Bellies" and "Keep 'nanas in the nursery!" Fights occur more and more often. P+J supporters come to school to find squashed bananas in their duffel bags, and the banana lovers find their lockers decorated with grape jelly. Fights occur more and more often and blood is shed. . . . gangs are formed. A banana loving extremist stands on the ledge of the three story accounting firm on Fourth and Main yelling not to come any closer because he must do this for the good of the cause. Rallies are held and SWAT teams must be called in to keep back the agitated masses. Riots break loose. Newspaper headlines are about drive-by shootings in which two banana eaters are knocked off by the jelly lovers in a Firebird. Ministers begin to pull their own beliefs into their sermons. Father Donald says that Jesus loves jelly eaters while Pastor Ted thinks that the banana lovers will make it to Heaven. Terrorists make bomb threats, and subway stations must be sealed off. Eighty-three-year-old women fear for their lives — they buy pit bulls and carry mace! Is this really the kind of crazy world we want to live in?!

In case you hadn't figured it out yet, I wasn't really talking about peanut butter and jelly vs. peanut butter and banana. It was symbolic. And for the most part, we, as teenagers in a small town in Maine, don't have to worry about the extreme effects of hate crimes and oppression. But we can still do our part to support diversity. We need to remember that variety is normal, and whether we like it or not, everyone, even we are different in some way. Tom W. might think that Susie F., who is Black, is so weird. But Susie may think that it is just as strange to have white skin. And although you may think it's bizarre to have blue hair, that person might think the same thing about your cheek piercing. But what everyone needs to realize is that these things have nothing to do with that person's personality. They might actually be one of the funniest or nicest or smartest people you have ever met. So when you think something about someone is strange, just realize that they might be thinking the same thing about you and ignore it. Get to know the person before you judge them and do it in a friendly way. If everyone would just try a peanut butter and banana sandwich, they might just realize that it isn't really so bad after all.

Following the assembly, students returned to their homerooms where DLI members and guests conducted follow-up activities as a means by which to process the comments made during the formal portion of the program. In the small-group discussion, students came up with and explored such question as:

What were the panelists talking about?
How did the experience feel for you?
What new learning occurred for you as a result of the panel presentation?
With what did you agree? Why?
With what did you disagree? Why?
What was the high point for you from the panel discussion?
What can you do to make a difference in the atmosphere at Madison High School and among the general public?
What can the faculty and administration do to help create this atmosphere?

The discussion on which I sat was lively, enthusiastic, and generally empathetic. Students talked about why some are tormented when kids are just joking with them. One student said that it is often hard to distinguish between kidding around and what is meant seriously. When kids have been teased a lot, of course, they are going to take things personally, she added.

Although not all students and faculty took the program to heart, many did. Among them was the guidance counselor for the elementary grades. Having attended the program and participated in one of the follow-up sessions, she was moved to create a Civil Rights Team for the school district. The Maine attorney general's office for hate crimes already helped over 150 schools statewide develop such teams. In September of 1999 all Madison area teachers were given an entire workshop day by the statewide coordinator of this program.

Developing Self-Actualization through the Arts

One of the avenues that enhances the growth of the individual is expression through the arts. This approach elicits within students not only an appreciation for different cultures and varied means of expression, but also evokes within individuals a new way how to see and express themselves. Therefore, it helps to build self-confidence so necessary in order to live harmoniously with others. This concept came to fruition through artist-in-residency programs I created for the school system.

It was in mid-September of my second year at Madison High School. My family and I went to the annual agricultural fair in Farmington. I was struck as several people disguised as oversized puppets came forth from behind a banner that read "The Blackbird Theater." Following their performance, I asked whether they would be interested in making masks and creating theater with my students should I be able to raise the necessary funding. They were delighted to do so. I was able to get a $300 grant from the newly created Maine Arts Commission for a three-day residency with the Blackbird Theater. All the school had to pay at that time were matching in-kind contributions.

One afternoon before their residency, several students and I took my Volkswagen van, shovels, and buckets to dig up blue clay near the town's water tower. With these materials they would make molds for masks and create skits with four members of this offshoot of Vermont's famed Bread and Puppet Theater. The residency climaxed as students together with troupe members performed their creations before the entire school by the students and members of the troupe.

Since that residency I have written numerous grant applications and established the Performing Arts Committee. It is now called the Fine Arts for the Curriculum Committee to fit in with the goals of the state's Learning Results. In spite of the fact that grant monies are harder to get, the committee continues to bring artists-in-residence to the entire school system for all grades and all students including those in special education programs.

Residencies at the high school included mime, storytelling, sculpture, paper making, puppetry, dance, movement, Franco-American culture: food, song, and dance, African drumming, traditional Cambodian melodies played on ancient-style instruments, classical music, and international festivals. A survivor of the Nazi Holocaust sang songs she had gathered while and following her incarceration at Auschwitz.

In 1982 I received a grant from the Maine Humanities Council entitled "The Asian Side of Art: A Humanities Project for Young and Old." A Japanese art historian gave several classes to interested high school students together with senior citizens from the community on Asian painting. (In fact, her husband, also Japanese, Masanabou Ikemyia, a noted classical pianist, did several residencies in the schools of S.A.D. #59 always culminating with a public performance by members of his group, the Arcady Chamber Players.) Her presentations included talks accompanied by slide and lively discussion. Students also practiced drawing with brush and ink.

The grant provided a chartered bus to take the group to view the Asian collection at Boston's Fine Arts Museum. We also made a stop at a museum in Salem that exhibited many items brought to New England in the 1800s by American sea captains and merchants taking part in trade with China. The participants were able to visualize an East-West connection that was a significant part of New England's and, of course, Maine's history. The project was determined a success by all participants. Laughter by both young and old on the trip to and from Boston and everybody's dedication for this project demonstrated the effectiveness of two very different age groups learning together.

Interest in Native American history resulted in a comprehensive, experience based project that cultivated and fostered understanding of and helped to preserve Native American cultures. This district wide project for all grades was funded by a significant grant from the Maine Community Foundation as well as funds provided by the school system itself. Barry Dana, a Native American, who had continued to preserve Penobscot skills since his youth on his nation's Reservation near Old Town, Maine, conducted this residency together with Katenia Keller, a modern dancer, who lived just outside of the school district in the small town of Solon.

In 1990 Barry founded a Native Studies Camp in Bingham, Maine, in response to a growing need among diverse people to find a connection with nature. Although high school faculty members frowned upon the idea, and the school board denied our students to spend an overnight at Barry's camp, Barry worked with students at the high school. In spite of this setback, the project became a truly interdisciplinary venture. With a technology class, using birch bark that he had harvested on his land, Barry directed students to build a wigwam. He taught students the art of bow-and-drill fire making using tinder instead of matches to create a fire. With English and American history classes storytelling, exploring native philosophies, making dream catchers, and drumming were all part of the residency. Katenia Keller and Barry Dana, together with students, choreographed and performed several Penobscot myths.

Incorporating movement as a form of self-expression was the theme for a residency the following year at the high school. For ten weeks a cross section of students grades nine through twelve explored self-expression using movement and modern dance. Students representing all three academic tracks, including some of the most alienated as well as popular students at the school, collaborated enthusiastically. Students also got in touch with their cultural heritage by recreating stories from the past and present through modern dance. These included stories of simple rural life, of immigrants from Eastern Europe, Italy, and French speaking Canada who came to work in Madison's mills.

Carl and Katenia, who had directed the previous year's Native American project, led this program. For 14 years Carl had been Madison's successful football coach bringing the team to win several state championships. Part of his success as a football coach and now as a modern dancer is his appreciation and respect for youths as well as his unyielding trust in them. As a freelance dance educator, choreographer, and performing artist, he succeeded to get some of the most "macho football type players" to enjoy movement and express themselves in ways they had never dreamed of before.

The Contact Movement programs he developed expressed his philosophy. They "emphasize creating community, celebrating diversity, exploring creativity and mindfulness, and involving authentic physical expressions of the self.... Anyone with an interest in exploring their own body, a willingness to offer compassionate support to others, a balance of curiosity and patience, and a healthy sense of humor will enjoy these dance classes" (from Carl Rudman's brochure "Contact Point Holographics").

In many ways this residency expressed what school is all about: self-expression, learning to live harmoniously with one another, and developing abilities that students never imagined they had. In addition, as students learn to develop and enjoy these qualities, they gain new leisure time activities. These are necessary for emotional and physical survival in a culture that demands a great deal of sitting and one as is predicted the work week will be reduced to four and three days within the near future. Also, several students commented on their newly discovered appreciation for fellow schoolmates toward whom they previously held disparaging attitudes.

As pointed out above, students were introduced to new ideas by directly meeting with individuals who held different views; they faced difficult situations that affected them by becoming actively involved in political action. Through self-expression students gained greater understanding of themselves, felt more comfortable with their bodies, and developed appreciation for the arts. Finally, a teacher within a democratic setting became a facilitator to nurture students in their search for a path in life that could bring them happiness and help them become concerned, caring, and responsible individuals.

The final chapter summarizes methods that help to prepare youths to become responsible, which means questioning, open-minded, and thinking, active citizens in a democracy, who are capable of accepting a wide diversity of ideas that are compatible with democratic principles. For this to happen, the hierarchical structure of our schools has to be modified. Greater harmony between all the elements that make up a community, which includes means by which each individual student is able to seek a balanced life, must be fostered.

10

SCHOOLING FOR HUMANITY

Since the emphasis of public education is upon economic viability, it is also necessary to focus on a more humane, democratic tradition. This appproach to teaching that focuses attention to human dignity, freedom, and social responsibility is commonly referred to as *postmodernism*. It fosters reflective thinkers, building upon the connection between the mind, the emotions, the physical world, and the cultural environment in which we live. It is also pragmatic in that it requires democracy. It is always open to asking questions and seeking answers. Its practioners try to reach beyond the cultural and social context in which they and their students have grown up.

By using the commonly expressed ideals as represented in *Maine's Learning Standards*, I believe teachers can develop their unique potential and creativity to inspire their students. As teachers tune into the various characteristics, temperaments, and needs of their students, their compassion and enthusiasm will excite students to acquire knowledge and wisdom. These qualities will enhance students' emotional and physical health as well as social and environmental consciousness and responsibility.

Focusing on the Humanity of Education

In order to become more confident with this approach, it may be valuable to examine a recent trend among some progressive, holistic educators to integrate humane and healing traditions that stem from ancient, Asian philosophies. They see aspects of this ancient culture applicable to dealing with contemporary American problems such as developing a sense of and appreciation for family and community. Others explore alternative ways to gain ultimate health and happiness through yoga, meditation practice, Tai Chi, and Chi Gong. Tai Chi is meditation in movement, teaching the mind to be silently attentive to the body, breath, and inner feeling. Chi Gong is the development of the body's energy circulation both to increase and control it. Many educators join scientists, environmentalists, and educators in acknowledging that the survival of Planet Earth depends on increased knowledge, understanding, and appreciation for different languages and cultural traditions.

These educators, of which I am one, support a nondogmatic, harmonious, nonhierarchical society in which people's lifestyles are balanced with one another and with the biosphere. In a heavily materialistic society as ours many cling to the idea that only money and material wealth can give us pleasure. Our contemporary society is personified by our desires and our fears. We encourage a form of awakening in which we are not afraid to explore the world of the unknown, while at the same time feeling a partnership with our fellow human beings. Because thoughts are impermanent, we still can have beliefs, values, and ideals, but know full well that these may continuously change and evolve as each person continues to explore. It is through reflection that we can break from the narratives that have been imposed upon us by our culture.

It was one of our own philosophers, my idol from my high school years, the transcendentalist Henry David Thoreau, who practiced meditation. He realized that a person knows more about himself, what he is doing, when he stops for a while, listens, watches, and understands. In *Walden* he concluded, "Only that day dawns to which we are awake."

In order to sow the seeds for a more harmonious, empathetic world, the practice of democracy and diversity should be applied to our public schools and classrooms. It is imperative to reverse the trend that has brought about the fragmentation of society since the First Industrial Revolution. This disintegration has triggered compartmentalization and standardization causing people to feel ever less connected with each other and with their natural environment. Our ecological environment has been devastated in the name of progress. Not only are our rivers and lakes polluted, our forests destroyed, our crops poisoned with herbicides, but many people live in large industrial cities where they live in fear and do not know their neighbors. A sense of community doesn't exist. An intimate connection with our biosphere has been dismantled. Therefore, as people become less sensitive and more impersonal toward one another, they easily become physically and emotionally abusive toward fellow human beings. Fewer people seem to feel a guilty conscience. Therefore, for example, laws have little impact upon them. Material wealth, instantaneous gratification, and reliance on the sensational for entertainment become the norm by which the majority of Americans seem to live. We take life for granted.

Already in the mid-1800s Emerson wrote, "The reason why the world lacks unity, and lies broken and in heaps, is because man is disunited with himself." Emerson, like Thoreau, Whitman, and Native American shamans did not take life for granted. They were, what practitioners of meditation today refer to as mindful, able to take in, appreciate, and cultivate an intimate relationship with the present moment. Mindfulness, according to Jon Kabat-Zinn, is the art of conscious living. In his book *Wherever You Go There You Are* he expressed the dilemma of being mindless:

> The habit of ignoring our present moments in favor of others yet to come leads directly to a pervasive lack of awareness of the web of life in which we are embedded. This includes a lack of awareness and understanding of our own mind and how it influences our perceptions and our actions. It severely limits our perspective on what it means to be a person and how we are connected to each other and to the world around us. (Kabat-Zinn, 1994, 5).

It should be, I believe, the intent of our schools to advance the humanity of which we speak. The idea of community service that now is a graduation requirement in many of Maine's public high schools certainly reflects a desire on the part of many people to cause young people to develop an appreciation for and feel a part of their community. However, by simply implementing another program, called community service, without challenging the forces of material greed expressed through the profit motives of multinational corporations, it is highly unlikely that the ideal of community can even be approached. However, a "psyche-based" decision making process that has been taking place since the early 1980s in a school system in North Glenn, Colorado, suggests the effectiveness of a less hierarchical more collaborative approach to community schooling.

Moving toward Egalitarian Decision Making

This system with 21,500 students, 25% of whom are minorities, was already in the 1970s on the forefront of education reform. It was practicing,

what has become today the basis of status quo reform, outcome based education. However, by the early eighties teachers were growing ever more frustrated by control coming from the central office. Many felt a need for change.

By 1982 James Mitchell was hired as superintendent. Although it took
him some time to win the faith of the teaching staff and the administration,
he won the support of the staff development people for the need to decen-
tralize the school system. He believed that since the make-up and the management style of each school and the community it represented was different, each site should determine its budget and how it should be used. Each
school should be responsible for the hiring process for its staff, including
principal, teachers, and custodians. Implementing the curriculum and select-
ing the materials for it should be the task of each school and its community.
The janitorial staff would be in charge of the facility's management.

The superintendent changed the name and nature of his cabinet. He
called it the district coordinating team to reflect more clearly the trend
toward decentralizing control. It included not only administrators, but also
teachers, support personnel, and even community representatives. Decision
making was based on consensus. No longer could his coordinating team lean
on him to make decisions.

Mitchell found it difficult at first to let others take part in the decision
making process. It meant that he was becoming vulnerable, but he described
vulnerability as a strength. By sharing decisions the school system became
stronger. Not only did this process cause principals, teachers, and people
from the community to gain greater faith in him, but also it filtered all the
way down to the students. By encouraging teachers to share in the administration of the school, principals gained greater respect and trust from their
teachers. Teachers respected and trusted their students more, allowing them
greater input into the management of their classrooms and the school as a
whole. Because of the success of and support for this approach, the few
remaining teachers who desired the traditionally more autocratic approach
were no longer able to stonewall the changes.

This approach, used in the school district that comprises North Glenn,
Colorado, can only be truly effective if principals and teachers become facilitators who make it possible for their students to find themselves on a course
that will bring them ultimate happiness. This means that the noble ideals of
the education reform effort, for instance of *Maine's Learning Results*, must be
upheld. These include cooperation versus competition. Interdisciplinary
learning that enhances an understanding of the relationship between people
and their natural connection to the biosphere must be fostered in contrast
to aiding and abetting the profit motive that is destructive to both humanity and the planet's ecology. It is these ideals that I have been trying to nurture in my classroom setting.

By consistently engaging students in gaining awareness of the institutional forces that have control over their lives, I have offered them means by which they can bring about change. They have been introduced experientially to democratic principles of problem solving. These include identifying the problem and trying among themselves to reach consensus on a solution. Then following the established, hierarchical protocol, they learned to approach the powers that be in a nonthreatening yet decisive manner. In order for teachers to go with the flow of the class when institutionalization requires standardization, bureaucratization, and regulation, it is important that they try in whatever way possible to uphold the **ideals** of the learning standards. The reader has already seen that by giving government/economic students projects in which they identify, explore, and try to solve a community or even statewide problem, they meet the guiding principles of the *Maine Learning Results*.

Teachers, I believe, should learn to distinguish critical thinking and problem solving from simply seeking solutions to problems defined by a standard curriculum in response to the corporate powers that appear to govern education. This culture of bureaucratic technicalization discourages teachers and students to "ask unique questions and to *detect* [emphasis is mine] problems as important aspects of higher intelligence" (Kincheloe and Steinberg 1993, 304). As teachers stimulate and challenge their students to examine their own cultural and social indoctrination by asking never before asked questions, students will become active in what Kincheloe and Steinberg, refer to as "problem detecting" (Kincheloe and Steinberg, 1993, 304). Students develop more sophisticated thinking, greater insight, and understanding of social justice and the forces that undermine it.

The new awareness that students have achieved as a result of this process is probably what Paulo Freire calls "conscientilzacao." It refers to the methods that educators can use to empower students to take action against the oppressive elements of the social structure that students encounter. In other words, teachers develop human relationships with demoralized youths to help them on their path to become empowered, self-actualized people, who will be able to create their lives in such a way as to bring them healing, happiness, and harmony.

Although teachers are considered as "public servants," who are supposed to represent the will of the people, the mission of our schools is to cause our students to become productively integrated into the set of values that reflect the status quo of American society. Unfortunately, education as a subversive activity that encourages students to look critically at their society, to raise questions, explore alternatives to transform it into a more beautiful, harmonious community is the antithesis of American education. Freire explains that the reason is that people for the most part fear freedom. Although they speak of it, defend it, "they confuse freedom with the maintenance of the status quo" (Freire, 1981, 21). It is scary to be creative, to ask questions, to seek answers, to take risks, and to express oneself in ways that others have not. The possibility to be misunderstood is considerable.

However, what is even more scary is that already in the mid-nineteenth century the transcendental philosopher, Emerson, said that we were disconnected from our bodies and our hearts. We had become so immersed in progress, trying to control and subdue nature rather than honoring and becoming a part of it, that we lost sight of ourselves. Instead, according to Jon Kabat-Zinn, we should be mindful.

> Mindfulness can help us to appreciate feelings such as joy, peacefulness, and happiness which often go by fleetingly and unacknowledged. It is liberating in that it leads to new ways of being in our own skin and in the world, which can free us from the ruts we so often fall into. It is empowering as well, because paying attention in this way opens channels to deep reservoirs of creativity, intelligence, imagination, clarity, determination, choice, and wisdom within us. (Kabat-Zinn, 1994, 9)

Since the ideals of the *Maine Learning Results* can be used to move us in this direction, teachers do not have to be controversial. They do not have to confront the administration but can make radicals out of their students. However, the radicals to whom I refer are not stereotypical persons who vehemently want to overthrow the existing order. Rather they are neither entrapped in leftist nor rightist ideology. In the words of Paulo Freire:

> The more radical [a person] is, the more fully he enters into reality so that knowing it better, he can better transform it. He is not afraid to confront, to listen, and to see the world unveiled. He is not afraid to meet the people or to enter into dialogue with them. He does not consider himself the proprietor of history or of men, or the liberator of the oppressed, but he does commit himself with history, to fight at their side. (Freire, 1981, 24)

This concept is really quite similar to that of those who practice meditation. Kabat-Zinn expressed it this way:

> The only way you can do anything of value is to have the effort come out of non-doing and to let go of caring whether it will be of use or not. Otherwise self-involvement and greediness can sneak in and distort your relationship to the work, or the work itself, so that it is off in some way, biased, impure, and ultimately not completely satisfying even if it is good. Good scientists know this mind state and guard against it because it inhibits the creative process and distorts one's ability to see connections clearly. (Kabat-Zinn, 1994, 39)

Mindfulness helps students to slow down and to focus on one task at a time. It allows them to feel connected to their body. It lets them deal with tension almost immediately as it arises in the body. Not only is this an effective way for the teacher to maintain classroom decorum known formally as good discipline, but it is also a means by which to get students involved in their work. Once they become excited about learning, the material over which they will be assessed will come naturally, and they will produce pleasing results on statewide assessments that are published in the media.

However, in order to sustain that beautiful sense of wonderment that small children have as they innocently and persistently ask questions, the teachers must be mindful of their students. They may not control their questioning opportunities. They must be aware of the cultural constructs that both they and their students encounter, be it printed, visual, or oral. With such understandings, the teachers will be open and able to support students as they challenge such cultural constructs based on the exclusions, misrepresentations, and stereotypes of gender, race, class, age, and sexuality.

When teachers are not mindful of their students, they stop asking questions. In the words of Kathleen Berry, "they are no longer agents of their own learning or action" (Berry, 1998, 31). Berry continued to point out the dangers of failing to nurture students to ask and seek answers to their questions.

> I find that each year a child is in school, it seems to remove both their initiative in asking questions, and also demand a conformity of thought. Teachers, even in the early years, seem to give limited time and credibility to students' questions. (Berry, 1998, 31).

All too often a teacher takes student questions, especially those that question the status quo, as disrespectful, disruptive, and as misbehavior. In order for teachers to reclaim and retain that wonderment about the world that young children initially have, they must cultivate and nurture the students to ask questions and seek answers in a conducive and safe environment. Students become hopeful as opposed to optimistic as they realize that their search for a beautiful and wonderful life is one of struggle.

Students' excitement for knowledge and wisdom can be enhanced through interdisciplinary learning that happens to be one of the standards of the reform initiative. Social studies teachers, for instance, can collaborate their efforts with the physical education instructor and the language-arts teacher. Together with a Native American storyteller, as we have previously seen, they can create dances out of Native American legends that may be taught in an English class. They can express the pain and suffering that brought about the Salem witch trials through movement that is "never an end in itself but always the outward result of inward awareness" (Miller, 1996, 114) according to the great dancer Isadora Duncan.

Since the teachers will be involved in this process together with their students, by learning together mutual trust and respect for one another evolves. Both teachers and students are becoming mindful, are taking risks, and are being creative and happy. When people feel comfortable with one another, they are less likely to get on each other's nerves and compete for attention by distracting fellow classmates and the teacher. Rather a sense of cooperation evolves that is productive both academically and socially.

I agree with the principal who, prior to the commencement of classes at the beginning of a new school year, tells his teachers of the importance of setting the tone as each class enters on the first day. That tone must be one of mutual respect, cooperation, and trust building.

It certainly is not easy to create an atmosphere of mutual respect when the administration demands that students from kindergarten on are taught to follow the commands of the teacher and never to rely upon their own intelligence and insight. Nor is it easy to practice cooperation when the direction of the school is competition: striving for high grades, vying for athletic championships against other schools, running for class office or student council. Finally, since students have been conditioned to be passively obedient or face disciplinary consequences, it is often difficult for some to develop the self-discipline to listen to other students, to offer their own thoughts, and to realize that their input has been taken seriously.

Just as James Mitchell, the Colorado school superintendent found it difficult initially to be vulnerable, the same holds true for the teacher in front of his/her students. Alfie Kohn wrote in his book *Beyond Discipline*:

> To be a person in front of kids is to be vulnerable, and vulnerability is not an easy posture for adults who themselves had to strike a self-protective pose when they were growing up. Moreover, to reach out to children and develop genuine, warm relationships with them may compromise one's ability to control them. Much of what is wrong with our schools can be traced back to the fact that when these two objectives clash, connection frequently gives way to control. (Kohn, 1996, 112)

However, a truly caring relationship with students is effective. They realize that the teacher cares about them and is able to attend to their emotional needs. At the same time teachers model for students the kind of behavior they expect from them. They listen patiently, show concern for others, admit if they don't know something, and apologize for something inappropriate they have said or done.

By understanding and coming to terms with one's own vulnerability, the teacher can work effectively toward creating a democratic classroom environment. The first step may be a discussion as to what democracy means and how it can be implemented within the setting of the teacher's own classroom. The teacher then, having set the stage as a facilitator, can explain his or her role in that position emphasizing, as the process evolves, that students themselves will be facilitating discussions. Teachers also need to demon-strate how academic work is part of this process whether it be solving prob-lems the class encounters, or integrating reading materials with experiential based projects within the community.

Rules are a necessity in creating the desired environment. However, these rules must be few in number, based upon mutual respect and common sense, and never punitive in nature. Particularly, the latter is at first some-times difficult to accomplish. After all, students have been conditioned to punishment throughout their entire lives if not at home then within the controlling, hierarchical parameters of the school. Therefore, teachers some-times have to bite the bullet if the class insists upon imposing punitive sanc-tions within rules they created, i.e., if a student misbehaves, he or she must sit alone for ten minutes in front of the room facing the blackboard. It does not take long for students to realize that this approach is ineffective. Successful teachers must not only be patient but also be good listeners. They should be able to adopt suggestions that class members have made. When several students want to impose their way, teachers need to acknowledge that opposing points of view exist. They would then facilitate a discussion that would move the class toward compromise.

Problems do occur as I have shown with my own experiences. Part of the problem solving process is to allow students to facilitate the discussion. If students are trained at conflict resolution, even if only one student can act as a mediator, they can facilitate the dialogue among those between whom conflict erupted. Only on rare occasions does it become necessary for the teacher to intervene. In such instances the student may be asked to leave the classroom either to go to the school library if he or she can calm down quick-ly, to the girls'/boys' room, or if necessary to the guidance office. Usually, when the student and teacher are calm, they can explore what the problem is and try to seek a solution.

Sometimes students continue to be disruptive and relentlessly challenge the teacher and other class members. Here is an opportunity to work with them either in developing and conducting a class, as I have described earli-er, or diverting their attention onto a meaningful project.

Although it is extremely difficult to establish a democratic classroom without the support of the principal, whose approach is often authoritarian, and without the championship of at least several colleagues, it still can hap-pen. When there exists a sense of community in the classroom, and students are part of developing and are effectively involved in an engaging curricu-lum, a democratic classroom exists. Teachers who are trying something dif-ferent in their classrooms and schools need support from colleagues.

Gathering Support for Democratic Schooling

Since teachers are overburdened with schoolwork, committee meetings, extra curricula activities, and recertification courses, it is hard to find the time to gather to explore different ideas and approaches to teaching. Since it is enough of a challenge to keep up with the daily workload, it is much easier for most teachers to simply adapt to the status quo. However, teachers never should lose sight of their ideals. Working collaboratively with teachers who hold similar values can help to maintain enthusiasm and reduce burnout.

One approach might be to work together with the staff development team. By cooperating with other school districts, especially if one's own is small, it might be possible to raise the funds to bring a keynote speaker for a workshop at the beginning of the academic year, who will talk about the ideas some are trying to implement. Alfie Kohn, whom I frequently quoted in this book, is one example. Others might include Michael Apple, bell hooks, and Neil Postman. Following the speaker's general address to the staff of the school systems involved, teachers could lead discussions around the ideas expressed in the respective speaker's books and articles. The school address could be followed up by a public talk at a community hall. Each teacher interested in attending would be encouraged to bring at least one parent along.

After such an event, the time might be right to develop at least one small group that would continue to explore similar ideas in education. It might be possible for teachers who participated in the continuing seminar to receive recertification credits. In order to gain the understanding and eventual support of administrators, they should be included in such discussions whenever possible.

Another way to build support among teachers is to introduce and explore ideas with the community at large. The newspaper's editorial page is one effective way in which to try to create a dialogue about education. When teachers, over the years, write to the local paper, their ideas will be seen. As ideas are examined from different perspectives, people who read the letters and guest commentaries as well as published responses, begin to think, "Maybe this person really does have something to say." Others will continue to think he is a crackpot. However, it is the exploration of different ideas that stimulates reaction, thought, and dialogue, all of which are necessary if education is going to change for the better.

In June 1998 Richard Haynie, pastor of the United Baptist Church in Madison, criticized educators for encouraging students to question authority. I offer his guest commentary to the *Morning Sentinel* and my response that appeared shortly afterwards.

Destructive Philosophies Are Building Violence

In light of the recent tragedies in schools, every parent and every student in every town and city across America must be concerned. This concern for the safety of our children is one that we never dreamed would ever happen. We have to be asking ourselves: "How could this be happening? How is it possible that students are killing students? Why should we have to fear to send our children to school, especially in Maine?"

Some would say that this fear could be relieved if we just got rid of the guns. After all, it is the guns that kill. We cannot be that naïve and narrow-minded. Weapons, whether they are guns or clubs, have always been a part of society and culture. There are some that will always abuse what is legitimate and useful with a society or culture. We need to always be concerned about the abuses but when the abuses become extreme, as in children killing children and teachers, we must look for answers.

We gain insight into these answers by seeing what has changed within our culture and by not removing what has been there. The presence of guns in our culture has not changed but an attitude of irresponsibility has invaded our society and culture. These attitudes and philosophies that are destructive to our society, are what need to be removed.

It is not a complete strain on the imagination to see why violence has invaded our schools. Educational philosophies have been in a constant state of fluctuation. There seems to be no standard that has endured the test of time. That which was a good method yesterday is not good today but may be good tomorrow. It is interesting to observe from statistics that we have the highest costs for education but not the highest scores worldwide. The high-priced educational philosophies have not been effective. I believe that along with ineffective educational philosophies have come destructive attitudes that are now rearing their ugly heads.

We have been teaching our children for the past 25 years to question authority, to express their individual freedom, if it feels good do it, that there are no absolutes, that I'm OK, you're OK. It is a very clear pragmatic observation that we are not all OK and that not everyone has the right to express him or herself in any way that they please. We desperately need to return to a standard of absolutes. The influence of moral revisionism is not compatible with society. We must have standards and accountability based on the unchanging principles of God's Word.

Let me give you an example. The Bible teaches a basic principle that is called sowing and reaping. A different variation of that principle could be expressed as "what goes around comes around." It is an absolute fact that if you plant green bean seeds you will grow green beans and not corn. We have been planting in the minds of our young people via TV, magazines, hard rock, acid rock, death metal, etc. the seeds of violence, anger, selfishness, irresponsibility, immoral behavior and a host of other undesirable attributes and attitudes. Is it any wonder that parents cannot control their homes and that the kids rule?

It should be no surprise as to what we are reaping. By removing effective discipline from schools, we have sown the seeds of anger and anarchy. We have lost the absolute meaning of right and wrong. It is tragic, but it should be no surprise that a student can enter a school building and think he can get away with murder.

We could probably go on and expand the cause of the problem but the bottom line is "What can we do?" The answer is not simple or quick. The problems have not arisen overnight nor will they subside overnight. We must, however, begin to reverse this destructive course. There are drastic short-term measures that may be necessary to make our schools immediately safer but let us also think in terms of the long term.

We as a nation, a community, a home, must return to the basic God honoring principles on which successful and enduring societies exist. We have seen where we are headed when God, prayer, and biblical principles have been thrown out of our schools. Where there is no reverential fear, respect, and awe of God, there will probably be no fear or respect for anyone or anything else. Authority must deserve, demand, and attain accountability and this must start in the home. Love and respect must be received as well as given. God has given and shown His love. We must respond and receive His love by acknowledging Jesus Christ as our Savior, Lord and Master.

If our nation or community or school had a majority of individuals and families that were committed to learning and practicing the absolute principles of God's Word, then there would be a noticeable, positive, safer change. I can guarantee that because God does. (*Morning Sentinel*, 2 June 1998)

I responded with the following commentary:

Freedom of Speech Is a Better Path
Than Blind Obedience

The Rev. Richard Haynie of Madison's United Baptist Church, like the rest of us, is deeply disturbed by recent tragedies in our public schools reported by the press. As a parent he is justifiably concerned about the safety of his and other children attending public schools.

However, he blames these terrible events on two factors: destructive educational philosophies that have spawned attitudes of irresponsibility and accountability, and a society that is not "committed to learning and practicing the absolute principles of God's Word."

Both of Haynie's conclusions appear to violate the democratic principles upon which our country was founded. He wrote that, "we have been teaching children for the past 25 years to question authority, to express their individual feelings." Although he admitted that for every freedom there is a responsibility, he added, "we desperately need to return to a standard of absolutes."

To prevent our government from becoming tyrannical, the framers of the Constitution established three branches of government: executive, legislative and judicial. These were tied together by a system of checks and balances. Still this was not enough. In order for the Constitution to be ratified, many including Thomas Jefferson insisted that the basic rights of the people must be added immediately. These were added as the first 10 amendments, otherwise known as the Bill of Rights.

The First Amendment, which guarantees freedom of religion, speech, press, assembly and petition, has undergone numerous tests. For example, in 1977 the American Nazi Party wanted to march on Skokie, Ill., a predominantly Jewish suburb of Chicago. Many of the residents were survivors of the Holocaust. The Nazi leader, Frank Colin, actually said, "I hope they're terrified (Jewish survivors). Because we're coming to get them again. . . . The unfortunate thing is not that there were 6 million Jews who died. The unfortunate thing is that there were so many Jewish survivors."

Although city officials tried to block the march, the American Civil Liberties Union defended the right of this group to parade. After all, the neo-Nazis promised to march for only 20 minutes, in uniform but limited to 25 participants, and without speeches and the distribution of leaflets.

As much as many of us find such organizations as the American Nazi Party deplorable, the court, I believe, ruled correctly. It said that prior restraint — opposing free speech before it happens — is illegal. The court felt it was better to have neo-Nazis express their hate in rhetoric than have the government decide what can or cannot be said.

Educators, particularly those of us who teach history and government, have an obligation to teach our students not only to question but also the process of questioning. This procedure includes learning to research, document and understand the point of view students want to present, as well as opposing viewpoints. This strategy teaches them how to express their position diplomatically, to follow the appropriate channels to bring about the change they desire. These range from speaking up at town meetings, writing to their legislators, voting and petitioning.

Haynie appears to defy the Constitutional principle of separation of church and state. By stating that "we must have standards and accountability based on the unchanging principles of God's Word," he implies that his interpretation of Christianity is the sole authority that should guide America. Such an explanation seems intolerant toward any other religion or faith that is conducive to democratic principles.

As a parent and a teacher I want young people to question. I want them to understand and practice the tenets upon which our country was founded. I want them to follow a spiritual path of their choice that will cause them to become self-actualized individuals. I want them to be able to live in harmony with their fellow human beings and their natural environment.

Unfortunately, when people blindly follow the words of leaders, tyrants like Hitler, Mao Tse Tung, Mussolini, Pol Pot and Stalin come about, I believe that neither Haynie nor I ever want such people to take on leadership positions.

A privilege of living in the United States is that our constitutional right to express opposing points of view is still alive and well. That Haynie and I may openly discuss divergent perspectives is healthy. In fact, we not only want our schools to be safe, we want a society in which such values as respect and responsibilities are fundamental. Our differences lie only in our approach to achieve these. Such discussion should help to sustain the ideals upon which this country was founded, principles we both hold to be sacred.

Sometimes a colleague places my articles on the bulletin board of the teachers' room. A fellow social studies teacher, who has been at the school for thirty-five years, born and raised in Madison, occasionally uses my pieces for discussion in his current-events classes. At least my concerns are being heard by some, even debated, and in some cases, just maybe, have had a positive impact on their thinking and actions.

If a teacher knows a sympathetic newspaper reporter or columnist, he or she might want to invite him/her to sit in a class. Particularly when students are discussing an issue that is of broad general interest, it is valuable for the community to see how this teacher tries to facilitate an informed and open-minded discussion. Sometimes, when a discussion is held with a guest speaker, it may be appropriate to invite the press. Needless to say, the teachers are expected to notify their direct supervisor of their intent.

The following article by columnist Gerry Boyle appeared in the 17 April 1992 edition of the *Morning Sentinel*. It introduces the public to people of different cultural and racial backgrounds who were just beginning to settle in central Maine. Even though the influx of newcomers to central Maine hasn't progressed beyond a trickle since the article was printed seven years ago, the need to accept and appreciate people of diverse backgrounds is imperative. Not only will more people of different backgrounds settle in rural, central Maine, but also many students will be living in cities that are culturally, racially, and ethnically very diverse. After all, by the year 2020 nonwhite minorities will replace whites in the United States as the dominant population.

From Maine to Miami

In Room 211 at Madison Area Memorial High School Thursday morning, a young woman named Marilyn was holding forth on the joys of living in beautiful downtown Miami. The street fairs. The Latino music. The regular weekend shootings. . . .

'When I thought I had enough, it was when one of my best friends was killed,' Marilyn was saying, as a dozen or so students listened. "He got three shots across his chest. Just for being in a club."

Marilyn is 19, married, with two kids. A Cuban-American who speaks Spanish, and English with a faint accent, she has lived for the past year and a half in the teeming metropolis of Anson.

Joining Marilyn for the class presentation Thursday was Zoe, who is 17 and a sophomore at Madison Area High School. Friendly and chatty, Zoe grew up in Orlando and Macon, Georgia, where she went to a middle school that had drugs, guns and police in the halls.

In her second year at Madison Area High, Zoe lives in Anson, too, with a friend and his family. Her father is from the Dominican Republic and lives in Florida. Her mother, who recently moved to Ohio, is from Puerto Rico, which is where Zoe was born.

Talk about being from away.

But away is where people like Marilyn and Zoe wanted to get. Away from mindless big-city violence that makes Maine look like one giant kindergarten. Away from places where crack addicts litter the streets and prowl the alleys. Where perfectly innocent little kids stand a pretty good chance of being shot, beaten, robbed, or if they're extremely lucky, just plain terrified.

On their way to school.

You know it must be bad if people from Latino Miami are even coming to Maine at all, much less all the way to Anson.

"My stepfather-in-law was up here when he was small," Marilyn explained. "He knew it here. We had just had enough. He picked us up and brought us to Maine. We had no idea where he was bringing us."

It did turn out to be Anson, a small town facing the paper mill across the river in Madison. Neither town has seen much in the way of a new ethnic group in nearly a century, unless you stretch things and count the hippies who came in the 60s.

Not that you could call two Hispanic families a group.

But it was enough of a phenomenon to get the attention of David Solmitz, the veteran Madison Area High teacher known as a crusader—and gadfly.

Solmitz's thing is racial or cultural intolerance, which he doesn't tolerate. The guy is tireless in his effort to get what he sees as prejudice out in the open. In this case, he said it was important to confront issues of tolerance before more people flee cities for Maine and run into problems.

When Solmitz introduced the topic to one class Thursday, one guy said, "Oh, my God," and stormed out of the room.

"I thought we was done with this stuff, Dave," another student, a big husky guy, complained. "I thought we was talking about Vietnam."

Solmitz said this was an indication that racial prejudice is an issue at the school. But the conversation tended to be more about big city vs. small town, than Hispanic vs. white.

Marilyn told horror stories about gang warfare, about parties where bottles and fists fly. She said her brother was in a gang, but was spared the beating that is part of the initiation. She said a gang was after one of her friends because he was a witness when her other friend was shot in the chest.

"He's just begging for us to get him a bus ticket here, even just until the trial," Marilyn said.

And so it went.

As the Maine kids listened, Marilyn and Zoe commiserated about how much they miss Latin music. Cuban, Salvadoran. About how the dance clubs in Central Maine are dead and the music is old. Zoe said she couldn't get used to the cold winter lasting through April.

"It's just boring," Marilyn said, smiling. "Many weekends I go to Boston. There's nothing here like I was used to."

"But this is Maine," one guy said.

Thank goodness.

Now, I've got to say I think it's good that teachers like Solmitz try to expose their students to all kinds of different kinds of people. Kids in Anson or Albion or Athens ought to know about this stuff. Hear the accents, and not just on TV. See the different shades of skin color. Know that salsa is more than something to dip chips in. That some cities in this wonderful country of ours are war zones.

It's a big world outside of Maine. And more and more, it's knocking on the door.

But I can't help coming from this sort of thing encouraged. Racial issues or no racial issues, you get the feeling that people can just get along. That most racial prejudice comes from being a lot naïve, a little ignorant.

At least in kids.

At least around here.

"In Georgia, they had this really pretty mall," Zoe said. "On Friday nights, the white people went. On Saturday night, it was the black people. I had to go both nights to keep my friends happy."

Integrating Eastern and Western Values

One of the beauties of living in a world where different cultures become more and more interconnected is that educators can learn from other cultures and adopt some of those ideas to make their teaching more human. The Indian philosopher Rabindranath Tagore, who created his own school in India in the early years of the twentieth century, had similar thoughts about the relationship of the individual to his or her natural environment as did Jean Jacques Rousseau in eighteenth-century France and Jon Kabat-Zinn recently. Tagore (1965) wrote:

[The human being] is born into a world which to him is intensely living, where he as an individual occupies the full attention of his surroundings, Then he grows up to doubt this deeply personal aspect of reality, he loses himself in the complexity of things, separates himself from his surroundings, often in a spirit of antagonism. But this shattering of the unity of truth, this uncompromising civil war between his personality and his outer world can never find its meaning in interminable discord. Thereupon to find the true conclusion of his life, he has to come back through this digression of doubts to the simplicity of perfect truth, to his union with all in an infinite bond of love.

Therefore, our childhood should be given its full measure of life's draught, for which it has an endless thirst. The young mind should be saturated with the idea that it has been born in a human world, which is in harmony with the world around it. And this is what our regular type of school ignores with an air of superior wisdom, severe and disdainful. It forcibly snatches away children from a world full of the mystery of God's own handiwork, full of the suggestiveness of personality. It is a mere method of discipline, which refuses to take into account the individual. It is a manufactory specially designed for grinding out uniform results. (Tagore, 1965, 113–14)

Therefore, the principle of lifelong learning must incorporate more than the need to prepare youths for the numerous careers, each requiring different skills, needed for a lifetime. Schools must prepare students for the reality that employment will be ever more scarce, that they will only work a three-day week at best, and that the government will not necessarily provide more services so all can live in reasonable comfort.

Students will have to learn how to be involved in the process of creating these changes for their own benefit as well as for future generations. Therefore, the ideas expressed by postmodernists and other philosophers before them of the need to experience the moment, not to be driven by future goals and fears, to live in harmony with one another and with the biosphere are especially important for today's young people. When schools encourage students to experience many different forms of expression: writing both prose and poetry, movement, theater, painting, sculpture, and music, they become better able to create their own meaningful use of leisure time. Uninhibited, students learn through many different forms of expression to effectively communicate their feelings, fantasies, and knowledge.

It is the purpose of the teacher, I believe, to nurture students, and to hold them silently with kindness and love while they develop their independence. Therefore, in order for our students to be able to grow into socially responsible, aware, self-actualized adults, teachers must give up the notion that they have to control every aspect of their learning, even their every move throughout the building and grounds. This concept Mark Epstein articulated in his book *Going to Pieces without Falling Apart* when he wrote:

> With too much interference from the parents [in our case the teachers], or too much absence, a child is forced to spend her mental energy coping, with her parents' [teachers'] intrusiveness or unavailability instead of exploring herself. This mental energy then takes over, leading to a situation in which the child's thinking mind becomes the locus of her existence and the child feels empty. . . .

When the relationship with a parent [teacher] is too fragile, a child naturally tries to compensate. This leads to the development of a precocious "caretaker self" that is tinged with a feeling of falsity. Besides feeling empty, a person in this predicament also fears emptiness. The fear of emptiness is really a sign of the fragility of the bond with the parent. We are afraid to venture into the unknown because to do would remind us how unsafe we once felt. (Epstein, 1998, 18–19)

Later Epstein explained that the teacher must learn how to *hold* a child not just physically but in silence. "In fostering a state of unintegration by being present but not interfering, a parent [teacher] creates a holding environment that nourishes a child" (Epstein, 1998, 38).

This is an extraordinarily difficult task for teachers, when they not only have a large number of students, but also are required to meet mandates established nationally, statewide, and locally. Not only are these standards demanded by the dominant force in America, large corporations, but also by the majority of citizens of most communities who have been conditioned to become producers and consumers. However, the rewards for the teacher, who is able to nurture and empower students, is truly magnificent.

So long as there is universal public education, there will be certain expectations that students are to achieve nationally throughout their twelve years of schooling. In a day and age when our consumerist society is geared toward instantaneous gratification and entertainment, it is particularly important to try to guide the school experience toward balancing the self-actualization of each individual with an harmonious, socially responsible and happy integration into the local, state, national, and international community.

In order to create a genuine sense of community the discrepancy between competition and cooperation must be addressed along with such other questions that examine our values as:

- Do we want our children to grow up conditioned to the notion that success can only be measured in dollars and cents? Do we want to focus on values that articulate the elegance of the automobile we drive, the number of luxury items available to us, i.e., from big screen TVs to ATVs (all-terrain vehicles), from comfortable campers to Caribbean cruises?
- Do we want our children to continue to demand instant gratification: be it from sensational TV shows to credit cards that will soon be issued to them, to instant contentment provided by drugs and alcohol?
- Do we want our children to fight in wars in developing countries to preserve resources so that we can continue our rampantly materialistic lifestyle? Do we want to be held responsible for the innumerable

deaths that may be caused by our military forces as well as the potentially enormous environmental damage created by such warfare? Do
we want our children to become scientists, engineers, and manufac-
turers of the weapons that create ultimate devastation?

These concerns and others can be effectively addressed if the community, through a partnership of students, teachers, school administrators, and
people representing all socioeconomic and cultural aspects of the community, determines the direction and curriculum of education in their community. In order to assure that the dominant influence in the community shares
power, meetings in different neighborhoods throughout the community
must take place.

Although school officials say that their doors are always open and that
they want parental involvement in their schools, many parents feel uncomfortable when they enter the school building. All too often the only contact
parents have with their children's school is when they are called to meet
behind closed doors with the principal and teachers because a child of theirs
has been in trouble. The first group of people to gather should be those who
are most alienated from the schools.

The process could begin as kindergarten and other teachers identify several parents, especially in a low-income section of the community, who
might be willing to attend a meeting at a neighbor's home or at a neutral setting in the neighborhood other than a school. Members of these families
would attend the initial meeting together with their children and concerned
teachers. As children are listened to with respect, they will be encouraged to
participate actively. Their voice should be equal to that of the adults. During
the first neighborhood conversation, the group might explore:

- feelings about school: what they like, what they don't like, their
  hopes, and their frustrations.
- focus on one or two concerns common to the group and begin to
  explore means by which to address these issues.
- explore their own visions as to the purpose for schooling and how the
  school and community could best implement these ideas.

At the initial meeting, a moderator from among the parents may be selected who will chair the meeting. No person shall be allowed to dominate the
discussion or the direction of the meeting. Before the session ends at a specified time, the moderator will make sure that the date, time, and location of
the next meeting is set. Tasks may be assigned and taken up by volunteers,
and a rough agenda for the following meeting should be set. As the group
develops a sense of comfort and congeniality, other teachers and administrators should be invited to become equal and active participants.

Eventually, similar neighborhood groups representing a complete cross-section of the community encompassing all socioeconomic and cultural groups, could develop. Parents in different neighborhoods throughout the city might be willing to host gatherings in their homes or at a neutral location in their neighborhood. The process for developing these groups would be similar to that of the first group that formed.

As these groups develop throughout the community, a steering committee consisting of two representatives from each group: a student and an adult, could meet to work on the concerns brought to it. It is imperative to have an independent moderator at neighborhood and steering committee meetings to make sure that no one person or group dominates the discussion.

Ideally, decisions should be reached through consensus. Although this is difficult to achieve, a modified version may be used. All those in favor of an idea, a project, or a program, would vote with thumbs up. Those who can live with the concept but aren't overly excited about it would vote with thumbs sideways. Those who are opposed would vote with their thumbs down and would be expected to make a counterproposal. For counterproposals the decision making process would be repeated until all are in agreement.

As a sense of partnership between students, teachers, administrators, and people representing all social classes and lifestyles within the community evolves, our public schools will become more democratic. Teachers and administrators will experience the support of people of all walks of life throughout the community. Students and parents throughout the city together with teachers, administrators, and school board representatives will actively participate and share in developing school policies, goals, curriculum, and hiring of staff. By the time the school board or the city council seeks community approval for the annual school budget, a lot of grassroots community support will be there to make sure the schools are properly funded.

Long before students reach high school, they could be responsible together with their faculty and staff for the daily cleaning and even the maintenance of the building and grounds. In rural areas they could grow gardens to support the school lunch program. Such projects can easily be tied into the curriculum. School maintenance certainly would necessitate an understanding of chemicals used in the cleaning process and their effects upon humans and the environment. Gardening easily ties into biology. An investigation of environmental damage created when crops are not rotated fits the realm of social studies. The subject of genetically engineered food will surely arise.

While students are involved in developing their curriculum together with teachers and parents, their sense of wonderment, which so often disappears when children enter kindergarten, and excitement for learning will be fostered. As they become older, they may seek and identify solutions to problems within their community ranging from developing recreation programs and facilities for youths to exploring a better support system for the mentally ill within the community. These projects would be interdisciplinary often using literature, history, and cultural studies, along with math and science. Through the arts: painting and sculpture, music, dance, and movement, students will discover new ways to express themselves and feel more comfortable with themselves and gain greater appreciation for others. As students become involved in decision making at all levels, they will be able to participate equally and effectively with other partners of the community in reaching the best decisions for their school. Above all, they tend to become lifelong, socially responsible and active participants of their community.

Concluding Observations

For thirty years as a teacher at Madison High School in the heart of rural, central Maine, I felt I was a lone voice in the wilderness crying against the corporatism of our schools. As I draw this book to an end, I realize that there are numerous thoughtful, thought provoking, and insightful and socially active voices throughout America resisting the powerful and cleverly manipulated strategies of corporate America to control the direction of American education toward their own needs. These include public and private school teachers, college and university professors, freelance authors, and concerned parents. I have also become conscious of the manner in which big business deeply penetrates not only the heart of education, but also the very fiber of American society to produce human capital as both skilled employees and rampant consumers for its purposes. A united grassroots effort of parents and educators is needed to stem the ravaging tide of corporate America by educating our children for humanity.

1. Although our public schools teach about democracy, they do not practice it. Our schools are hierarchical in structure, controlling teachers and students to assure compliance to school, community, state and national standards demanded by corporate America. This is accomplished in Maine, as in other states, too, through a curriculum mandated by the state legislature and assessed regularly at the local and state levels. In order to create this new curriculum along the guidelines established by big business and industry, the Governor of Maine as well as his commissioner of education sought teachers, business professionals, and legislators to create the curriculum that soon would become law. By involving people from different professions, it was hoped that there would be little resistance

to this plan. Since many teachers believe that the purpose of schooling is to prepare students to become self-reliant, productive citizens of a capitalist economy, they appeared to have no qualms in supporting the *Learning Results* they helped develop. The same holds true for the assessment aspect of the new curriculum—controversial high stakes tests. Many teachers feel honored by being asked for their input into the assessment process and rewarded when asked to read the grade four, eight, and eleven assessments.

2. Schools use the same strategy of false ownership that is used by corporate America to win student compliance. Corporate America gives its employees the feeling but not the actuality that their voice is accepted and acted upon favorably by management. School leaders, working together with parents, business leaders and police officers pervade and invade the psyche of students in order to accomplish compliance. By appearing to be more understanding, compassionate and less authoritarian as opposed to strictly punitive they are better able to build the self-esteem and win the compliance of students to school standards.

3. The manipulative language of advertisement used by business and industry to give people the feeling that they are concerned and caring has been adopted by state mandates legislating educational standards. Such expressions as global stewardship, critical thinking, problem solving, interdisciplinary learning, cooperative learning, lifelong learning, and diversity education touch the humanitarian chord in teachers while in reality they represent skills needed for the newest paradigm of corporate America to make great profits often at the expense of their employees and the natural environment.

4. Emphasis upon different learning styles and Individual Educational Plans (IEP) sound as if schools are really concerned about the individual child. Really, these are monitoring devices to make sure that each child will meet the required standards at the local, state, and eventually at the national levels.

5. Although the current wave of education reform stresses cooperative learning and teaming, it is still very competitive. For instance, if Maine students do poorly on statewide assessments, the children, their teachers, school administrators, and even the school board take the blame since the results of each school system are published in the press statewide. Furthermore, the whole purpose of the education reform movement appears to be to upgrade America's corporate ability to compete successfully in the international market. This intent of education was substantiated in the *Boston Globe* of 24 May, 2000. The Massachusetts Board of Education just voted unan-

imously to administer competency tests to some math teachers because, in the words of Governor Paul Cellucci, "The MCAS [the Massachusetts equivalent of the Maine Educational Assessment] results in math these last two years have set off alarm bells that too many children in too many schools are not getting the math education they need to work in the leading industries of our state." This evident lack of trust has a debilitating and demoralizing effect upon teachers and students alike. Since knowledge of a subject matter is just one of many factors that make for a good teacher, demeaning and insulting regulations as these placed on already overburdened teachers quickly diminishes the ranks of fine educators.

6. Our educational system fails to acknowledge the reality of social class. Students who are of middle- or upper-class backgrounds have much greater opportunities for success than the poor and the majority of those belonging to minority cultures. This is because they live in communities that receive adequate funding for schools. Therefore, class size is reasonable, learning materials from books to computers are at least adequate, extracurricular activities such as drama and debate are supported fiscally and encouraged by parents and staff. Teachers are better paid. They have greater freedom to be creative in the classroom as they are preparing middle- and upper-class students for leadership roles in society. With both parental encouragement and expectations along with academic preparation, these children have better opportunities to get into college and therefore succeed professionally and materialistically within the middle and upper classes. Conversely, those from poor families and cultural minorities who live in the poorer sections of large cities do not have the same opportunity to succeed because their neighborhood schools lack adequate funding, have large classes, prepare students with lesser skills to lead subordinate lives, and expect students to do poorly academically. They often have low self-esteem exhibited by behavior problems. This is because they are considered to be failures and are at least subconsciously labeled by many of their teachers and classmates in the higher tracks as youths destined to a life of poorly paid menial jobs, welfare recipients, common criminals, who sometimes drop to the rank of the homeless. Their teachers often have a harder time to relate to these students because they come from middle-class families, did well in school, and complied with the aspirations expected of them as middle-class students.

7. Many students, regardless of social status, experience pain and alienation from their families, school professionals, and even the community at large. Lack of nurturance, excessive pressure from

overly busy parents, control without understanding, lack of communication with important adults within the family, and dysfunctional home life all contribute to emotional pain and often to alienation. If students do not adhere to the status quo, if they question authority, and dress in Gothic or other unconventional styles, they are ostracized, condemned, and even punished by those in authority. Since those in charge of the schools fail to acknowledge that their appearance is frequently an indication of depression and oppression, they alienate them further. Little wonder some students turn to violence as a means by which to release their anger and pain.

8. With increasing pressures on teachers and school administrators to meet local, state, and national standards to which both their students and jobs are held accountable, students are held tightly in reign to meet rigorous academic demands. Any opportunity to explore their own interests, make new learning experiences, i.e., through movement, drama, art, and music, that will help them to find a lifestyle and career that bring them optimum happiness is considered superfluous.

9. The need to create democratic public schooling is imperative for the ultimate success of both our students and the country as a whole in an ever-shrinking, interdependent world where a balance between economic affluence, individual self-actualization, and preservation of the biosphere is at risk. As important as private schools may be ranging from those offering a religious orientation to experimental "free" schools that map the way to a more holistic and healthy education, well-funded public schools for all children regardless of their economic background are mandatory. Without an educated citizenry a democratic nation cannot survive. In non-centralized school systems, participation is balanced between all elements of the community. Administrators and teachers gain strength through vulnerability when they are open to suggestions from parents, students, and colleagues. When teachers and students have the opportunity to select their principals and teachers and their classrooms are conducted democratically, students become healthier, energetic, caring, socially responsible and active participants of the society.

10. To achieve these ideals students must be actively involved in their learning experiences. Government, as I have tried to demonstrate in this work, can be taught through hands-on experience in which students are actively involved in identifying and trying to resolve local and statewide problems through research and fieldwork. Learning to read and relish literature allows students to become

engrossed in books that allow their imagination to develop and provides them with new understanding of their own and other cultures.
This is particularly relevant as leisure time will continue to become
more plentiful due to replacement of jobs by technological advancement.

11. Americans can learn from Eastern philosophy in which a balance of
opposing forces are necessary for the very existence and survival of
our planet, i.e., fire and water, as opposed to the Western concept of
competing forces whereby the strongest wins. By balancing the educational and emotional needs of each student with the requirement
of living harmoniously in a community, the individual can become
who she or he is while embracing and being embraced by the community.

12. Teachers, as John Dewey recognized, are artists — persons who use
their imagination to create beautiful ideas into satisfying and fulfilling results. Their passion allows them to develop a feeling for beauty and experience emotional fulfillment. They have a purpose for
what they are doing and are able to bring about satisfying results by
integrating the various parts to create a beautiful whole. In the
words of the contemporary philosopher, Cleo Cherryholmes, "the
aesthetic is receptive, loving, passionate, holistic; it involves sur-
render, cares deeply, includes immediately felt relations of order and
fulfillment, and is concerned with the integration of the parts"
(Cherryholmes, 1999, 3).

The full potential of teachers as unique individuals who share irreplaceable
gifts with their students need be acknowledged by all of us. After all, the
classroom teachers are the only group of people who know what is going on
in our schools and with our children — kindergarten through twelfth grade.

To begin to alter the present course of national and global obliteration,
schools must become as lush as the Maine forest in early June. They need to
strive to achieve its phenomenal, balanced diversity of life ranging from
many species of plants and trees to a great variety of insects, birds, and mam-
mals. This does not ignore the fact that there is much violent and vicious
conflict in the natural world.

It is the responsibility of our schools to balance the growth of students'
inner lives with their intellect. As students ultimately become healthy and
self-actualized individuals, their own inner peace radiates happiness and
empathy for their fellow human beings.

This process of learning to live at the moment while at the same time
exploring and exchanging different ideas and opinions in a never ending
search for the truth, nurtures a set of values that foster tolerance and accept-

ance of differing beliefs, viewpoints, and cultures. This ability to accept yet disagree cultivates a sense of equilibrium between all peoples and the natural world we all share. The process is called schooling for humanity.

REFERENCES

Anyon, Jean. 1980. Social class and the hidden curriculum of work. *Journal of Education*. 162:67–92.

Apple, Michael, W., and James Beane. 1995. *Democratic schools*. Alexandria, VA: Association for Supervision and Curriculum Development.

Avidsen, John C. 1989. *Lean on Me*. Warner. Film.

Beem, Edgar, A. 1989. From farm to mall: The architecture of the new Maine school. *Maine Times*.

Beezer, B. G. 1991. *North Carolina teachers' professional competencies handbook*. Durham, NC: Academic Press.

Berman, Sheldon. 1997. *Children's social consciousness and social responsibility*. Albany, NY: State University Press of New York.

Berry, Kathleen S. 1998. Reclaiming wonder: Young students as researchers. *Students as researchers: creating classrooms that matter*, edited by Joe L. Kincheloe and Shirley R. Steinberg. London, England: Falmer Press.

Bither, Roy. 31 March 1976. Memorandum to David Solmitz.

Booth-Athenian. 4 June 1999. Graduation Address.

Boston Globe. 24 May 2000.

Bowles, S., and H. Ginitis. 1976. *Schooling in capitalist America: Educational reform and the contradiction of economic life*. New York, NY: Basic Books.

Boyle, Gerry. 17 April 1992. From Maine to Miami. *Central Maine Morning Sentinel*.

Boyle, Gerry. 9 March 1997. School paper runs afoul of grandma. *Central Maine Morning Sentinel*.

Briscoe, Felicia. 2000. Discipline. *Knowledge and power in the global economy*, edited by David Gabbard. Mahwah, NJ: Lawrence Erlbaum.

Brosio, R. A. 1994. *A radical democratic critique of capitalist education*. New York, NY: Peter Lang.

Brunswick Record. 5 May 1965.

Brunswick Record. 20 July 1965.

Brunswick Record. 8 January 1961.

Central Maine Morning Sentinel. 1 May 1999.

Central Maine Morning Sentinel. 14 August 1999.

Cherryholmes, Cleo. 1999. *Reading pragmatism.* New York, NY: Teachers College Press.

Chia, Mantak. 1984. *Taoist secrets of love cultivating male sexual energy.* Santa Fe, NM: Aurora Press.

Clinton, William. 1990. Foreword to *Schools for the 21st century: Leadership imperatives for educational reform,* by Philip C. Schlechty. San Francisco, CA: Jossey-Bass.

Conant, James B. 1959. *The American high school today: A first report to interested citizens.* New York, NY: McGraw.

Cornford, Francis M., 1957 trans. *The republic of Plato.* New York: Oxford University Press.

Cremin, Lawrence A., ed. 1957. *The republic and the school: Horace Mann on the education of free men.* New York: Teachers College Press.

Dewey, John. 1944. *Education and democracy.* New York: The Free Press.

Dewey, John. 1963. *The child and the curriculum. The school and society.* Chicago, IL: University of Chicago Press.

Dostoyevsky, Fydor. 1950. *Crime and punishment.* New York: Random House.

Epstein, Helen. 1979. *Children of the holocaust.* New York: Bantam Books.

Epstein, Mark. 1998. *Going to pieces without falling apart: A Buddhist perspective on wholeness.* New York: Broadway Books.

Farber, Jerry. 1967. *The student as a nigger.* Los Angeles, CA: Los Angeles Free Press.

Fine, M., L. Weis, and J. Addelston. 1986. On shaky grounds: constructing white working-class masculinities in the late twentieth century. In *Power, knowledge, pedagogy: the meaning of democratic education in unsettling times,* edited by David Carlson and Michael Apple. 1998. Boulder, CO: Westview Press.

Freire, Paulo. 1981. *Pedagogy of the oppressed.* New York: Continuum.

Gabbard, David, A. 2000. *Knowledge and power in the global economy: politics and the rhetoric of school reform.* Mahwah, NJ: Lawrence Erlbaum.

Galvin, Robert, W., and Edward W. Bales. 1996. Foreword to *Teaching the new basic skills:Principles for educating children to thrive in a changing economy*, by Richard J. Murnane and Frank Levy. New York: The Free Press.

Gandhi, Mohandas, K. 1940. An *autobiography: The story of my experiences with truth*. Boston, MA: Beacon Press.

Gazecli, William. 1997. *Waco: The rules of engagement*. Sam Ford Entertainment. Film.

Gibboney, Richard, A. 1994. *The stone trumpet: A story of practical school reform 1960–1990*. Albany, NY: State University of New York Press.

Giroux, Henry, A. 1997. *Pedagogy and the politics of hope*. New York: Westview Press.

Goals 2000: Educate America Act. 1994. Washington, DC: U.S. Government Printing Office.

Green, Andy. 1997. *Education, globalization and the nation state*. New York: St. Martin's Press.

James, William. 1956. *The will to believe and other essays in popular philosophy and human immortality*. Boston: MA. Dover.

Harrington, Michael. 1994. *The Other America: Poverty in the United States*. New York: Macmillan.

Haynie, Richard. 2 June 1998. *Destructive philosophies are building violence. Central Maine Morning Sentinel*.

Hennigar, James, W. 9 January 1978. Letter to David Solmitz.

Hennigar, James, W. 8 September 1978. Letter to David Solmitz.

Hennigar, James, W. 3 October 1978. Letter to David Solmitz.

A Harvard Magazine Roundtable. 1999, November/December. Strengthening the Schools. *Harvard Magazine*.

Holt, John. 1974. *Escape from childhood: The needs and rights of children*. Boston, MA: Holt Associates.

Irvin, John. 1987. *Hamburger Hill*. Facets Multimedia. Film.

Jameson, F. 1992. *Postmodernism or the cultural logic of late capitalism*. Durham, NC: Duke University Press.

Kabat-Zinn, Jon. 1994. *Wherever you go, there you are: Mindfulness meditation in everyday life*. New York: Hyperion.

Keen, Sam. 1988. *Faces of the Enemy:Reflections of the hostile imagination.* San Francisco. CA: Harper & Row.

Kincheloe, Joe L., and Shirley R. Steinberg. 1993. A tentative description of post-formal thinking: The critical confrontation with cognitive theory. *Harvard Education Review.* 63: 296–320.

Kincheloe, Joe. L., Shirley R. Steinberg, Nelson M. Rodriguez, Ronald, E. Chennault, eds. 1998. *White reign: Deploying whiteness in America.* New York: St. Martin's Press.

Kohn, Alfie. 1996. *Beyond discipline: From compliance to community.* Alexandria, VA: Association for Supervision and Curriculum Development.

Kovick, Ron. 1976. *Born on the fourth of July.* New York: Mcgraw-Hill.

Kubrick, Stanley. *A Clockwork Orange.* Warner. 1971. Film.

Kubrick, Stanley. *Full Metal Jacket.* Warner. 1987. Film.

Lax, William. 1996. Narrative, constructionism, and Buddhism. In *Constructing realities: meaning-making perspectives for psychotherapists,* edited by H. Rosen and K. Kuehlwein, K. New York: Jossey-Bass.

Lee, Gordon. C., ed. 1961. *Crusade against ignorance: Thomas Jefferson on education.* New York: Teachers College, Columbia University Press.

Lehne, Gregory, K. 1976. Homophobia Among Men. In *The forty-nine percent majority,* edited by D. David and R. Brannon. Reading, MA: Addison-Wesley.

Lesson in Tolerance. 1986, March. *Playboy Magazine,* 43.

MacLeod, Jay. 1995. *Ain't no makin' it: Aspirations & attainment in a low-income neighborhood.* Boulder, CO: Westview Press.

Madison Bulldog. 1973, October.

Maine's common core of learning. 1990. Augusta: ME. Maine Department of Education.

Maine Sunday Telegram. 1 September 1999.

Maine Times. 20 October 1989.

Malloy, Caitlin. Speech on harassment at Madison High School. 8 April 1999.

Mann, Horace. 1957. Second Annual Report, State of Massachusetts. *The republic and the school: Horace Mann on the education of free men*, edited by Lawrence A. Cremin. New York: Teachers College Press.

Mann, Horace. 1957. Twlefth Annual Report, State of Massachusetts. *The republic and the school: Horace Mann on the education of free men*, edited by Lawrence A. Cremin. New York: Teachers College Press.

McLaren, Peter. 1994. *Life in schools: An introduction to critical pedagogy in the foundations of education*. New York: Longman.

McLaren, Peter. 1998. Revolutionary pedagogy in post-modern times rethinking the political economy of critical education. *Educational Theory*. 48: 441.

Meltzer, Milton. 1967. *Bread and roses: The struggle of American labor 1865– 1915*. New York: New American Library.

Miller, John, P. 1996. *The holistic curriculum*. Ontario: OSIE Press.

Moufee, Chantral. 1995. Radical democracy or liberal democracy? *Radical Democracy*, edited by David Trend. Florence, NY: Routledge.

Murnane, Richard J., and Frank Levy. 1996. *Teaching the new basic skills: Principles for educating children to thrive in a changing economy*. New York: The Free Press.

National Commission on Excellence in Education. 1983. An open letter to the American people: A nation at risk: The imperative for educational reform. *Education Week*. 27 April 1984.

National Education Association, American Association of School Administrators. 1940. *Learning the ways of democracy: A case book of civic education*. Washington, DC: Educational Policies Commission.

Ohanian, Susan. 1998. *Standards, plain English and the ugly duckling*. Burlington, VT: Phi Delta Kappa Educational Foundation in cooperation with the John Dewey Project on Progressive Education

Payne, W. H., 1926. Trans. *Rousseau's Emile*. New York: D. Appleton.

Payzant, Thomas F. 1996. Foreword to *Teaching the new basic skills:Principles for educating children to thrive in a changing economy*, by Richard J. Murnane and Frank Levy. New York: The Free Press.

Portland Press Herald, 12 June 1962.

Postman, Neil. 1995. *The end of education: redefining the value of school*. New York: Vintage Books.

Real, Terrence. 1998. *I don't want to talk about it: overcoming the secret legacy of male depression.* New York: Fireside.

Rifkin, Jeremy. 1995. *The end of work: The decline of the global labor force and the dawn of the post-market era.* New York: G. P. Putnam's Sons.

Robinson, William. 1996. Globalization: Nine theses on our epoch. *Races and class.* 38: 20–21.

Rosenau, P. 1992. *Post-modernism and the social sciences: Insights, inroads and intrusion.* Princeton, NJ: Princeton University Press.

Rudman, Carl. 1997. Contact Point Holographics: Transforming movement and bodyworks. Brochure.

Schlechty, Philip, C. 1990. *Schools for the 21st century: Leadership imperatives for educational reform.* San Francisco, CA: Jossey-Bass.

Shapiro, H. Svi. 2000. Empowerment. *Knowledge and power in the global economy: Politics and the rhetoric of school reform,* edited by David A. Gabbard. Mahwah, NJ: Lawrence Erlbaum.

Sizer, Theodore, R. 1985. *Horace's compromise: The dilemma of the American high school,* Boston, MA: Houghton Mifflin Company.

Sizer, Theodore, R. 1992. *Horace's school: Redesigning the American high school,* Boston:, MA: Houghton Mifflin Company.

Solmitz, David. 1973, October. To be a non-conformist. *Madison Bulldog.*

Solmitz, David. 17 June 1998. *Freedom of Speech is better than the path of blind violence. Central Maine Morning Sentinel.*

Solmitz, Walter, M. 1939. Report on Dachau. Unpublished manuscripts translated by David O. Solmitz.

Spring, Joel. 1991. *American education.* New York, NY: McGraw-Hill.

Staley, Betty. 1988. *Between form and freedom.* Landsdown, Stroud, UK: Hawthorn Press.

State of Maine learning results. 1997. Augusta: ME. Maine Department of Education.

Steinberg, Shirley, R., and Joe L. Kincheloe, eds. 1998. *Students as researchers: creating classrooms that matter.* London, England: Falmer Press.

Stone, Oliver. 1986. *Platoon.* Orion. Film.

Stone, Oliver. 1989. *Born on the fourth of July.* Universal. Film.

Stone, Oliver. 1993. *Heaven and earth*. Warner. Film.

Studebaker, John W. 1939. Education moves democracy forward. In *Education for democracy: Proceedings of the Congress on Education for Democracy*. New York: Bureau of Publications, Teachers College, Columbia University.

Taffel, Ron. 1999 September/October. Discovering our children. *Networker*, 24–35.

Tagore, Rabindranath. 1965. *Personality*. London: MacMillanan.

Tozier, Steven. 2000. Class. In *Knowledge and power in the global economy*, edited by David A. Gabbard. Mahaw, NJ: Lawrence Erlbaum.

Thoreau, Henry, David. 1965. *Walden*. New York: Harper & Row.

Trend, David, 1995. *Radical democracy*. Florence, NY: Routledge.

Triandis, Harry, C. 1995. *Culture and social behavior*. Blacklick, OH: McGraw Hill.

Tyack, David, and Cuban, Larry. 1998. *Tinkering toward utopia a century of public school reform*. Cambridge, MA: Harvard University Press.

Waskow, Arthur, I. 1966. *From race riot to sit-in: 1919 and the 1960s*. Garden City, NY: Doubleday and Company.

West, Cornel. 1991. *Prophetic thought in postmodern times: Vol. I: Beyond eurocentrism and multiculturalism*. Monroe, ME: Common Courage Press.

Wolk, Steven. 1998. *A democratic classroom*. Portsmouth, NH: Heinemann.

Wyman, Jasper. 9 February 1985. Letter in *Central Maine Morning Sentinel*.

INDEX